Going Our Way

by Becky Perry Brown
with Roxane Atwood

My life with Jim Ed Brown

Grand Ole Opry legend and member of the Country Music Hall of Fame

Going Our Way

©2018 by Becky Perry Brown

Published by Clovercroft Publishing, Franklin, Tennessee

Published in association with Larry Carpenter of Christian Book Services, LLC
www.christianbookservices.com

Edited by Roxane Atwood

Copy Edit by Isabella Brown

Cover and Interior Design by Caryn Baker

Printed in the United States of America

Hardcover 978-1-948484-00-8

I've always respected the quiet reserve of Becky Brown. Once you get to know her and learn how extremely talented she is you realize that her demeanor actually reflects her personal creativity with measured confidence, whether it's her unique and illustrative ability to paint, her fluid and coordinated mobility for dance, or simply her genuine dedication to her family and friends. Becky Brown is someone you'll be happy to know.

by Patsy Crutchfield
wife of music producer, Jerry Crutchfield

Becky Brown is a force all her own. She is brave and sensitive. I think you will enjoy this book.

by Jeannie Bare
wife of Country Music Hall of Fame member, Bobby Bare

Becky Brown has led an extraordinary life in the country music world. Sometimes in the background but always involved. This is a must read.

by Pat Chesnut
wife of songwriter, Jerry Chesnut

This book is such an inspiration for other wives in the music industry, and Becky's faith in God to do this project, is truly a blessing.

by Mary Larkin
wife of the late Nelson Larken

A professional dancer, great tennis player, beauty queen, and wife of a country music legend, Becky was leading a storybook life. However, this strong-willed woman has also mastered some very challenging storms. What a story!!

by Areeda Schneider-Stampley
wife of Joe Stampley

To my grandchildren

I would like to thank my children, Buster and Kim, for their love and support. Roxane Atwood for the many hours writing, and Caryn Baker for the many hours illustrating this book.

My dear friends Donna Rolin, Patsy Crutchfield, Mary Larkin, and Cindy Yarbrough for their words of encouragement. My childhood through life friends Gloria Williams and Barbara Anderson Caruthers.

Last but not least my twin brother and sister-in-law, Reggie and Susan Perry, and my sister, Lynda Murdock Courtney.

Foreword

I love the saying, *Hard times don't build character, they reveal it.* If I spent the rest of my life trying to define my mom's character, I would never do a better job than Proverbs 31:10-31 NIV. Dad could often be heard saying, "the Lord has been good to me," and that was the absolute truth. Quite possibly the best blessing ever bestowed on my dad was my mom, because it is indeed true, *she is worth far more than rubies.*

At times writing this book wasn't easy for her and I am sure that after you read it, you will understand why. I hope you will also understand why I am so proud of her for putting her life on paper. So often we forget that the hard lessons we experience are important to share, because they teach the next generation that you can fight and win against any and all obstacles. It just requires faith, a belief that all things are indeed possible when you have the Lord on your side. If she ever wavered in her faith, I never saw it. She has always been a warrior like no other; always ready to face whatever this world could throw at her.

This is a love story about survival, perseverance and forgiveness. If you ever questioned their love, all you had to do was watch her walk in the room. Dad was always excited to see people, but there was a very special twinkle in his eye that was reserved just for her. She never entered a room that he didn't tell her she was the most beautiful woman in the world. She could have been sweaty from a tennis match or all dolled up ready to go out. It just didn't matter. To him, she was everything. She was his rock.

Like I said, I could spend my life telling you how amazing she is, but I will let you discover that for yourself. I will leave you with this because she truly is *worth far more than rubies... She is clothed with strength and dignity; she can laugh at the days to come. She speaks with wisdom, and faithful instruction is on her tongue. She watches over the affairs of her household and does not eat the bread of idleness. Her children rise and call her blessed; her husband also, and he praises her: Many women do noble things, but you surpass them all. Charm is deceptive and beauty is fleeting; but a woman who fears the Lord is to be praised.* Proverbs 31:25-30 NIV.

One more thing before I go. Against a lot of advice, she left out some stories that I feel should have made the book. There was the time she brushed her teeth with deep heat. In her defense, the tube did look like toothpaste and smell like toothpaste. I can't forget about the time she thought my car alarm had a motion sensor and she froze for 10 minutes while I went into the movie store. There was also the time she was scared half to death by her own reflection. She also sprayed her hair with what she thought was hairspray, but was in fact, bathroom cleaner. I could go on, but I won't. I mean she will probably cut this part out any way, but every book needs a little humor. And after all, what kind of daughter would I be if I let her get away with not at least mentioning them?

Kim Brown Corwin

The Becky Brown Story

Introduction

I believe in the power of prayer. I always have.

As I look back at my life, I know there were times when my talks with God were the only thing that gave me the courage to put one foot in front of the other.

I believe God hears my prayers, and HE answers them—in HIS time.

My faith gives me the strength to face my tomorrows in both joyous times and troublesome times. Spring 2015 was a troublesome time.

My name is Becky Perry Brown, and my husband of fifty-four years was Jim Ed Brown, perhaps the only man in the world to embody three successful careers in the field of country music: as a member of a family trio, as a solo artist, and a duo. On March 25, 2015 at a press conference in Nashville, Tennessee, the CMA announced that Jim Ed Brown and The Browns would be the newest members of the Country Music Hall of Fame.

To be a member of the Country Music Hall of Fame was Jim Ed's dream come true. It was a dream he carried in his heart for decades. But that spring, as I sat beside my husband's hospital bed in Franklin, TN, I began to doubt that he would live to realize that dream. The official Medallion Ceremony to induct The Browns into the Hall of Fame was in October. This was June and Jim Ed was dying.

You see, in September 2014, Jim Ed was diagnosed with cancer—a word I know only too well. After sixteen rounds of chemo, weeks of radiation, and eight re-constructive surgeries later, I can stand today and say I am a seven year survivor of breast cancer.

I never shed a tear when my doctor told me I had cancer, and I never questioned God as to why I would have to fight this demon in my body. However, three years after my diagnosis and treatment, from the moment Jim Ed received his own diagnosis, I knew in my heart that I had traveled my own cancer journey to better understand what lay ahead for Jim Ed and to help him fight his fight. It all makes sense to me now.

Jim Ed was diagnosed with small cell lung cancer—a form of cancer with an entirely different set of demons than mine. At first, this type of cancer responds well to chemo; however, when it resurfaces in the body, chemo doesn't help at all. Only 1% of the people diagnosed with this cancer survive twelve months past the diagnosis and treatment. Jim Ed's demons weren't just knocking on his door, they were trying to knock his door down.

Ten months had passed since his diagnosis, and during that time, I watched my husband lose his hair. I watched him lose weight and grow frail, and I watched him lose his stamina and vitality. However, through all the trials and debilitating injustices that he faced in the fight of his life, he never lost his ability to laugh and to make others laugh. He trusted God, and even with the trials before him, he had incredible peace.

At the end of May 2015, Jim Ed's oncologist Dr. Ruth Lamar broke the news to us that Jim Ed's time was short. The end was growing near. Still, he held on to the hope that he might somehow make it to the day that he and his sisters would be official members of the Country Music Hall of Fame. He wanted to be there when his dream came true. He wanted to be that 1%.

In June, Jim Ed was hospitalized once again. At the time, we didn't know this would be the last time. For ten days, our daughter Kim held court by her dad's bedside as his child and his protector—leaving the hospital only once to go home and take a shower. She was there for her dad 24/7. I worried about her, but I knew she was strong, and I knew how much he needed her—almost as much as she needed to be with her dad. She was our angel.

Our universe, as we knew it, seemed so surreal. I was trying to grasp the fact that my husband, the man I loved and made a vow before God to cherish when I was 19, may never come home again. It is never an easy thing to let go. We had talked about death, and Jim Ed knew he wouldn't be around much longer.

Somehow through it all though, we comforted each other. While I was reassuring him that everything would be ok, that he was headed for a glorious place, he was reassuring me that I was going to be ok.

He said, "Becky, you have such faith. I don't know where you get such faith. It's unwavering. You're going to be fine, Becky. You are the strongest person I know."

I said, "J.E., I hope you're right. Sometimes I don't feel so strong."

What I wanted more than anything else in the world was more time with our family together, but I wasn't in charge of the clock. It was in those moments I'd have a heart-to-heart talk with My Lord and Savior.

I'd ask God to help us...to give him peace...to take away his pain. If God had to call him home, I prayed God would to allow him to hold on at least another four months until he could see his dream fulfilled—the dream of becoming a member of the Country

Music Hall of Fame. The Lord knew Jim Ed earned that honor, and HE knew how much it meant to Jim Ed.

Day after day, I'd watch him grow weaker, and I continued to pray to God. Even in our darkest hours, I had faith my prayers would be answered.

They were answered, not necessarily in the way that I would have ever imagined. Not in the way Jim Ed had dreamed, but they were answered.

There we were. Some might call it holding vigil. We were with him at his beside at Williamson Medical Center.

Kim spoke to Dr. Lamar on Thursday morning, and after watching her father grow weaker, asked the question no daughter ever wants to ask.

"Dr. Lamar, in your professional opinion, how much longer does my Dad have to live?"

The doctor's answer took Kim's breath away. "I don't expect him to be here on Monday... Tuesday at the latest."

It was then that the phone calls began.

Jim Ed and I had talked about death and dying. It's a conversation most couples dread or even ignore. But I think it's one of the most important conversations you'll ever have...to know the wishes and beliefs of your spouse.

Weeks before this hospital stay, while we were seated at our kitchen table at home having breakfast, I asked Jim Ed, "J.E., are you good? Are you ok with knowing you're going to die? Would you have rather not known your time was near, and go quickly? Just go?"

He turned to me with the sweetest smile on his face and said, "Becky, I'm glad I know what God has in store for me. I'm good. I want to see all my friends before I go. I want to tell them how much they've meant to me. In a way, it's a gift."

Once Kim received the devastating news from Jim Ed's doctor that Thursday morning, she immediately began to reach out to every one of his friends. People she knew he would want to see while he could still talk and enjoy their company. People she knew he would want to say "I love you" to one more time. One of those people was his publicist Kirt Webster.

Kim called Kirt and told him Jim Ed's time was near. The doctor expected that God would call him home in two or three days. A few hours passed and Kirt called Kim back. He told Kim he had a surprise and asked that the family sit tight. He and some friends were on their way to the medical center.

An hour later the door to Jim Ed's hospital room opened and in walked Kirt Webster and right behind him was Grand Ole Opry President, Pete Fisher. Both men were smiling from ear to ear. Both said they ran into each other in the hallway. It was a crazy coincidence that they arrived at the same time to check on him. He had been on their minds.

Low and behold, a few minutes later the door opened again and in walked the lovely Sarah Trahern, Chief Executive Officer of the Country Music Association. A few steps behind her was Kyle Young, Director of the Country Music Hall of Fame. They laughed and seemed surprised to see Kirt and Pete.

Sarah leaned down and gave Jim Ed a kiss on the cheek. He smiled. The twinkle in his eyes was still there even though he was struggling for every breath he took. He was on forced oxygen, and an IV bag dangled from a stand next to his bedside keeping the pain at bay.

For a few moments everyone made small talk. The country music family had rallied around Jim Ed.

Sarah said, "You know you're loved, don't you?"

He tried to sit up a little straighter in his bed. With difficulty, he grinned and sputtered, "Yes I do. A lot."

Sarah touched his hand and replied, "I like your hat. I can't think of a hat more special than that."

Jim Ed was wearing a baseball cap to keep his head warm. The logo on the cap read *Country Music Hall of Fame*.

Once again the door to his hospital room opened and in walked our good friend and fellow Grand Ole Opry member, Bill Anderson. Bill said, "What are all of you folks doing here? It looks like you're having a party!"

More small talk. Then as if on cue, a hush fell over the room. The only noise we could hear was the constant shush of the oxygen machine. That low hiss filled the room. Kyle Young began to read a short, historical biography on the career of The Browns. His voice quivered with emotion. Jim Ed breathed deeply into his oxygen. Everyone was listening intently. Tears began to fill eyes.

Then Bill Anderson spoke. Wrought with emotion Bill began. "Jim Ed, as you know, it is customary when one is inducted into the Country Music Hall of Fame that an existing member of the Hall of Fame do the honors." Bill's voice cracked as he continued, "Jim Ed, I am here today...right now...(long pause) to induct you...(barely a whisper)...into the Country Music Hall of Fame."

With those words, Jim Ed knew.

We all knew.

Jim Ed was being inducted into the Country Music Hall of Fame.

At that very moment.

Not as he had imagined.

Not before a crowd of thousands. But before a handful of his peers whom he admired and loved.

No shining spotlights. Only the harsh glow from the florescent lights above his hospital bed.

Not dressed in his best red suit; standing tall. But in a hospital gown; confined to his bed.

But this moment, with these people, was absolutely beautiful. It was beyond beautiful. It was perfect.

The feeling of love in that room was almost tangible.

When he realized he was actually being inducted into the Hall of Fame, tears began to fill his eyes. His face contorted with emotion, glimpses of gratitude and pride.

Jim Ed began to cry.

Bill Anderson began to cry.

The bond of sixty years of friendship forged between these great entertainers was so apparent.

I don't think there was a dry eye in the room.

Over and over in my head I was thanking God. God had indeed answered our prayers. After sixty-three years in the music business, Jim Ed had reached the pinnacle, and he was still alive to enjoy the view, if only for a few days. Never before had anyone been inducted into the Country Music Hall of Fame outside of the proper ceremony. This was a first. One for the history books. I heard myself say out loud, "God, we give you the glory! Thank you God!"

As the ceremony continued and our family and friends embraced each other and wept in bittersweet joy, I watched my husband's face. His breathing was labored, but his eyes danced with excitement. He was overwhelmed. I could see he was tiring, but I could also see the happiness this moment brought him. The love in that room was medicine for his soul. This day was truly a gift.

So many thoughts began to race through my mind. I couldn't shut them out. You know how they say your life flashes before your eyes. I saw those flashes, snippets of our time together, our lifeline. I thought how in the world did a young couple from Arkansas get here—to the Country Music Hall of Fame? It seemed like a lifetime ago that we met and fell in love. Then again, it seemed like a blink of an eye. One thing for sure, Jim Ed and I traveled this road together. There were some bumps in that road along the way, but we made it to our destination side by side.

I closed my eyes, and I thanked God for our journey. My goodness, it was quite the trip.

Chapter One

Even after all these years, the memories come flooding back. I had a wonderful childhood...mostly because of my hard working parents who always made us feel loved... and partly because of the times.

I was born Rebecca Sue Perry in 1942 on the top floor of the Davis Hospital in Pine Bluff, Arkansas, and I wasn't alone. I made my worldly debut just fifteen minutes before my twin brother Reggie made his entrance.

I have to tell you, it was pretty great being born with a partner in crime...and dare I say it? We were a handful! Rebecca Sue and Reginald Hugh. Consider the fact that my sister Lynda was only eighteen months old when we came on the scene, and you can only imagine the chaotic activity in our household—especially when that household was attached to our place of business.

My parents owned Perry's Grocery & Poultry Market right on Main Street in Pine Bluff. We lived in a small apartment in the back of our store. When Reggie and I began to walk, my mom actually placed each of us in a harness just so she could take care of the customers. Sometimes, it was the only way she could do business. I'd take off in one direction; Reggie would toddle in another; two-and-a-half year old Lynda would crawl around mom's feet playing with her dolls, as Mom would work the register. That must have been quite the sight.

When we were a little older, Reggie and I would play together for hours on end in a loft that my father built in our apartment. The loft shared a wall with the store, and lo and behold, that wall had a secret window! A small hole in the wall was covered by a metal sign advertising Sunbeam Bread. If we moved that sign ever so slightly, we could see directly into the store.

In a way, that secret window was our safety net. If we got frightened, we could peek through that hole and know our parents were only a few feet away; but more than that, it made us spies! We could spy on anyone in the store and become secret agents.

Back in the 1940s we didn't have iPhones, video games, or laptops. We entertained ourselves with pure imagination, and boy, did Lynda, Reggie and I have active imaginations.

As children, our regular trips to the movie theater nourished those developing imaginations. Oh, how I loved the movies!

Pine Bluff back then was such a wonderful place to live—a quaint, thriving town of 49,000 people on the Arkansas River. It had magnificent old buildings and beautiful, pre-Civil War homes that took my breath away every time I'd walk past them. Though my hometown began to grow after World War II, and our economy began to once again prosper, the one thing that remained unchanged in Pine Bluff was a state of innocence that allowed us to have a fabulous childhood.

Those idyllic times allowed the three young Perry children to walk safely by ourselves on Saturday mornings, out the front door of our store, and down the street to one of four movie theaters in town: The Saenger Theatre, The Strand Theatre, The Community Theatre, and The Malco Theatre. For the cost of a mere twenty-five cent ticket, the big screen brought a world of possibilities to Pine Bluff.

I can't tell you how many times we played cowboy after watching a Saturday matinée western. We'd pretend to be one of our silver screen idols—Rex Allen, Roy Rogers or Gene Autry—taking turns being the bad guys because we only had one sheriff's badge. We didn't just act the part, we looked the part; we were riding the range on little stick horses complete with cowboy hats, toy guns and holsters.

I remember watching Charlton Heston and Betty Hutton in the movie that brought the Ringling Brothers—Barnum & Bailey Circus to life. It was called *The Greatest Show on Earth*, and watching that big screen in vivid color with all of the exotic excitement, I thought it truly was the greatest show I had ever seen. I was especially fascinated by the beautiful costumes, poise and artistry of the trapeze artists, and I thought, I want to do that. Then I was introduced to the grace and skill of Fred Astaire and Ginger Rogers. The two of them dancing together, were pure magic, and I thought, I WILL do that.

The movies made me a dreamer, and I dreamed BIG. Thank goodness God blessed me with parents who encouraged me to reach for the stars.

My mom was Vera Hudson, the youngest of nine brothers and sisters...a green eyed beauty from the small community of Faith, Arkansas. It was on faith that my mom ventured over to Vivian, Louisiana, where she met my dad, Arthur Perry, in a diner he owned and operated. The story goes that it was love at first sight for my mom. She flipped over Dad, after all he was a fine dresser and a good looking man. Dad used to tell us kids that Mom began chasing after him; however, I think it was more like that old saying, "he ran and ran 'til he caught her."

They were an attractive couple, and to this day, two of the hardest working people I've ever known. My mom was the more serious of the two. We knew she loved us, but she didn't outwardly express her love the way Dad did.

When my parents married, Mom was twenty-seven and Dad was forty. He had a lot more living under his belt. In fact, Dad said when he was growing up, he was considered the black sheep of the group. In a prim and proper family filled with lawyers and judges, he exhibited an adventuresome spirit that often left his family dismayed. As a young man my father liked to hop trains just to see where they would take him. He always made his way back home, but those little escapades often left his family shaking their heads.

With the turn of the 1920s, however, dad gave up his hobby of riding the rails for college and studied business at Louisiana State University. My dad was an LSU Tiger!

He'd often tell us kids about his glory days as a cheerleader for LSU. Then one day we were browsing through his old college yearbook, and for some reason we couldn't find him in any of the pictures of the LSU cheer leading squad. We knew it wasn't true!

My father loved practical jokes and had the best sense of humor. The reason we all thought he actually was an LSU cheerleader was because even into his 40's, my dad could do the best cartwheels. He could even stand on his head. His joy for life was a constant source of delight for Lynda, Reggie and me. He really was something else. With his movie star good looks, I'm sure he could have sold ice cubes to an Eskimo.

As it was, Dad and Mom sold groceries and chickens, lots and lots of chickens! Perry's Grocery and Poultry Market dressed as many as 1,500 chickens a week. My parents didn't raise the chickens. My dad sold the chickens wholesale to other grocery stores. He'd place an order with the grower; the chickens would come to us in crates, then be sent immediately to slaughter. At any given time, we'd have up to thirty people working in assembly line fashion to dress those chickens to get them ready for market.

When I first met our now good friend Gus Arrendale, President of Springer Mountain Farms Chicken, I was so excited. If you'll pardon the expression, in a way we were birds of a feather. I said, "Oh my gosh, Gus! My dad dressed chickens too! When I was a little girl, I worked the gizzard table. Cleaning those gizzards was a dirty job. Do people still work the gizzard table nowadays?"

With a twinkle in his eyes, Gus put his hand on my shoulder and said, "Becky, we still have those gizzard tables. That hasn't changed one bit."

Working both the grocery store and the poultry business was a 24/7 job for Mom and Dad. In retail, even when the store is closed there is so much to do to get ready for the next business day. There's clean up, restocking shelves, book keeping, placing and filling orders. The responsibilities are never ending. Most of the time my parents spent their Sundays preparing for the week ahead.

Aunt Florence was my mother's sister who lived nearby and, for whatever reason, never had children of her own. Aunt Florence had dark hair, streaked with gray, that she always wore on top of her head—either in a bun or in a high twist. Her barrel like figure was usually clad in a dress, and she wore what I called big, clunky-heeled Granny shoes that laced up the front. To top it all off, whenever she'd leave the house, she'd carry her pocket book over the crook of her arm. I can still see her so clearly in my mind, and when I do, I also see her bright smile and kind eyes.

Because our parents worked through the weekends, Aunt Florence was in charge of our early Christian foundation, and she made sure that foundation was solid. My whole family loved the Lord, and although Mom and Dad couldn't go to church with us very often, they made sure we knew the love of Jesus.

Mom and Dad were Baptist, but Aunt Florence was Lutheran. So off the three Perry children went to the Lutheran Church on Sunday mornings—Reggie holding one hand, me holding the other hand, Aunt Florence in the middle with that pocketbook on her arm, and Lynda hanging on to the tail of Aunt Florence's dress. I loved Aunt Florence. She was more than an aunt. She was a second mother to us, and I loved going to church with her every Sunday. Heavens, I loved church!

I enjoyed hearing all the Bible stories; I enjoyed hearing the choir sing. I'll never forget, one Christmas I heard a soloist from that choir sing *O Holy Night*[1], and I thought that it was the most beautiful song I'd ever heard. Jesus was in my heart.

As the years passed and my parents' business continued to grow, we moved several times with each expansion—always in the center of Pine Bluff activity. My Mom and Dad then began to go to church with us occasionally and we became members of The Baptist Church. My love for God continued to blossom there.

The day I gave my life to Christ, accepting Jesus as my personal Savior, is a day I will never forget. I didn't plan for it to happen that day, it just happened.

At this time in our lives, we attended The Second Baptist church in Pine Bluff, and our minister was Brother George Pirtle. Brother Pirtle was the opposite of the preacher at The First Baptist Church. The minister there would slam his fist on the pulpit as he preached, jump up and down, yell, holler and turn red as a beet as he screeched about hell fire and damnation. Brother Pirtle was easy going, mild-mannered and kind. He preached from a place of love.

I was in the sixth grade. My parents were working in the store that morning, but my sister and I put on our freshly pressed dresses, fixed our hair, hurried Reggie along and walked the short distance to the church. I sat in a pew beside my best friend Gloria Miley. I remember I felt the love of Jesus in Sunday School that day, and by the time I got to the sanctuary, my heart was overflowing with emotion.

Brother Pirtle began to preach. I wish I could remember the message he shared with us that day, but something he said during that sermon just hit me hard—right in the heart. It's hard to explain, but I felt a change taking place inside me. It was so powerful, almost overwhelming. Just before the benediction, the pianist began to play. The choir began to softly sing:

Softly and tenderly, Jesus is calling.

Calling for you and for me.

See, on the portals, he's waiting and watching;

Watching for you and for me...

Come home...Come home...[2]

Tears filled my eyes. This place, these people, and this unconditional love from God, touched my heart. I heard the call. I couldn't sit in that pew any longer. I remember walking to the front of the church with bowed head; tears freely running down my cheeks. At the front of the alter I looked around and saw Reggie standing beside me. He felt the calling too. It was so special. My twin brother and I gave our lives to The Lord on the same day.

Accepting Jesus Christ as my Lord and Savior was such a liberating feeling. It was so freeing. I was humbled. I was filled with joy.

Looking back, I realize that I didn't fully understand what God's will was that day. But the more I studied The Word, the more I realized that it's not about me. It's not my will. It's God's will.

Little did I know then, that accepting God's will as truth, would help me make some hard decisions and hurdle some major obstacles in my future. However, all I knew as my twelve year old self, was I loved Jesus. I wanted everyone to know I loved Jesus, and that Jesus loved me!

Twins: Rebecca Sue and Reginald Hugh. Oh how I love this picture of him.

Reggie, Lynda, and Becky standing by Perry's Grocery and Poultry Market—1947

Reggie, Lynda and Becky—wow no perms.—1946

Lynda and Becky have perms, and a very lucky Reggie

Reggie, Lynda and Becky at Grandmother Hudson's—she cooked on a wood stove.—1946

*Becky and Lynda at
Lutheran Church—1952*

Chapter Two

I was a young girl when I first heard the classic gospel hymn, *Farther Along*.[3] There's a line in the song that reads, *We'll understand it, all by and by*. As I grow older, I have come to understand and accept the truth in that lyric. For it is only with the distance of time that we are bestowed the gift of reflection.

I've often thought of life as a jigsaw puzzle. As events were happening in my life, they were simply pieces of my puzzle—a work in constant progress. But as the years passed, those pieces began to connect. There are still pieces of my puzzle yet to be placed, but now, as I look back at my life, I can see the big picture.

I understand the significance of childhood friendships, family gatherings, chosen activities and even first encounters. They are all pieces to my puzzle. Those pieces made me who I am today. Connected, they form a picture of my life. They are a part of God's plan; a plan I will understand *all by and by*.

I've mentioned that my parents were hard workers. They worked long hours to provide for us kids. They wanted to give us an even better life than they had. It's a work ethic that's instilled in me to this very day, a piece of my puzzle.

I learned at an early age that you didn't go to sleep one night, dream the American Dream, wake up the next day and prosper in the Land of Milk and Honey. The American Dream was built on sacrifice, determination and grit. So, I learned to cherish those special, everyday moments with my family. Another piece of my puzzle.

Isn't it funny how some of the smallest things in your life, upon reflection, end up being some of your biggest memories? The borders of my puzzle.

Before we owned a car, deliveries from my dad's store were made by a delivery truck to larger retailers, and by a commercial bicycle with a basket in the front for neighborhood grocery runs. After work, my dad would often place me in the basket and ride down the street. Maybe we'd visit a neighbor; maybe we'd visit my mother's other sister Aunt

Bea who also lived close by. But no matter where we went, I loved being in that basket with my dad pedaling away on that bike, my hair blowing wildly in the wind, my cares blowing wildly away.

Most of the time, it was the three of us scrunched together in that bicycle basket—Lynda, Reggie and me. My dad made a little seat so the three of us could ride at the same time. My goodness! Thinking back now, that must have been a very large basket. I can still hear the laughter and squeals of delight as we'd egg Dad on. With childlike abandonment we'd plead, "Go faster, Dad! Pedal faster!"

Whenever the carnival or the circus came to Pine Bluff, you could feel the excitement in the air. Back then, practically the whole town would show up at these events. They made an ordinary day extraordinary!

One carnival stands out in my mind more than the others because of the rarity of the day. On this particular day, Mom and Dad walked away from the store and the poultry business, gathered us kids, and headed for the fairgrounds.

My dad was a music lover, and he was especially fond of the music of Al Jolson and Vaughn Monroe. On this day, however, my Mom and Dad left work behind to see a special show at the fairgrounds performed by a nationally known group originally from Sparkman, Arkansas who had come to call Pine Bluff their home.

I was a young girl, but I remember this day. There we were as a family, seated in the grandstands. A gentleman walked out to center stage, stepped up to a microphone and made an announcement that echoed through the fairground speakers. "Ladies and Gentlemen, please put your hands together for country music hit makers...Pine Bluff's finest...THE BROWNS!" The applause was thunderous.

I can't remember if it was just Jim Ed and Maxine, or if Bonnie had joined them as part of the famous trio, but I do remember how much I enjoyed their music. I had no way of knowing back then, but The Browns would soon become one of those all important corner pieces of my life.

I guess you could call me energetic when I was growing up. I couldn't sit still. There was so much to do, so much to see, and I wanted to do and see it all.

I loved getting all dressed up and looking my best. I was petite and blonde and had big blue eyes, and I hate to say it, but I thought I was just too cute. That feeling didn't last very long, though. I remember going through a not so cute stage too.

By the time I was three, Mom would send Lynda and me to the local beauty parlor down the street to get perms. There we'd be, two little girls, wearing little capes that swallowed us whole over our clothes, sitting quietly in those beauty parlor chairs that went up and down kind of like a see-saw. I was too small for my legs to dangle over the edge of the chair, so my legs stuck straight out in front of me.

Not once did Lynda or I complain about the torture we had to go through to achieve our curls, nor did we complain about the rotten-egg-smell of the perming solution. We just held our breath, sat as still as we could while the beautician methodically pulled and twisted our hair, and we sucked it up.

I learned early on in life, that complaining about something is mostly a waste of time and breath. If you're striving for a goal, sometimes you have to do things you don't like to do in order to attain the anticipated results. Can you believe my curls taught me all that? Well, they did. And the moment our curls began to grow out, back to the beauty shop we would go.

I loved my curly hair, and I loved wearing nice clothes. Mother always made sure her children had presentable clothes to wear. The Perry kids were a smart looking bunch. Then again, my mother, being in the daily public eye as a store keeper, dressed well too. My first remembrance of my mom is seeing her dressed in a fitted suit with shoulder pads. She had on platform shoes with a fashionable hat placed slightly askew atop her perfectly coiffed, 40's style hairdo. She was so beautiful.

I spent many an hour looking in the mirror as a young girl, fixing my own hair and playing dress up. However, as much as I loved wearing my nice clothes as a child, I liked taking them off equally as much.

When I was ten years old, my mother had a hard time keeping a shirt on me. I wanted to play outside with my twin brother, Reggie, and our friends. I'd usually run around barefooted, my hair in pigtails, and wearing a pair of jean shorts.

My poor Mother would yell out the door, "Becky, put that shirt back on! Little girls can't go outside without a shirt!"

I tried my best to ignore her. I didn't understand why I had to put on a shirt. The boys didn't have on shirts. I looked just like those boys, except for the fact my hair was longer.

I think that was an early sign of wanting to be equal. I considered myself to be a Tomboy, but i was also a girly girl. I loved playing with my dolls and playing house. That is why I loved going to Grandmother Hudson's. I had the best of both worlds. I could climb a tree as fast as Reggie and make mud pies when I played in my make believe kitchen.

Even getting to Grandmother's house was an adventure. My mom's parents, William and Elizabeth Hudson, lived in Yorktown, Arkansas, about twenty-five miles or so outside of Pine Bluff. They lived in the country, on a hilltop, surrounded on one side by a living, breathing bayou. If we took the short cut, we had to park our car on the other side of Bayou Bartholomew and walk the rest of the way to their house—that meant crossing that old swamp on a foot log that ran all the way across the bayou. That foot log was LONG too. At least in my memory it was long. It seemed to go on forever.

I felt like I was in a Tarzan movie whenever I had to cross that makeshift bridge. In my mind I could hear Johnny Weissmuller yell his famous cry, "Ahhhhh Aaaa Ahhhhh Aaaa Ahhhhh Aaaa Aaaa!" Tarzan was telling me the coast was clear. "No snakes or alligators today. It's safe to cross, Becky!"

Whenever I think about my grandparents, I can just about hear the crowing of their rooster in their backyard. That rooster was loud. As soon as night began to tip his hat to the dawn, that old bird would start to Cock-A Doodle-Doo! No sleeping late here. We were up with the chickens—literally. Of course, getting up at sunrise meant going to bed at sundown, but I didn't mind. I loved all those wonderful things to do in the middle. Each morning, Reggie and I would eat a hearty breakfast of grandmother's biscuits and home made jelly, and then we'd take off full tilt.

Grandpaw Hudson was a cotton farmer who worked his land with a team of mules and a plow. We often played in a room in the barn where Grandpaw stored his cotton seeds. Over and over again, we'd climb a ladder to the barn's loft and jump right in the middle of those seeds. We never had a lack of things to do.

Reggie and I would spend much of our days running through the cotton fields and climbing fruits trees where we would eat to our heart's content. At the end of the day we'd run back to the farmhouse, constructed from unpainted barn wood, and devour a big supper prepared by our grandmother over an old cook stove. Sometimes we'd eat peas that we shelled ourselves sitting at Grandmother's feet. Life was great.

Lynda, on the other hand, was usually homesick during our week long stays at the farm. I seem to remember her crying a lot, and for the life of me, I couldn't understand why. We were having so much fun, and the best part was we only had to take a bath once a week; and then, it was in a big washtub outside on Grandmother's back porch. Oh the glory of it all!

Of course, no electricity and no plumbing meant we'd have to make a trip to the outhouse if we had to go to the bathroom in the middle of the night, but I didn't mind that either. Grandmother would take me by the hand and lead me outside. We didn't need a lantern. The night sky lit our way.

I just thought I'd seen stars in Pine Bluff, but I never really saw stars until I spent time in the country. I couldn't believe my eyes. Those twinkling stars looked like a blanket of sequins in the sky. Somehow I felt even closer to God out on that farm.

My mother's parents lived a very simple life. Years later, as my own life began to get more and more complicated, I began to think there's a lot to be said for simplicity.

In contrast, my father's parents, Curry and Ruby Perry, were prim and proper educators from Ida, Louisiana—approximately two hundred miles from Pine Bluff. My Grandmother

Perry was a Sunday school teacher, and my grandfather owned a Mercantile in Ida in the early 1900s. In later years, he became the Principal of the Bethsaida School. Sadly, Grandfather Perry passed away in 1940, three years before I was born. So I never had the opportunity to get to know him.

I do, however, have two pictures of my grandfather, which I dearly cherish.

The first photograph is a picture of my grandparents standing together on their front porch in 1904 surrounded by fifteen girls in gorgeous white dresses practicing a fan drill for a commencement exercise.

The second picture appears to be taken at a baseball game. In this photo, my grandfather, a state senator, is standing alongside Sgt. Alvin York from Tennessee, the most decorated US Army soldiers of World War I and Kenesaw Mountain Landis, the first Commissioner of Baseball and a federal judge.

Sgt. York is wearing his Army uniform, while my grandfather and Judge Landis are each attired in nice suits. My grandfather is holding a fedora in his hands. Judge Landis is holding what appears to be a ten-gallon cowboy hat. I've often wondered about the story behind this photograph. What brought these three very different men together for this picture? I really would love to know.

I remember visiting my grandmother at her home in Louisiana as often as we could. She lived in a lovely "breeze way home" or "dog trot house" as some people used to call it, comprised of an open air hallway that ran from the front of the house to the back of the house. Even now, I can visualize a pristine, shingled roof home with gingerbread trim and a charming front porch that was perfect for catching a faint breeze on a warm Louisiana springtime afternoon.

Grandmother Perry was very soft spoken and very kind, with beautiful long hair that had grown well past her rear end. One of my favorite things to do on our visits was watch grandmother style her beautiful hair. With swift, yet methodical precision, she would braid her long tresses into one big braid down the middle of her back, then she would wind that braid into the most stunning top knot. It was glorious!

Even more glorious was to watch her take her hair down in the evening. I couldn't take my eyes away. I was mesmerized.

Inch by inch, as grandmother released her beautiful hair from the confines of the braid, an undulating series of soft, shiny waves cascaded all the way down her back, practically teasing the floor. When country star Crystal Gayle first came on the music scene years later with her trademark tresses, I thought Crystal Gayle doesn't have a thing on my Grandmother Perry.

Grandmother Perry taught me many things.

By example, she taught me how to live my life; but more importantly, she had no fear of death.

When I was twelve years old, my grandmother was hospitalized. She never recovered. Before she died, however, my parents brought me and my siblings to her bedside there in the hospital to see her one last time. Many of Dad's family members thought this was no place for children. I suppose they thought we were too young to be exposed to death. But Mom and Dad, wanted us to know that death was a part of life, and nothing to fear.

My memory of that day appears to me now in flashes—little snapshots of time—but I can remember that even in illness, Grandmother Perry looked beautiful. She turned her frail, prone body toward my dad. He leaned toward her and gently stroked grandmother's glorious hair and she whispered, "I love you, son."

We all told Grandmother how much we loved her that day. There was so much peace in that room.

I thought, if you're right with The Lord, death's not that bad. It's not that scary.

If my Grandmother Perry can die with so much dignity, then when my time comes, so can I.

Back Row: Arthur (my Dad), Grandmother Perry, Uncle C.L. Middle Row: Kay Perry, Lynda, Vera (my Mom) Susanna Perry, Reggie, Aunt Carrie, In Front: Becky

Grandfather Curry L. Perry with Sgt. Alvin York and Judge Kenesaw Mountain Landis in the mid '30s

Vera (my Mom), Lynda and Arthur (my Dad)

Becky at her first piano recital

When Jim Ed wasn't working, he was singing.

School picture of J.E.

Jim Ed's high school basketball team. J.E. is on front row #77

Chapter Three

I was one happy little girl growing up. Maybe because my parents gave me every opportunity to explore my passions; and I was passionate about everything. From the time I was small, I took dance lessons, piano lessons, tumbling lessons, art lessons and swimming lessons.

My Dad loved the movies so much and going to the picture show was something we often did as a family. I saw quite a few Ester Williams films in my childhood. I enjoyed those fabulous aqua-musicals from the 1940s. I was fascinated at how Esther could rise out of a swimming pool on a mechanical platform; belt her heart out in song surrounded by twenty swimmers extending their bodies above the pool's surface with ballerina grace and precision, barely making the smallest of splashes or ripples in the water.

I didn't want to be Ester Williams when I was little, but I sure wanted to master the art of swimming. I usually started on Thursday afternoon asking my mother how many more days until Monday. Every day, I asked the same question. "How many more days now, Mother?"

You see, Monday was the day I took swimming lessons. I would walk my six year old self to the corner, catch the bus all alone, and then ride all the way to the park about ten miles away.

I would then proceed to the ladies locker room at the community pool, change into my swimsuit, take my swimming lesson, change back into my casual clothes and with the appearance of a drowned rat, I would hop the bus back home.

You could do that during a Pine Bluff summer in the 1940s. Today I wouldn't let a small child venture past the drive way, much less out of eyesight. It truly was a kinder society back then.

Before the summer was over, I was swimming like a fish. My lessons were a success. Come to think of it, I didn't fail at too many things when I was younger—except maybe memorizing Bible verses in the first grade at my Lutheran Church grade school (Our teacher required us to memorize one new Bible verse every day. Let's just say, I stayed after school a lot.) Then there was that infamous school year better known as second grade. Can you believe I failed the second grade!?! Reggie and I both "repeated" the second grade.

Our second grade year was the year my brother and I caught every childhood illness imaginable, at least it felt that way. We had measles, chicken pox, whooping cough and colds. You couldn't graduate to the next grade if you were never in class. So my teacher suggested to my parents that Reggie and I repeat the second grade.

No one ever really wants to repeat a grade in school, but looking back now, I see God's plan. Holding me back a year, placed me squarely in the paths of three girls, who to this day, are life long friends.

There's something special about the friendships we make in childhood. We experience and share many of our "firsts" with childhood friends: first days of school, first heartbreaks, first triumphs, first dates (My first date was with Freeman Sawyer in the fourth grade. He met me at the door with a pretty wrist corsage. We were going to a formal dance at Pine Bluff Country Club.).

As we grow older, we also experience and share many of our "lasts" together—like saying goodbye to your dying husband—things we'd never begin to think about as children when we had life by the tail. Things we think about now, however, as reality hits us squarely between the eyes.

Sixty years, and I continue to stand tall through my faith in God, but when times are tough and I need someone to lean on, my friends are there.

I first met Gloria Miley in fifth grade. She was so smart. She actually skipped a grade in school. I thank my lucky stars we were placed in the same class. Gloria was there the day I accepted Jesus Christ as my Lord and Savior and has remained all of these years, a part of my inner circle of friends.

I admired Gloria so much growing up. When she styled her hair, I'd style my hair the same way. If she changed her hair color, I'd change my hair color. We went to school together; we went to church together; we lived in the same neighborhood. Reggie was my twin by birth, but you would have thought Gloria and I were the twins the way we acted.

I can remember many times watching TV together curled up on the couch side by side sharing a bowl of radishes. Radishes! Most people would snack on a bowl of popcorn or chips, but not the two of us. There we were enthralled in those television programs of the day and eating our radishes.

Gloria is now a successful Realtor in Melbourne, Florida and remains quite the character. For a while it looked like my precious friend was trying to give Elizabeth Taylor a run for her money. Gloria has been married at least six times.

Cheerleading threw Barbara Anderson and I together, and I'm so glad it did. After grade school, I attended Pine Bluff Junior High which was a melting pot of all the local grade schools in Pine Bluff. The size of our 7th grade class swelled to 350 students. Barbara and I tried out for cheerleader that first year.

In preparation for the tryouts, I mastered a jump where both of my feet touched the back of my head, and I practiced and polished my gymnastics and dance skills. First, we had to audition in front of our teachers who chose four girls from each class to try out in front of the student body. I made it to that second round.

You know how Dolly Parton felt when her mother made her the famous coat of many colors. Well, I felt the same way at my auditions. Grandmother Hudson made me a skirt to wear at tryouts from a flour sack. I was so proud of it! But then I remember looking around the room at all of the cute girls trying out for cheerleader, and I thought, I'll never make it. I auditioned in front of the entire student body and hoped for the best.

I was in gym class at the end of the day when a friend of mine came running to find me. In a high, shrill voice she exclaimed, "Becky! Becky! You made it!"

My legs wouldn't hold me. I sat right down on a bench in that locker room and I cried. I remember my gym teacher sat down beside me and put her arm around me. She brushed the hair away from my face and softly asked, "Becky, why are you crying?"

I wiped my eyes, but the tears kept coming. I said, "Because I am so happy. I am thanking God. This wouldn't have been possible without HIM."

I loved being a Pine Bluff cheerleader. I was a cheerleader for all six years—from junior high school through my senior year, and so was Barbara. Back then, being a cheerleader was almost like being a part of Pine Bluff royalty. Our community was a tight-knit group. Not only did the entire student body know who we were, but so did their parents and most of the town. I'm not bragging. That's just the way it was back then.

Barbara was a good athlete and one of the most popular girls at Pine Bluff High. Our friendship has continued to grow stronger with each passing year. Even today when we attend a high school reunion together, our classmates continue to say, "Our cheerleaders, Becky and Barbara are here."

My other soul mate was Dorothy Vanlandingham. Dorothy oozed personality out of every pore. Dorothy was a petite little beauty with long dark hair and piercing green eyes who lived in nearby Dollarway, Arkansas where The Browns would eventually build their Trio

Club. We didn't go to school together, but we did become fast friends through dance class, and eventually we became professional dance partners. It was on one of those professional appearances at the age of twelve where Jim Ed and I officially crossed paths.

I was performing that night with a group of tumblers in a Minstrel Show put on by The Lions Club at the high school auditorium. After I finished my part of the show, Dorothy was waiting for me, and we climbed the steps to the balcony where we sat down in the audience to watch the rest of the entertainers.

A nice looking young man with dark hair turned around in the seat in front of us. He was wearing his Army uniform and smiling from ear to ear. He looked at me and spoke in a loud whisper to be heard above the music playing on stage, "I enjoyed watching you perform. You were amazing!"

I smiled back at the young man and politely said, "Well, thank you." The handsome soldier turned around in his seat and once again began to watch the show.

Well, Dorothy recognized him, and she punched him on the shoulder. "Hey! Aren't you Jim Ed Brown?" she asked.

He seemed amused, as he turned his head toward her and mouthed the word, "Yes."

For once in my friend's life, she was speechless. Dorothy might have been in shock. She was surely in awe. Once she gathered her wits, she pointed to me, then pointed repeatedly to the soldier, "That's JIM ED BROWN!" she said in quiet excitement—over and over—JIM ED BROWN. She made a funny face as she silently and dramatically over-enunciated his name.

I had to laugh. Of course I knew who Jim Ed was. Who didn't? He was a rather famous resident of Pine Bluff, after all. By this time, he and his sisters Maxine and Bonnie already had hit records on the charts as The Browns. But I wasn't in to country music back then, at least not the way Dorothy was.

I was familiar with country music; it just wasn't my favorite. Once my Grandmother Hudson got electricity on the farm, I'd watch all of those Saturday television shows with her, like *The Wilburn Brothers Show* and *The Porter Wagoner Show*. I enjoyed them too. But my favorite artists were singers like Nat King Cole, Johnny Mathis and The Platters.

Dorothy on the other hand LOVED country music. Every time I'd go to her house she'd have the radio in her room blaring on a country music station. Just to get her goat, I'd say, "Dorothy, can we change the channel to a rock-n-roll station?" She'd shake her head no, and we'd howl with laughter.

Dorothy was the friend I dreamed those girlish dreams with. I remember from the time we were very young, we'd talk about who we thought we were going to marry and what our lives would be like.

I told Dorothy I was sure I would marry someone with a FABULOUS last name. She thought that was so funny.

"Yes, indeed, Dorothy, I'll have a fabulous last name. You just wait! Something with a ring to it that people will remember. My husband's last name will be grand!"

We'd laugh until our sides hurt. Dorothy already had a grand last name. After all, it didn't get any grander than Vanlandingham.

My teen years found me busier than ever. My dance teacher Dorothy Harrison introduced me to that professional group of tumblers who were impressed with my flexibility. They taught me how to do back handsprings, front handsprings and aerials. They even convinced me to be the top rider in their multi-tiered unicycle routine. But the most important thing they taught me was how to take a fall.

As I look back, I think I was twelve at the time, and I was rehearsing for a show with that group of professional tumblers and acrobats who had retired from the circus. I was jumping extremely high to throw a double tuck, opening into a layout. I decided not to throw it at the highest point of my jump and I came straight down on my neck, bounced a couple times, then right into the springs and on to the floor like a rag doll.

My spotters were in shock. They rushed over to me and asked if I was alright. I was a bit shaken, but I said, "Yes, I am OK." They encouraged me to jump again and I did. I had no fear and I loved working with these great acrobats.

Try as they might, they could not convince me to apply for a scholarship for a program called *Flying High Circus* offered by Florida State University. I might have enjoyed watching the movie *The Greatest Show On Earth* when I was a little girl, but now that I was older, I didn't want to run away and join the circus. The circus was their dream. My dream was to dance.

In the summer, when I was 16 or 17, I traveled to Chicago and New York to study dance. My favorite classes were with jazz master Gus Giordano in Evanston, Illinois. I also began to earn extra money with part time modeling jobs.

One of the oddest modeling jobs I ever had was for a beautician who needed a model to pass her state boards. She wanted to impress the board with a hairstyle that was unique and innovative, so she decided to do something wild.

She dyed my hair red, but not just any red. This lady dyed my hair fire engine red. She back combed my hair so it stood high atop my head; then she used an entire can of Spray Net to keep it there.

I'll never forget; I had to go to school the next day and dance at an assembly. My hair didn't move! I'm sure my classmates' eyes didn't move from my hair either. How could they have possibly looked away? Today kids go to school with all kinds of colors in their hair, but back in the early '60s, this was not something we did.

Well, the beautician liked her fire engine red creation, but she wanted to try something even bolder. She promised me she wouldn't damage my hair with the bleach she was using, and this time when she was done, she had her masterpiece. She colored my hair LAVENDER. I wore a lavender dress with lavender makeup. It was something to see, and caused quite a stir.

I was always willing to step outside of the box and do things. I did things without over thinking them. I was never concerned what other people thought. In fact, it just never occurred to me to be concerned.

So there I was going to school, making good grades, cheerleading, modeling, dancing, performing and going to church. My childhood and teen years were almost storybook perfect. I was a mover and a shaker who still made time to go to dances, eat out with my friends and on Saturday nights do what normal teenagers do who are too old to sit home with their younger siblings, but not old enough to venture into the clubs— I'd cruise up and down the streets with my friends in my parents' car.

One night my girlfriends and I were dragging Main Street in my family's station wagon. I was the chauffeur, and the car was full of girls laughing and cutting up with the radio blaring. I was sixteen years old, and life was good. Suddenly we noticed that a handsome young man had pulled up beside us in his white and turquoise '56 Chevy.

He really was a sight to see. The girls recognized him immediately. It was Jim Ed Brown.

Jim Ed was flirting with us big time, and the girls were eating it up. I can't remember what he said exactly, but I do remember that sly smile and how he winked his twinkling eyes at us.

I said, "Don't look at him, girls. Don't pay him any attention." And to the dismay of most of the girls in the car, I drove away. At the time I thought it was kind of funny—leaving a flirting romeo in the dust.

I bet it surprised Jim Ed, too. I'm not sure how many other carloads of girls had left him behind in the past, but this car load sure did.

Fate is a funny thing, however.

Soon I wouldn't be driving away. Soon I would be cruising those same Pine Bluff streets seated right next to Jim Ed Brown.

Through my teen years, I entered many beauty pageants. The pageant circuit was exciting to me.

As it turns out, I was injured from that trampoline fall. But I didn't discover the injury until years later when my chiropractor Dr. McBride asked me to enter the Miss Correct Posture Contest as his representative for the state of Arkansas. This wasn't your typical beauty pageant. As I walked the runway in my swimsuit, there were large screens on stage that displayed oversized x-rays of my spine for the audience to see. Crazy but true.

When Dr. McBride first examined my x-ray months before the competition, he couldn't believe what he saw. Somewhere along the way, I had suffered a terrible spinal injury to the cervical area. In no way was my neck in line with the rest of my spine.

Dr. McBride couldn't believe I was not in chronic pain. I assured him I was not.

Through multiple treatments and following daily instructions at home—like sleeping a certain way and carrying my school books on one side of my body—my condition improved. I even walked away with third place in that state competition. I was named Miss Jefferson County and still have the diamond ring and trophy to prove it. I was also selected Miss Champagne Music of Arkansas which led to a television appearance on *The Lawrence Welk Show* where I danced to the music of Mr. Welk's Orchestra.

The summer after my high school graduation, I was a contestant in The Miss Pine Bluff Pageant. I knew a year in advance that I was going to run for Miss Pine Bluff, so I started making preparations early.

Dancing for the talent portion of the competition would be the natural thing for me to do, but I enjoyed exploring new opportunities to broaden my horizons.

I sang at church, and I actually loved it, although I didn't consider myself a singer. So for a solid year, with some tutelage from our choir director at school, I practiced singing.

The night of the pageant I sang *Can't Stop Lovin' That Man*.[4] Then I danced to a medley of songs from the musical *Show Boat*.

I did well; but in the end, I fell just a little short. I came in First Runner Up in The Miss Pine Bluff Pageant.

It just so happened, however, that Jim Ed Brown was in the audience that night. Jim Ed was a member of The Junior Chamber of Commerce, and his organization sponsored the pageant.

Two weeks after the contest, I was home when the telephone rang. I picked up the phone and put the receiver to my ear.

"Helloooo," I said.

A velvety smooth voice questioned, "Is this The Perry residence?"

"It is," I replied. That voice sounded oddly familiar.

"May I speak to Becky Perry, please?"

With hesitation I said, "This is she."

"Becky, this is Jim Ed Brown. Would you like to have dinner with me?"

NEW JEFFERSON FAIR QUEEN

Becky Perry, right, was named winner last night of the Miss Jefferson County Fair Queen contest at Hestand Stadium. Crowning the new queen is Cheryl Henry, last year's winner. Becky, 18, is the daughter of Mr. and Mrs. A. F. Perry of 1605 Nebraska. Sponsored by the Seventeen Home Demonstration Club, Miss Perry won over 16 other contestants. Sheila Black was runner-up.

1961 Miss Pine Bluff Pageant

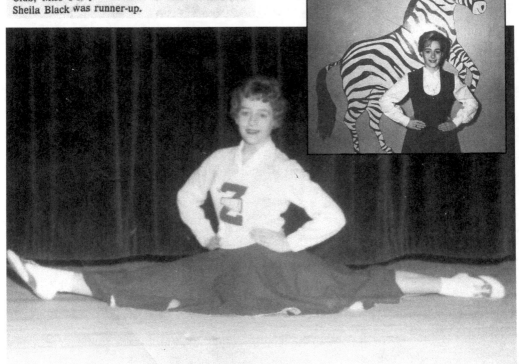

Go Zebras!—Pine Bluff High School—1959

30

Back Row: Kathy Shinell, Carol Taylor, Catherine Caldwell, Rhonda Oglesby, Peggy Browning, Front Row: Barbara Anderson, Becky Perry, Mary Anne King, Olivia McClaran

Archery is fun, especially if you hit the target.

Christmas photo shoot for Ben Pearson Bow and Arrow Factory

Miss Champagne Music of Arkansas greeting Lawrence Welk and the Lennon Sisters—1960

Becky and dance partner Dorothy Vanlandingham—1961

Chapter Four

For the first time in my life, I understood the meaning of the expression *You could have knocked me over with a feather.* I'm not sure who I expected to be on the other end of that telephone, but Jim Ed Brown wasn't it. He wasn't even on my radar.

By this time, Jim Ed had been recording hit records with The Browns for over seven years. Two years earlier their song *The Three Bells*[5] topped the country charts for ten straight weeks. It also went #1 on the pop charts, and became a top ten R & B recording as well. If I wasn't very familiar with Jim Ed Brown when I first met him—back when I was that twelve year old girl—I was certainly familiar with Pine Bluff's most prominent celebrity now.

But how in the world did Jim Ed track me down? Why me? If he wasn't on my radar, how in the world could I have been on his? Besides, he was eight years older than me. I was eighteen, about to turn nineteen in a few weeks. Jim Ed was twenty-seven.

"Becky, are you there?"

"Yes. I'm here," I replied.

"I asked you if you wanted to go to dinner with me Friday night, but I haven't heard a yes—or a no. Well, would you like to go out with me, Becky Perry?" Jim Ed inquired.

 Another pause.

Without a doubt, I had my share of boyfriends, dates and crushes, but up to now, my dates usually centered around groups of friends. We'd go to Teen Town for a night of dancing and fellowship—maybe a night of bowling. We'd go to the movies, or we'd grab a burger at one of our local diners. No one had ever asked me out to dinner.

"Becky, are you there?"

Finally I answered. "Jim Ed, if you can hold on for just one moment, I need to check my calendar and see if I'm free Friday night."

I heard a low, throaty chuckle as he waited.

"Yes. Friday looks fine. Thank you. I'd like to have dinner with you."

He said, "Great! Let me write down your address, and I'll pick you up at eight. Becky, I'll be looking forward to Friday."

I could hear the smile in his voice as he said goodnight.

When Friday night rolled around, I looked at the girl in the mirror. She appeared perhaps, a little more confident and put together than she actually felt.

I checked the color of my lipstick to see if it matched the dress I'd selected from my closet earlier that day. A cloud like mist began to settle as I applied a light spray of Aqua Net to my hair, and for good measure I rubbed some of my favorite perfume on my inner wrists and behind my ears.

The girl in the mirror wasn't exactly nervous. But she was a little anxious—maybe even a little excited—wondering what this night would hold in store. I was fastening the lock to my favorite necklace when I heard the knock on the door.

He arrived on time and looked very dapper in a suit and tie. I had forgotten just how handsome Jim Ed was.

I observed him as he engaged my parents. One of the things I liked the most about Jim Ed was the way his smile reached his eyes. When he smiled, his eyes twinkled.

I also appreciated the way he treated my parents. Not only was he charming to my mother and dad, he was also genuinely respectful.

I remember him placing his hand gently on the small of my back as he escorted me to his car, and like a true gentleman, he opened and closed the car door for me, making sure I was comfortable before we pulled out of the driveway. I can't remember what we talked about on our drive to dinner, but I did discover something I hadn't anticipated. Jim Ed was a little shy.

Alone in the car, he was much quieter than I expected, and he even seemed a little nervous. Somehow his faltering self confidence seemed to bolster my own.

My eyes widened, however, when we arrived at our destination. He told me he was going to prepare dinner for me. But assuming you are going to his home, and going to his home, are two different things. This was a new experience for me. Jim Ed wasn't one of the many boys I had dated, Jim Ed was a man.

Jim Ed lived behind the Trio Club. I glanced over at the club as we pulled into his driveway. I knew the place well. The Trio Restaurant and Supper Club was owned and operated by Jim Ed's parents—specifically his mom. The name of the club was a nod to Jim Ed, Maxine and Bonnie who together formed the famous trio who America had come to know as The Browns.

The Trio Club hosted some of the country's best entertainment including Elvis Presley, Harold Jenkins (who later became Conway Twitty) and so many of The Browns' artist friends from *The Louisiana Hayride* and *The Ozark Jubilee.*

Even I had performed at The Trio Club. The band that backed me in The Miss Pine Bluff Pageant, Todd Ward & The Moonliters, asked me to be a regular in their group. The boys in the band liked my voice, and I had fun singing torch songs with these guys. The Trio Club was one of the places we performed. Again, it's strange how a simple sequence in your life, in retrospect, becomes a piece of your puzzle.

I closed my eyes and took a deep breath as Jim Ed walked around and opened my car door. Now he seemed a little more confident, and I seemed a little more nervous.

The house itself was a beautiful ranch style home of light colored variegated brick. Inside, everything was state of the art. His kitchen was equipped with every modern gadget imaginable, and each room was connected by an intercom system.

I was in the office, admiring his trophies from his days as a high school and college athlete, music awards for his hit records and pictures with some of his celebrity friends when I noticed Jim Ed was no longer in the room. I looked around again, and there he was—only something was very different.

Gone were his coat and tie—replaced instead by a smoking jacket. I had never seen anything like this in my life, except maybe in the movies. I didn't know whether to be in awe, or burst out in laughter. Truthfully, I didn't know what to think. The jacket sported a black and gray pattern of odd geometric shapes with black satin lapels and cuffs and tied at the waist with a black satin sash. Jim Ed reminded me of a young Clark Gable from *Gone With The Wind.*

I mentioned to him that some of the awards on his wall had the name James Edward on them while other awards read Jim Edward. I asked him what he liked to be called. He said his friends and family called him J.E. and he hoped that I would feel comfortable enough to call him J.E.

He found a station on the radio with some light instrumental music and played it softly in the background as he led me to his dining room where we sat down to a meal of salad, baked potato and filet mignon—accompanied by a mouth-watering dessert—all served beautifully on a perfectly set table adorned with a white linen table cloth. Jim Ed served each course himself—disappearing into the kitchen and reappearing with a course more delicious than the one before.

I often wondered if he had someone prepare the meal from The Trio Club and bring it over to the house as if he cooked it. But in all, of what ended up being, our fifty-four years together, I never once asked him that question. I like to think he did it all himself. Everything was over the top fabulous!

When we finished eating, he invited me back to the den where we looked through his albums and found some common favorites. It was then that I learned I wasn't the only one in the room who could dance. He actually caught me off guard when he extended his hand

and pulled me up to jitterbug. I can't remember the name of the first song we danced to. All I can remember is that he was an unbelievable dancer. He was so light on his feet. The man had moves. I was having so much fun; I didn't want the music to end.

We danced song after song, and then the music changed. On came The Platters, and he pulled me close as we swayed to the song *Twilight Time*.[6] I went from being breathless, to him taking my breath away. It was all so surreal. It almost seemed like a scene in the movies. Just me, Jim Ed, low lights and soft music. I felt my heart skip a beat or two during that dance.

Oh no! This wasn't in my plans at all. I wasn't looking for a steady relationship.

On the drive back to my parents house, he said, he wanted to show me something. When I agreed, he made a detour to Atkins Lake about eight miles outside of Pine Bluff. He stopped near a quaint A-frame lake house that he used to own, but recently sold. I thought this is just a ploy to "park." As it turns out, I was right, but he sure picked the night for it.

He couldn't have painted a more romantic picture if he tried. I wondered if he had possibly called in a favor from God. The evening itself was absolute perfection. Not too hot. Not too humid. A galaxy of stars winking at us. Alone in the darkness, overlooking water bathed in moonlight. More soft music playing low from the speakers of the car, intermingled with the crickets' serenade and the beating of my own heart.

It was then that he leaned forward and kissed me. A slow, long, gentle kiss. He pulled me closer, and kissed me again. This time with passion. Jim Ed knew how to kiss. I thought it was best to go home at that moment, and I told him so. He smiled and started the engine.

On the drive home, in the back of my mind, I was thinking I'm too young for this. I have so many things I want to accomplish in my life, and I'm just getting started. Besides, Jim Ed had a playboy reputation. Girls just threw themselves at him, and he never had to work very hard for the attention. I didn't want to go there. I didn't want to be one of many. I was dating other people, and I didn't want to give up my social life. I was busy!

When Jim Ed walked me to my door, I said, 'Goodnight, J.E. I had a wonderful time."

He looked into my eyes, and he said, "Becky, may I call you again"

I said yes.

He called the very next day, and the next, and the next, and every day thereafter.

––––––––––––––––––––

J.E. was in hot pursuit. He immediately asked me out for a second date, but I wasn't so quick to accept his invitation. I thought this could get out of hand real quick. He made no bones about the fact that he wanted a relationship.

I finally relented and began to date J.E. on a casual basis, but I was leery. It wouldn't have bothered me if he were dating other people, because I was dating other people, and I told him so. He said he understood the situation. But he also said he had found the woman he wanted to be with, and I was that woman. So with that understanding, we began to see each other. This arrangement worked well, for a short time, a very short time.

J.E. moved to North Little Rock, forty-five miles away so he could be near his Dad's base camp. His father operated a logging business, and whenever he wasn't singing, he helped his father with the logging operation.

J.E. heard that Dorothy and I were performing at a church luncheon one afternoon, and he asked if he could drive over and tag along, just as a friend, and watch us dance. Of course we said yes.

Afterward, J.E. and Dorothy came to our house to hang out. I thought he would get tired and go home, but he stayed. One hour lead to two hours. The later in the day it got, the more fidgety I got. Finally, six hours had past. J.E. was still there when there was a knock on our door. Right away I knew who that was. I ran for my bedroom and my twin brother Reggie opened the door.

I had scheduled a date with another boy for 7pm. I was praying that young man had forgotten that we were supposed to go to the movies together. No such luck. He was right on time.

With a big goofy grin on his face, Reggie escorted my date into the den to sit with J.E. Reggie then came back to my bedroom where I was hiding with Dorothy and tapped on my door. I only opened the door a crack—enough to frantically point over and over again from the living room to the front door. I thought my meaning was perfectly clear. I wanted Reggie to send one of those fellows home.

He was no help. I turned to Dorothy in exasperation. She was no help. Both Reggie and Dorothy were laughing their heads off. They were enjoying my predicament. I was embarrassed and horrified.

I don't know why I felt like I had been caught red handed, but I did. J.E. had invited himself to our church luncheon. I had no idea he was going to stay all day. Maybe I should have called the other boy and explained to him that J.E. was visiting from Little Rock. Maybe I should have confessed to J.E. that I had a date at 7pm. But I did neither.

Now, here I sat. Locked in my bedroom. Wringing my hands. Pacing the floor.

Neither boy would leave. They were trying to out wait the other. Reggie practically skipped back into the living room and gleefully began to hold court. There they sat— Reggie, my date and J.E. —and the only one with a smile on his face was Reggie. Finally after thirty minutes had elapsed, it became excruciatingly obvious that I wasn't going to leave my bedroom.

The only thing they could do was go home. Both men decided to walk out my front door together. Both men got in their cars and drove home without so much as a single goodbye or a kiss my foot from me.

With their departure, I exhaled a long, slow breath. I don't think I ever heard from that young man again. J.E. called me the next day.

Years later, J.E. continued to refer to these shenanigans as "The Day I Double Booked." I'd shake my head and remind him that I did no such thing. I only had one date booked for that night. I simply had two men waiting in my den.

The mere thought of that night always brought a smile to his face. He knew he made it impossible for me to date other people. He had set his sights on me, and he wanted to be with me all the time. Truthfully, I began to enjoy all the attention. I liked being with J.E. too.

J.E. singing to sister Norma

J.E. and Maxine

A 22 year old, J.E. off to Germany for a year, then to the Pine Bluff Arsenal

This picture of J.E. makes me laugh. Pictured with Maxine and Bonnie.

I was about 17, at this time J.E. and I were not a couple, we had yet to meet.

J.E. was around 25 years old here.

Date unknown, but the clothes and hair tell it all for both of these photos.

Chapter Five

J.E. and I began to see each other exclusively. His mom and dad began to tease him, saying he was burning a lot of rubber driving back and forth between Little Rock and Pine Bluff. My own mother thought J.E. hung the moon. I think he swept Mother off of her feet before he swept me off of mine—but I could feel myself falling.

Sometimes he would take me on the most extravagant dates. Twice he chartered planes and took me to Dallas and again to New Orleans to see Arkansas play college football. But most of the time our dates consisted of going to his parents' home for dinner.

We became somewhat of a fixture at the Brown's house. We'd sit around the table together—eating what Jim Ed called Momma's good ole country cookin'. No one cooked like Momma Brown. She had a gift in the kitchen.

While Jim Ed's dad, Floyd, ran the logging business, it was Mrs. Brown who oversaw the operations at The Trio Club. She also filled in as a sort of surrogate mother to all of his music friends—young entertainers making a living singing on the road away from their own families.

So many of those young performers would call her late at night, and say, "Mrs Brown, we'll be coming through. We'll be there about one o'clock in the morning," and Mrs. Brown would get up and head for the kitchen. By 1a.m. she'd have a feast for a king prepared and set out on the table.

She understood these kids were homesick, and they missed their mothers' home cooking. She also knew that the expense of living on the road ate up most of the money these young artists had earned the night before. Many times they would end up on her doorstep with empty pockets, as well as empty stomachs.

She'd feed them a huge meal, and send them off again with a bag full of goodies for the next leg of their journey. Many a time Elvis Presley, Bobby Bare, Johnny Cash, Jim Reeves, The Davis Sisters (Skeeter and Bee Jay) or Conway Twitty left her kitchen table with a sack full of ham and biscuits, cornbread or maybe slices of homemade cake to eat on the way to their next gig.

The day after one of those late night escapades, I'd often drive Mrs. Brown to the grocery store to restock her pantry. You don't even want to know how much her weekly grocery bill was back then. She fed everyone. It was unbelievable.

Mrs. Brown had one of the best hearts of anyone I'd ever met. I loved sitting around the table with J.E. and his family. I loved how they interacted with each other. I loved the respect I saw in his eyes for his parents, and I loved to hear them talk and tell stories. Rarely did we talk about the music business during those long, southern meals. Truthfully, most of the chatter centered around family, the logging business or hunting.

J.E. and his dad could talk about hunting for hours. When he was born, his daddy made his living as a hunter and trapper before turning to farming and eventually logging. He passed his love for hunting and his vast knowledge of trapping wild game on to J.E., and he was good at it.

Mrs. Brown confided that when he was a small boy, she'd send him off to the woods, alone with a gun, and tell him to come home when he had quails or squirrels that she could cook for supper. That was a big responsibility for such a little boy, but rarely did J.E. come back empty handed.

J.E.'s aunt gave him the name J-bird because he whistled like the birds. He was a happy child and he whistled everywhere he went.

However there was one horror that haunted him in his dreams—a tragedy that continued to replay itself in his head at the oddest times for the rest of his life. He told me about the day his little brother Raymond died in a terrible accident right before his eyes, and he couldn't do anything to stop it.

Raymond was only seven years old. J.E. was only nine. The year was 1943. They were with their dad on a logging job—trying to haul huge timbers loaded on a truck from the woods to the mill. The ground was wet from a recent rain.

J.E. and Raymond were in the cab of the truck thinking how lucky they were to be out in the woods with their dad when the tires to that big truck began to spin on the damp forest floor covered in mud and slippery pine needles.

Raymond stood up on the front seat and stretched his body out the open window trying to get a better look at the spinning tires. Somehow, the door to the truck flew open. Raymond fell out. The truck spun sideways in the mud and came to a stop on top of Raymond's small frame. J.E. saw it all.

It happened so fast. The wails of despair that came out of his daddy as he and the men tried to push the truck away—trying to rescue Raymond's limp body from beneath the weight of the vehicle—were like nothing J.E. had ever heard. He was crying and calling Raymond's name. "Raymond! Don't die! Raymond! RAYMOND!"

But Raymond was gone.

It felt like the world was moving in slow motion. Nothing made any sense.

J.E. remembers riding home in the back of a wagon with his dad and Raymond. As they approached the house, his daddy began to yell his mother's name—over and over.

Then he saw his momma's face void of color, contorted in pain as she ran out of the house. He heard her mournful cries and screams—almost animal like—when she saw her husband standing in the back of the wagon, tears streaming down his face, holding Raymond's lifeless figure in his arms. So helpless. So distraught. So inconsolable.

Those images—those sounds—were permanently etched in his heart. A boy should never have to witness something like that, no one should.

That was the day that J.E. was stripped of his innocence. He drew even closer to his sisters—closer to God.

The congregation at the little Methodist church down the road embraced the Browns in their time of sorrow. J.E., his siblings and his parents were baptized. The knowledge they would see Raymond again eventually brought them comfort.

The death of a child is one of the most horrific things that could ever happen to a family. I can't imagine the pain the Browns felt from the loss of their beloved Raymond.

I hope I never have to experience that loss myself.

It's not the way we are brought up to think. A child shouldn't die before a parent. That's not the natural order of things. How can anything good come from such tragedy?

I guess the glimmer of light in one of the darkest days of J.E.'s life was knowing this experience cemented his relationship with God. At the age of nine, J.E. found faith. Years later, it would be that faith that would lead him back to the righteous path when he stumbled.

———————————————————

More and more I was getting to know the Brown family. They were such hard workers, such good people. J.E. adored his family.

My family was close, but we didn't hug like the Browns did, and we didn't tell each other "I love you" every time we turned around. Nor did we talk as freely or as openly about everything under the sun the way the Browns did. I had never met anyone quite like the Browns.

I was familiar with his younger sister Norma. She was a year younger than I was, and for a short time, we attended Pine Bluff High School together.

Norma was an attractive girl with long brown hair. She was kind of on the quiet side. She and Dorothy were classmates and friends.

Bonnie, his younger sister by three years, was already married to her husband Brownie when I first met her. Brownie was a handsome young doctor with a practice in

Dardanelle, Arkansas, about eighty miles northwest of Little Rock. Together they made the most striking couple.

By this time they already had their first child Kelly. Somehow they managed to juggle a young doctor's hectic schedule plagued with long, grueling hours, with bouts of Bonnie working the road for weeks at a time with The Browns. I'm not sure how they did it, but they did.

There's no other word to describe Bonnie Brown Ring except "gorgeous." Bonnie was a dark haired beauty who exuded warmth and friendliness.

Elvis Presley himself fell in love with Bonnie, and at one time the two flirted with the idea of marriage. But God knew what he was doing when he placed Brownie in Bonnie's life. Those two were meant to be.

Bonnie and Brownie welcomed me to the family. They acted like they were truly glad J.E. had found someone special, and they made me feel special.

And then there's Maxine.

Maxine was a force of nature.

She was tall and attractive, and I thought she had such an air of sophistication about her. Whenever I saw Maxine, no matter where it was, Maxine was dressed to the nines. Perfectly coiffed. Not a hair out of place. She accessorized every outfit with just the right jewelry, and she wore dark lipstick to accentuate her full, beautiful lips. When Maxine walked into a room, you knew it. Chances are, however, you heard her before you saw her.

Maxine had a voice that carried, and as much as she looked like a lady, her quick wit and often bawdy delivery of quips and comebacks made her one of the guys. Maxine's vernacular could be, shall we say, "colorful" at times.

Back in the day, out of respect to women, when men told jokes of questionable content, they excused themselves and walked a few steps away from the ladies forming an all male huddle. They'd speak in hushed tones with heads slightly bowed—silly grins on their faces.

So many times over the years, I'd see Maxine in the center of those huddles. She wasn't just listening to those jokes either. She appeared to be telling them!

Maxine could always make every one in the room laugh. I think she loved the sound of laughter as much as she loved the sound of music.

Maxine was a true character. I often thought of her as a cowgirl in the wild west. Because when it came to business, she could take the bull by the horns.

When it came to spending time with me, however, she was more like a bull in a china shop. I don't think Maxine liked me much at first. Then again, I don't think Maxine would have liked anyone who threatened to take her little brother away. The Browns were a tight-knit group, and Maxine was holding on the tightest.

Maxine often made snide remarks whenever I was around, sometimes under her breath, but mostly to my face. I've always respected the fact that I knew where I stood with Maxine. There was never any beating around the bush with Maxine Brown.

One day while J.E. and I were dating, out of the blue, Maxine turned to me and said, "You do realize that Cadillac J.E. drives is in all three of our names—J.E., Bonnie and me. All three of us own that car."

I guess Maxine thought I was some kind of gold digger. I don't think she realized I couldn't give two hoots what J.E. had or didn't have. I was spending time with J.E. because I enjoyed his company, and he enjoyed mine.

My family had a very successful business. I watched it thrive and was able to enjoy wonderful opportunities because of that success.

Like J.E., I had a tremendous work ethic and had been making my own money for years. I was a professional dancer, singer and model. I had my own plans.

After J.E. and I married, Maxine and I found our footing. I came to love Maxine and understand her.

Even today, when I'm sitting around the table with my children and grandchildren, some of our favorite memories start with the words, "Remember when Maxine..." No matter what story is about to be told, we know if Maxine is involved, it's going to be a good one.

When we were dating, J.E. shared with me that it was because of Maxine that the phenomenon known as The Browns got its start. As children, the siblings were always singing together. It's simply what they did on Sunday afternoons or after a hard day of work. Singing was their main source of entertainment. Early on, the children learned to harmonize.

His Uncle Cecil gave J.E. his old Sears and Roebuck guitar strung with strings from Grandma Brown's old pump organ.

On Saturday nights, the Browns gathered around their battery-powered radio and listened to The Grand Ole Opry. That old radio brought Roy Acuff, Minnie Pearl, Eddy Arnold and Bill Monroe right in the middle of their living room. Many times, Jim Ed would pull out his old guitar and strum along with his Opry idols.

I think one of the proudest days in his life was the day he became a member of The Grand Ole Opry and claimed each one of those idols as his friends and colleagues.

Many times, I'd try to imagine the dreams J.E. had dreamed as a small boy? What was he thinking sitting there with his family playing along to the radio? Was he secretly wishing that he could be on that stage too?

I was by his side that night in 1963 at The Ryman Auditorium when The Browns became members of The Grand Ole Opry. It was quite a journey from Arkansas to The Opry stage. I'm so thankful I was there to share in J.E.'s elation.

The boy's dream became a man's reality. It all started eleven years earlier when Maxine Brown, unbeknownst to J.E., entered him in an amateur talent contest sponsored by a Little Rock radio station for a spot on *The Barnyard Frolic*. J.E. didn't win the talent contest even though he brought the crowd to their feet that night, but after the show, on his way out the door, he was asked to become a *Frolic* regular. This was the beginning of Jim Ed's professional career, and the beginning of what would soon become The Browns.

Jim Ed was a hit. His smooth voice and southern charm made him a fan favorite of the older folks in the *Frolic* crowd. His tall, lean frame, country boy smile, and twinkling, deep brown eyes made the young girls in the audience jump to their feet.

Jim Ed was a crowd pleaser, and one night it pleased him to call a surprised Maxine out of the audience to harmonize on a song they'd rehearsed together at home, *Are You Missing Me?*.[7] The crowd loved them, and gave them an encore that night. They knew they were on to something big.

Even though they were fast becoming *Frolic* favorites, they knew they couldn't continue to sing other people's songs if they wanted to have a career of their own. They needed their own material. That's when Jim Ed and Maxine recorded a song that Maxine had written after Maxine overheard their nine year old sister Norma explain to their momma that she got in trouble at school because she was looking at a cute boy in her class when she should have been doing her school work.

Norma cried, "I was just looking back to see if he was looking back to see if I was looking back to see if he was looking at me." It was a song inspired by one Brown, written by another Brown and performed by two Browns. There just might be something to this family thing.

Jim Ed's and Maxine's recording of *Looking Back To See*[8] on Fabor Records, their first recording ever, made it to the top ten in the country music charts. He was on the map! He began setting his course for Nashville.

Package shows with Jim Reeves as the headliner followed. In between those shows, Jim Ed and Maxine would perform two years of grueling one-nighters, anything it took to make their audience grow.

This was before the Internet, before social media and YouTube were even thought about. My goodness! This was thirty years before Mark Zuckerberg, creator of Facebook, was even born. If you wanted to be a household name back then, you had to be visible to a lot of households, and the only way to do that was to hit the road.

When I began dating J.E. in 1961, The Browns had already toured Europe and had performed in just about every major venue in The United States. They had also made appearances on just about every major television show of our day including *American Bandstand, The Ed Sullivan Show, The Arthur Murray Show* and *The Jerry Lewis Telethon.*

With the release of their hit single *The Three Bells* in 1959, The Browns became the first group to cross over from the country music charts to the pop charts and secure the #1 spot on both of those national charts simultaneously. At its height of popularity the single of *The Three Bells* sold between 30 and 40 thousand copies a day in record stores—making it The Browns' first million selling record.

Two other back to back million sellers followed: *Scarlet Ribbons*[9] and *The Old Lamplighter.*[10]

When J.E. wanted something, he went for it. Now he had his sights on me.

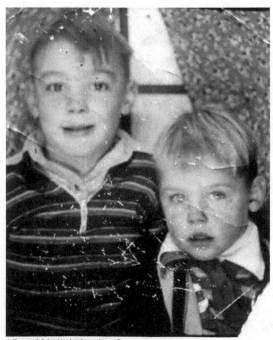

J.E. and his little brother, Raymond

*Maxine has said something funny.
I can tell by the expressions on
Bonnie and Jim Ed's faces.*

50

One of my favorite pictures of Maxine and J.E.

Jim Ed with Jim Reeves, Bonnie, and Charlie Lamb

Dee Kilpatrick, Del Wood, Hack Locklin, Maxine, Eddie Arnold, Hank Snow, Bonnie, Tom and Billie Perryman and Jim Ed.

The smoking jacket J.E. wore on our first date. Pictured here with Bonnie and Maxine.

Chapter Six

At the age of twenty-seven, J.E. was ready to settle down and start a family. At nineteen, I wasn't sure if I was ready to settle down. He had become a big fish in a big pond. As a known dancer and singer, primarily in Pine Bluff and surrounding areas, I was a big fish in a little pond. He had seen the world. I was just lacing up my traveling shoes.

J.E. confided that as a young man he would ride into Pine Bluff with his dad to get the log trucks serviced. It just so happened that the garage they used was Glover Motors, which was located across the street from my dad's store.

Although it's hard for me to believe, he said he can remember on several occasions a little blue eyed girl with spirit and pluck playing in front of the store—her blonde hair blowing wildly in the wind. That little girl had found a place in his heart. He never was able to get her out of his mind.

He said, "That little girl was you, Becky. I've been waiting for you to grow up."

Over and over he would tell me that God had sent me to him. I was the one with whom he was destined to be with. In the back of my mind, I thought, "If this is so, then who am I to question?"

Like me, J.E. had immense faith and an unwavering trust in The Lord. He probably knew every song ever published in the *Baptist Hymnal*[11] by heart, and when it came to the Bible itself, he was a true scholar. He read his *Bible* regularly, and he could find scriptures quickly and easily.

He also knew every book in the Bible in order. Now I had a problem with that. He could recite them in less than a minute.

I was convinced something was wrong with my copy of the Bible. Surely his Bible had less books in it than mine did.

He would laugh at me as I sat in frustration thumbing my way through the pages. "Oh where in the world is Ecclesiastes? Is it after Psalms or Proverbs? Oh my! Where in the world was Proverbs? Is I Thessalonians in the Old Testament or the New Testament?"

More often than not, the preacher would be finished reading the scripture before I had found the book much less the chapter and verse.

And memorizing Bible verses? Well, you could forget it. J.E. had almost perfect recall and could recite away. Not me. I couldn't recite a passage of scripture perfectly to save my life, although I did believe that understanding those scriptures and believing in the word and love of Jesus Christ would SAVE my life. In that thought, he and I were on the same page.

With his professed love for me, and his belief that God wanted us together, J.E. was beginning to talk about marriage. He wasn't asking me to marry him, mind you. There was never a question, as in, "Becky, will you marry me?"

He would make definitive statements that started something like, "Becky, when we get married, we'll live in Little Rock near my parents."

Becky, when we get married and have children, I bet our kids will be beautiful like you."

"Becky, we will be married sooner than you think. I can't wait. I would love to marry you!"

I'd shake my head in disbelief. We had only known each other a few short months. How could he be so sure?

But then I knew.

It was Christmas time. J.E. and I were extremely busy. We saw each other every chance we got, but those opportunities were few and far between now. He was performing all over the country with his sisters. I was singing with The Moonliters and working dancing engagements with Dorothy.

We had signed with a booking agency in Atlanta that booked us for a week's worth of dancing engagements at a military base in Huntsville, Alabama as part of Vaughn Monroe's show. Vaughn Monroe was a big band leader and singer who put over 70 songs on the music charts—primarily in the 1940s and '50s. Mr. Monroe was one of my dad's favorite singers, and during that time, he became a father figure to me and Dorothy. My dad was bustin' buttons at the thought of his little girl performing with one of his music heroes.

We soon followed that week in Hunstville with performances the entire week of Christmas in 1961 at the world famous Gus Stevens Restaurant and Supper Club in Biloxi, Mississippi. Gus was a man of Greek descent who believed good food, good drink and a memorable evening made for lifetime customers.

Many famous entertainers like Andy Griffith, Mel Torme, Rudy Vallee, Jerry Lee Lewis and Jane Mansfield filed through Gus' doors on a regular basis. I thought it was pretty cool that the names Becky Perry and Dorothy Vanlandingham would be added to that list.

I was excited to perform at Gus Stevens' Supper Club, but I was also feeling a little melancholy.

I remember so vividly sitting at a table in the club one evening having dinner before our performance. Christmas music was playing in the background. All of the customers were looking their holiday best. I looked around and saw the smiling faces. I heard the laughter. I saw a man and woman exchange little presents in a private moment. I saw tables filled with friends and family—everyone talking just a little too loud—drinking and eating just a little too much. Everyone looked so happy. Every now and then I'd catch the pine scent of a real Christmas tree; its big colorful bulbs illuminating a dark corner of the club in reds and greens.

And then it hit me. The band began to play *I'll Be Home For Christmas*.[12] That did it. I was homesick. I was missing my parents, missing my brother and sister, missing my friends and my town, but most of all, I was missing J.E.

You should have seen my face the next day when I received a visit from J.E. He was sure a sight for sore eyes.

He had just completed a couple of road dates with his sisters. He dropped them off in Little Rock, then jumped back in his car and drove 450 miles down to Biloxi to surprise me. He hugged me so hard, I thought he was going to break a rib. I thought he'd never let go. Truth be told, I didn't want him to.

He could only stay a short while in Biloxi because he had to be back in time to celebrate Christmas with his family in Arkansas. He cherished his family. Family meant everything to J.E., and I loved his loyalty.

I playfully chastised him for driving such a long way for such a short time with such little sleep. He said he could sleep later. He had to make sure his girl got her Christmas gifts before the big day.

You know how as years go by, you can't name what gifts you received on any given year at Christmas. Well, I can tell you exactly what J.E. gave me our first year together.

First I unwrapped the most beautifully decorated box with a big, full bow. Inside was a cashmere sweater. A cashmere sweater back then was like getting a fur coat.

The second package was much smaller. Inside was an exquisite diamond watch. He placed it around my wrist, and gave me a kiss. In return I gave him my heart.

I was in love with J.E.—not because of the gifts he had given me—but because of the way he wooed me, the way he treated me, and the way he treated everyone he met. He was a good person, and this good person was determined to win my affection. And he did. I was feeling like a ship tossed at sea sitting in Biloxi without him. J.E. was my harbor.

He informed me it was time to wed. He never did officially pop the question. But he knew the answer was yes when I pulled out my calendar, and we began to compare schedules.

Finding a date to marry wasn't going to be easy. I had a month of work obligations on the books, and he had even more. He was also helping his dad in the logging business. Although his dad got around amazingly well, Mr. Brown had lost his leg in a logging accident years earlier. J.E. pitched in with assistance anytime he could. He was a good son.

Miraculously we found a couple of hours in the books that we were both free. Without thinking, we hopped in the car and drove to a Justice of The Peace about ten miles outside of Little Rock. Just like his sister Bonnie and her husband Brownie, J.E. and I eloped.

It was a beautiful, brisk Friday afternoon—January 5, 1962. The temperature was about fifty degrees as I slid out the passenger side of the car and walked the few steps to the JP's front door. I vaguely remember the JP saying that on Sundays he was the preacher for the community too.

Admittedly, I was a little nervous. J.E. and I didn't tell a soul we were tying the knot. Our only witness that day was provided by the JP.

Of course we were both dressed up for our informal ceremony. I said, "I do" in an outfit I had sewn on my sewing machine: a little beige suit with an animal collar and animal buttons that I accented with little beige, boot like shoes. J.E. made a dapper figure in a suit and tie. We kissed and held hands and laughed like carefree kids.

Not a single picture was taken that day. There were no flowers or long flowery speeches. In fact, J.E. forgot to bring the wedding ring to the ceremony. He felt terrible about that, too, but I assured him it was ok.

We said our vows, and he turned to me with the biggest grin I'd ever seen and said, "Well hello, Mrs. J.E.! Hello, Mrs. Brown!" We were so excited.

Jim Ed sang his entire life. He had a song for everything, and our wedding day was no exception. Back in the car, my very own country music crooner with million selling records of his own, turned to me and sang a song composed by Frank Loesser, *A Bushel and a Peck*,[13] from the Broadway musical *Guys and Dolls*.

I love you a bushel and a peck

A bushel and a peck and a hug around the neck

A hug around the neck and a barrel and a heap

A barrel and a heap and I'm talking in my sleep.

I love you a bushel and a peck

A bushel and a peck though you make my heart a wreck

Make my heart a wreck, and you make my life a mess

Make my life a mess. Yes a mess of happiness.

I thought it was the most beautiful love song I had ever heard. Suddenly I was grinning bigger than he was when we said our I dos....but it wasn't so much the song as it was my wandering thoughts that put that big smile on my face.

I was thinking how Dorothy Vanlandingham was going to tease me when she found out J.E. and I were married. When we were girls hanging out having slumber parties, I was the one who liked rock-n-roll music and vowed to marry a man with a fabulous last name, and "Brown" wasn't exactly the grand name I had hoped for.

Here I was married to a COUNTRY music singer with the one syllable last name of BROWN. Dorothy Vanlandingham was going to have a field day.

I also thought about my first date with J.E. less than six months ago. A short time after we began to see each other, he confessed that the reason he called to ask me out in the first place was because his friend, Howard Peters, who was also at The Miss Pine Bluff Pageant that night, had dared him to give me a call and ask me out.

Can you believe it? My entire fifty-four year relationship with J.E. started on a dare! Well...I guess good things can come when one chooses to be daring.

We didn't break it to our families that we were married right away. For a couple of days, we simply basked in the fact that we had our very own little secret. Although, admittedly, most of that basking was done over the telephone.

J.E. and I didn't have a proper honeymoon, at least by most people's standards. We said our "I dos" and a few hours later we said our "goodbyes." It was a miracle we found a couple of hours in our day in which we were both free. We actually spent our first night as a married couple in separate towns.

I still had engagements on the books, I was teaching dance in Pine Bluff, and I had a million loose ends to tie up before I could make the move to Little Rock. J.E. had to get back to perform a show that weekend.

It was so frustrating! Eloping was crazily, wonderfully insane! He was so anxious to get married. Once I said I'd marry him, he insisted on getting married immediately.

So here we were without any real plan — Mr & Mrs. Brown. Now what?

We were anxious to start our lives together as husband and wife, so we decided to work as hard as we could, as fast as we could, to get me to Little Rock.

A few days into our marriage we broke the news of our elopement to our families. I told my family. J.E. told his. Both sets of parents were pleased that we had pledged our love to each other although maybe a little disappointed that we didn't have a church wedding where they could have witnessed our union.

Among J.E., Bonnie and Maxine, Maxine was the only sibling to have a church ceremony. Maxine was also the most vocal family member to voice her doubts about our elopement. I don't think she was ready for him to settle down. Maxine was losing her playmate on the road.

Breaking the news to Maxine was one conversation I was glad I didn't have to be a part of first hand.

It took several weeks before I was able to call Little Rock home, and when I did move in with J.E. our first home was a trailer. It was more like an RV really—used by the Brown family as a comfortable base camp that they would move from location to location as needed for their logging operation.

Even now I can close my eyes and see the layout perfectly. The space was confined and took a little getting used to for a full time residence, but it actually was a nice motor home. There was a bedroom up front and then a pretty large living area and kitchen. In the back of the trailer there was another bedroom, a bathroom and a closet. Again, the space was small, but newlyweds in love don't need a lot of space.

So here we were. In our new home. A cozy trailer. Just the two of us. J.E. and me. Me and J.E. How romantic can you get? It was indeed a very romantic time for us—for a few days.

Then a funny thing happened. There was laundry to do. There were dishes to wash. The bed needed making. The floors needed mopping. The toilet needed cleaning. The shower needed scrubbing. The clothes needed ironing. The garbage needed to be taken out. And I was a perfectionist.

Whenever J.E. walked back in the door from a singing engagement or a day out helping his dad, I made sure the house was spotless upon his return. Every task was done to the letter, but all those tasks were time consuming. When was I going to find time for my career?

And then there was the cooking! Remember. J.E. was used to his momma's cooking. All of his life, he'd had the best home cooking in twenty counties. I grew up with a family who owned a grocery store. Whenever I was hungry, I'd pull something off of a shelf, open a can and heat it up.

Oh my goodness! Did I sign up for this? No one told me marriage would be this much work. You can't wear a diamond watch and a cashmere sweater when you're cleaning a toilet!

This nineteen year old dancer/singer/gymnast/ model was a lot of things, but Betty Crocker wasn't one of them. However, if I needed to be a domestic goddess to make this marriage work, then bring on domesticity!

I started by setting the alarm clock for 5am every morning. Bleary eyed with no makeup and tangled hair, I'd head for the kitchen. J.E. didn't like sandwiches. He liked fried chicken for lunch. That made me very happy, because I was good at frying chicken. After all, I did grow up in a family that owned a poultry market! So there I'd stand in my pajamas, up before the rooster, frying chicken for him at our little stove in our little RV humming a happy tune.

J.E. would soon be headed out the door to help his dad with the logging business. I'd start the chicken; then I'd wake him up. He'd get dressed, give me a kiss at the door, and off he'd go into the early morning with my freshly fried chicken in his lunch box.

I'm not sure whatever happened to all that chicken I fried so painstakingly at 5am every morning. Jim Ed might have eaten it; he might not have. I soon learned that he was toting two lunches to work.

His momma also prepared a lunch for him everyday and sent it to him by way of his dad. Momma Brown didn't trust me to feed her only son properly. That had been her job for twenty-seven years, and she enjoyed spoiling J.E.

I truly didn't mind that she wanted to prepare her son a daily lunch. I just minded that I was getting up at 5am to fix him that superfluous meal when I could have slept for at least two more hours. I was beginning to think that marriage may not be for me. Surely I could squeeze a career in somewhere!

I was too busy sifting flour. He probably loved his momma's biscuits better than anything in the world, and he wanted me to learn how to make them.

I don't know how many times, I'd call her on the phone and say, "Momma Brown, this is your favorite daughter-in-law. I need help. I'm trying to make your biscuits, and I'm not doing something right."

With each call, Momma Brown would patiently share her recipe and give me tips on how to make my biscuits better. With each new batch of biscuits, J.E. would say, "Becky, these biscuits don't look anything like Momma's biscuits, and they sure don't taste like Momma's biscuits."

J.E. wasn't upset. He was just perplexed.

I'd say, "J.E., what do you want me to do with these biscuits?"

He would laugh, put his arm around me and say, "It's ok, Sweetheart. You can just try again."

I loved his good-natured teasing. We teased each other a lot. It reminded me that we were in this marriage together through better or worse...and those rock hard biscuits were some of the worse.

I finally learned to make those biscuits to perfection, but it took a lot of practice. I actually went over to Momma Brown's house and watched her make her biscuits in her kitchen. Then I made the biscuits while she watched. I thought we were a pretty good team.

I learned so much from Momma Brown, and I think I was a constant source of amusement for her.

Momma Brown made a wilted leaf salad that was so good. It was one of my favorites. One day I called her and asked her where in the world I could buy wilted lettuce to make that salad. I thought she was going to hurt herself she was laughing so hard. She couldn't catch her breath.

She explained to me that the salad was made with a leaf lettuce, green onions, radishes and bacon. The salad dressing was made from the warm bacon drippings and vinegar. Pour the warm dressing over the salad, and the lettuce wilts.

Sometimes I just accepted the fact that I'm a natural blonde.

J.E.'s Mom and Dad, Birdie and Floyd Brown

Soon after we married in 1962

Chapter Seven

Something isn't right.

I don't feel well.

What in the world is wrong with me?

For days upon days, this was my routine. Even the thought of food turned my stomach.

I was young, but I wasn't stupid. I kept a close account of my menstrual cycle, and I knew I had missed a period. I was pretty sure I was pregnant.

How could this happen? Well, I knew how this could happen, but how could this happen to me?

I was nineteen years old. I was a newlywed. I was trying to make a marriage work and trying to find time to fit in my career. Motherhood wasn't in my plans. Not right now. But then I took a deep breath and realized this was God's plan. I picked up the telephone and made an appointment to see a doctor in Little Rock.

I remember my doctor had the same last name as a character on a television series— McClintock. Somehow that made me feel more at ease. Dr. McClintock was a young doctor with a wonderful bedside manner. He was so kind.

I told him my symptoms, and he ordered a blood test. When the results of the test came back, Dr. McClintock walked in to the examination room smiling from ear to ear. "Congratulations, Becky! You're pregnant! You're going to be a Momma."

For a split second my world was frozen in time. My mind was empty of thought. I couldn't think at all.

Then my mind began to race.

I was shocked, but not too shocked. After all, I thought pregnancy was a big possibility, didn't I? Wasn't that the reason I was here? But to hear it said out loud. "Becky, you're pregnant!" Wow! Just wow. I was going to be a mother. I was excited. But at that very moment, Dr. McClintock seemed more excited than I was.

It was slowly sinking in. In less than a year of marriage, the two of us would become the three of us, and what if I had twins? Twins do run in my family.

I'm rolling the word around in my head.

I vowed then and there that I was going to be the best mother I could be. I have months to go before I meet my baby. But I already know. I love this child.

I remember driving home that day and waiting for J.E. to get home from work. I wondered how he was going to take this news.

When he walked through the front door, I didn't do any of the clever things that young wives do today to reveal to their husbands that they are about to become parents. Instead I used the straight forward approach.

J.E. came home, put down his lunch box and gave me a hug. I backed up a foot or two so I could see his face, and then I just blurted it out.

"Guess what!" I beamed.

"I'm pregnant!"

Now look who had the shocked expression!

Just like me, for a split second, he was frozen in time. Then his mouth flew open as the news was sinking in, and in the blink of an eye, he began to grin from ear to ear.

He had confided to me numerous times that he wanted a family of his own. He was ready. He wanted to have babies with me and watch them grow, he wanted his children to have our grandchildren and watch them grow, and he wanted to grow old with me as our entire family grew older together. It was a beautiful dream, but I didn't know that dream would become a reality just a few months into our marriage. And yet, that was exactly what was happening. Since J.E. was eight years older than I was, and Maxine and Bonnie had already added a few branches to their family trees, Uncle J.E. was eager to become a dad.

The first thing a jubilant J.E. said to me after I delivered the news that I was pregnant was, "I sure hope it's a boy!" I didn't say it out loud, but I thought to myself, "A girl would be nice too."

———————————————

Things just got a little more hectic in the Brown household. I didn't think that was possible.

I continued to teach dance classes in Pine Bluff. The extra money would come in handy with a baby on the way. J.E. continued to help his father in the logging business when he wasn't on the road, although he still toured regularly with his sisters.

The Browns last two singles *The Old Lamplighter* and *Send Me The Pillow You Dream On*[14] fell short of the country top ten. But they did earn respectable charts positions of #20 and #23. Whenever The Browns performed, they were fan favorites.

There was just so much to do, and on top of it all, we began to make preparations to move to a larger home. The cozy trailer was fine for the two of us, but it was no place to raise a baby.

Perhaps my greatest challenge during this time in my life was the morning sickness. It only hit me once a day now. But like Connie Smith sang in her yet-to-be-released country classic, that queasy feeling hit me *once a day, every day, all day long.*[15]

For the life of me, I couldn't gain any weight. I knew the baby needed nourishment, but it was difficult to supply that nourishment when everything I ate wanted to come back up, and usually did. I fought nausea for the entire length of my pregnancy.

That first year of our marriage was a balancing act. Although looking back at it now, I wouldn't change a thing.

Most of our socializing as a young married couple was with J.E.'s parents. Come to think of it, when he and I were dating, we never once went bowling or to a movie like most couples do. We even did most of our courting at the Browns' home.

We spent most of our time with his parents because when we went out in public, Jim Ed would be bombarded by other diners in the restaurants who recognized him as the lead singer of The Browns. He was a celebrity, and invariably we'd be approached by well wishing strangers right about the time our waitress was serving our food.

Poor J.E. I don't think he was able to eat very many hot meals back then, but he never once complained.

He remembered those times when nobody knew his name. He remembered how much work it took to make his name a household name in country music, and he understood that we were enjoying the life we had because of those fans.

If a stranger wanted to talk with him, he made time for them—even if that time was dinner time—and every time, that stranger walked away from his table a friend.

The other reason why we spent so much time at the Brown's house was J.E. just loved his momma's cooking. My own cooking had greatly improved. I went from opening a can of pork and beans, to being able to produce a steaming pot of pinto beans just the way he liked them. But in a strapping boy's mind, there's no cooking like Momma's cooking, and Momma Brown loved to spoil him.

She honestly catered to his every whim. He never took advantage of her kindness. But let's just say, he knew he had it good.

When J.E. was in his early twenties, he and Elvis enlisted in the Army about the same time. After a hitch in Germany, he was assigned to the Arsenal in Pine Bluff. I never asked him if his family pulled strings to get him back home for the remainder of his service, but I always suspected that he managed to secure this duty just so he could be close enough to home to eat his momma's cooking most nights.

Momma Brown was constantly inviting us over to dinner. If she had it her way, we'd have been there every night.

I honestly didn't mind—at first. My day started at 5am cooking J.E. a breakfast and a lunch to see him through the day. Cooking dinner was one less thing I had to think about—especially when my morning (all day) sickness kicked in, and I was feeling queasy from even the smell of food. I knew I had it good too.

One night J.E. came home with a surprise for me—a dinner guest. We seldom had company in the evening because we were usually at the Brown's home.

Our guest was Howard Peters. Howard was the friend who dared him to call me after The Miss Pine Bluff Pageant.

The house was absolutely spotless, and I was ready for dinner when J.E. and Howard waltzed in. J.E. quipped, "Hey, Good Lookin'! What ya got cookin'? We're starving!"

Everything was going fine until it was time to serve my dinner. In my defense, I wasn't prepared to entertain. A phone call and some advanced warning would have been nice.

You should have seen J.E.'s face when I served him and Howard a Chef Boyardee Pizza!

For the life of me, I didn't know why he had such a look of dismay. I cooked!

I couldn't help it if our pizza started out in a box. I made the crust by putting a powdery package in a bowl and adding water and vegetable oil, and I opened the can of pizza sauce and spread it out over what appeared to be dough. I even sprinkled on the little packet of Parmesan Cheese and popped it in the oven for 20 minutes. To my way of thinking, I had provided a delicious, home-cooked meal.

J.E. let me know real quick that a box mix of Chef Boyardee Pizza wasn't an acceptable meal. He tried to be "Man of The House" stern, but he just couldn't pull it off.

I thought the three of us would never stop laughing.

I felt horrible and continued to apologize, "J.E., I'm sorry. I feel terrible that's what I cooked tonight. I'm sorry."

Of course I was apologizing through bouts of giggles.

"I'm sorry, J.E." More giggles.

Howard and J.E. just wouldn't let it go either. Howard kept saying, "J.E., you've got big trouble on your hands. BIG TROUBLE!"

Once the laughter subsided, we settled in to eat my master piece. It was awful! No. Saying it was awful would be a kind statement.

It was then J.E. confided to me that it wouldn't have mattered if this pizza was topped with some of his favorite fried chicken. He still wouldn't have liked it. He didn't eat pizza at all. He never did like pizza. That night was a live-and-learn experience for these newlyweds. The laughter started again.

The situation became ridiculously funny.

Today I smile whenever I see a Chef Boyardee label.

Pizza was never one of his favorites. He learned to tolerate it in those later years with kids and grandkids, but it would have to have anchovies on it for him. Unlike that funny night with Howard Peters as a dinner guest. That night became one of our favorite memories.

It was during our first year of marriage, before our baby was born, that J.E. and I drove down to Henderson, Texas to spend some time with perhaps two of the finest people I have ever had the honor of knowing—Tom and Billie Perryman. J.E. wanted so badly for us to become good friends.

He need not have worried. Talk about loving two people instantly. They became part our extended family.

In the 1950s, Tom was a disc jockey who did a lot of the booking for *The Louisiana Hayride*. Tom was friends with Jim Reeves, and it was Jim who introduced Tom to The Browns. Like me, The Browns took to Tom instantly.

According to J.E., whenever The Browns were anywhere within a hundred mile radius of the Perryman family, they'd stop by Tom and Billie's home, and the two of them welcomed Maxine, J.E. and Bonnie with open arms. The Perryman's made sure The Browns had a home cooked meal to eat and warm beds to sleep in—even if it meant making a pallet on the floor for the kids. The Perryman household was home away from home for the Brown family.

Eventually Tom became an agent and personal manager for The Browns. The family trusted him that much. Tom introduced The Browns to a young Elvis Presley. And it was Tom who booked a tour of Texas with Elvis and The Browns—giving The Browns top billing.

On the drive down to Texas in 1961, J.E. was entertaining me with stories about Tom Perryman—how Tom helped get them out of a bad recording contract, how he helped them secure a new label, how he booked numerous one-nighters for The Browns in the southeast, and how he always made them laugh. Tom Perryman was a character.

When I first met Tom, I knew he was special. He was a lanky man—tall and thin, with a thick head of dark hair. He wore glasses, even in his thirties, but those glasses couldn't hide the mischievous twinkle in his eyes. And talk! Goodness! Tom could have talked Matt Dillion out of his marshal's badge. Tom and his Texas twang were a little loud, sometimes a little brusque. But those eyes were always twinkling, and it seemed Tom could get away with saying just about anything without offending.

His wife Billie is an olive skinned beauty—full figured with wonderful curves and a tiny waist. I just about passed out the first time I heard Tom drawl, "Come on, you big tub of lard. We got to get going!" Billie, just smiled, popped an equally quick quip back at Tom and off they went.

As of this writing, the two have been married over 70 years.

When I met Tom, he was General Manager and business partner with Jim Reeves as co-owner of radio station KGRI in Henderson, Texas. With Billie's support, Tom went on to become General Manager of WMTS in Murfreesboro, TN, which went on to become the CMA Station of The Year under his direction. He later became Vice President of Jim Reeves Enterprises and was inducted into the national DJ Hall of Fame.

The greatest honor Tom and Billie ever bestowed upon J.E. and I was their friendship.

To this day we are still faithful friends. We know where most of the bones are buried, and chances are we buried some of those bones together.

J.E. and I were building a life together. I enjoyed meeting his friends, and I was ready to make the move to our new home. With a baby on the way, we were going to need more space.

We decided to move a short distance away to a home that had been Maxine's home at one time in North Little Rock. It was a three bedroom / one bathroom 40's style home on Lakeshore Drive with a nice sized, eat-in kitchen and a living room window that overlooked the lake across the street. I loved the fact that our new home was perched on top of a small hill, and I could see the sun's reflection on the water in the late afternoon.

One of the most unique things about our Lakewood Neighborhood was the location of the famous Old Mill that attracted tourists to our area. The Old Mill was located one block from our house. The mill was built in 1934 as a recreation of an 1880s water powered grist mill. What made the Old Mill famous was its strategic presence in the opening scene of an Academy Award winning classic, the 1939 movie *Gone With The Wind*. It was and still is a Little Rock landmark.

Back when we lived on Lake Shore Drive and I needed to give directions to someone new coming to the house, all I'd have to say is, "Do you know where The Old Mill is? You do? Well, you're practically at our front door!"

I'll never forget when Mr. and Mrs. Brown gave us furniture they had in storage from a previous move to help us furnish the Lakeshore home. Most of the furniture in the trailer were built-ins. We were starting from scratch. That kindness made things so much easier on us. Instead of searching for beds, couches and tables, I was able to concentrate my efforts on decorating the nursery.

I had no idea in 1961 if our baby was going to be a boy or a girl, but I decided to paint the nursery light blue. I then found a picture that I liked of a boy and girl on bended knees; their eyes closed; their heads bowed reverently in prayer. I put those art lessons to use that I had in my childhood, and I set about creating a mural for the nursery wall.

I've always been able to lose myself in my art. Creating something is almost a form of meditation for me. I can block out all other thoughts and think solely on the project at hand. In this case I'd think about what the picture itself represented.

With every stroke, I'd think how my baby was going to wake up every morning and see this painting of these two children in conversation with God. I'd think about the love I had in my heart for J.E. and this baby I had yet to meet—our baby.

There was so much to do to get ready for Baby Brown, but I did manage a few outings during this time for pure fun. One of those occasions was the time Momma Brown decided to take us girls to the horse races in Hot Springs—Maxine, Bonnie and me. Lord have mercy, we must have been a sight to see.

I wasn't the only one pregnant that day. All three of us girls were pregnant at the same time! Two babies were due in November and one baby was due in October.

Can you just picture it? One matriarch and three pregnant women sitting in a box seat at the race track surrounded by a bunch of screaming men urging their horses on, and the one screaming the loudest was Momma Brown.

And I just wish I had a picture of us after the horse races, as we were going to dinner, before we made the drive back to Little Rock. There we were waiting to be seated in a nice restaurant. Finally our table was ready and the waiter asked us to follow him. I remember walking to the table in a single file line behind Momma Brown.

Can you just see those three pregnant silhouettes passing your table in a single line? I bet we looked like a line of baby ducks obediently following right behind Momma Duck in a funny kind of stair step way—tallest to shortest—Maxine, Bonnie and me...baby bellies bulging.

Come to think of it, we were probably walking like ducks. The mental image of it all still makes me giggle—especially as I recall my sister Lynda was pregnant at the same time as we were. There was actually four of us due at about the same time.

Jim Ed and Becky celebrate Vicky Perryman's wedding to Gary Petty, with Jimmy and Mae Newman.

Jimmy C. Newman, Tom Perryman and Jim Ed at Vicky Perryman's wedding to Gary Petty

Chapter Eight

In the 1950s, some psychologists devised a personality test that categorized a person as either an A-Personality or a B-Personality. An A-Personality was defined as someone who was outgoing, aggressive, impatient, anxious, rigid, and overly competitive; whereas, a B-Personality was characterized as someone who was more relaxed, easygoing, harbored less stress and was usually more creative.

Although I enjoyed competing in various events and competitions, I never got upset if I didn't win. I always tried my best, and I was proud that I tried. I thought the journey was just as important as the destination.

So, I consider myself a B-Personality type. I'm an easy going person who is usually happy going with the flow. I don't want to upset the applecart unless I absolutely have to, but when I do speak up, and that small A-Personality part on myself surfaces, I hope someone is around to catch those apples.

I've admitted that the first six months of our marriage were an adjustment. However, I also believe those first months of any marriage are an adjustment for newlyweds. This is the time in a marriage when you're learning new things about your partner. Sometimes you learn new things about yourself in the process.

You have to remember our courtship lasted less than six months. We didn't even know what we didn't know about each other, but we made a vow that we had a lifetime to learn.

I loved J.E. and he loved me, and we loved being married. We were happy. But in truth, I was a nineteen year old perfectionist ready to pave our own road as a married couple. J.E. was a twenty-seven year old man ready to pave an additional lane in the family highway.

Even as a young woman, I knew that the foundation for a good marriage was built on compromise. However, in the beginning, it felt like I was doing most of the compromising. I was the one always saying, "I'm sorry." And because I was that B-Personality, and wanted every one to be happy, I went with the flow. Until I couldn't.

I felt like it was my responsibility as J.E.'s wife to make sure our house was spotless, the meals were prepared to his liking, and I was waiting for him when he came home after work. If this sounds a little like a scene out of *Leave It To Beaver*, then so be it. Maybe it does sound a bit like that when you put it in print, but that's the way it was.

The big difference between me and June Cleaver, however, was the fact that I also worked outside of the home. But I never felt like my "responsibilities" were a chore. I loved doing things for J.E., and he loved doing things for me.

We still spent a lot of our evenings at the Browns' house. Momma Brown continued to pamper J.E. But as I observed and learned, she loved to pamper all of her children.

I think the loss of their beloved son Raymond all those years ago was always in the back of her mind. With the intimate knowledge that someone you love could be ripped from your life, Mrs. Brown made a concentrated effort to show her love in a variety of ways daily.

I remember one night, in our newlywed stage, my own heart was broken. I had no intention of saying a word, but my tears inevitably gave me away.

J.E. and his father had slipped into a semi-regular routine of going out after a hard day of logging and having a few drinks. By the end of the day, I was ready to see my husband and spend some time with him. I missed him while he was gone, but I accepted the fact that father/son enjoyed their bonding time. So I never spoke up.

On this particular evening, I was sitting by myself on the sofa flipping through a magazine when they returned to the house after 9pm with Mrs. Brown in tow. I was surprised to see Momma Brown with them. J.E. explained they called her on the phone to join them. My phone never rang.

J.E. walked over to me and gave me a kiss hello. He said he was starving, and needed something to eat. I told him I had prepared him a nice dinner, and I wrapped it up and saved it for him in the oven. I was trying to keep it warm.

Momma Brown said, "Come on back to our house, J.E. I'll fix you something good and hot!" ...and he went.

After they left, I sat there on the couch for a minute in stunned silence. Then the tears began to flow.

Now in his defense, I never said, "Don't go." I never said, "I've been patiently waiting for you. I miss you." I just smiled and stood there until they walked out the door.

I also knew that Momma Brown wasn't trying to undermine me. She would never do that.

I promise, Momma Brown never thought that taking J.E. to her house at 9pm and cooking a meal for him was overstepping any boundaries. There were no boundaries. This is what she had always done, and all she knew to do. She loved taking care of everybody. She hadn't fully realized yet, that taking care of her son was my job now.

I don't remember how long he was gone, but when he came back, I was still waiting up for him. Still crying. I couldn't seem to stop. My face was swollen. My eyes were red. I felt like a rag mop. I was hurt, and at the same time, I was a little mad at myself for feeling hurt. How could I be hurt? He was going over to his family's house to have a late dinner for goodness sakes. But I also heard this soft, little voice in my head asking, "Where do you fit in, Becky?"

He took one look at me, and it was as if someone had switched on a light bulb. He gently put his arms around me and rocked me back and forth. He wiped away the tears from my eyes as tears began to well in his own eyes.

J.E. never said he was sorry. Instead he whispered, "I love you, Becky. I love you so much."

Over and over I heard those words. "I love you, Becky."

It's amazing how big hurts seem to melt away with those three little words—I love you.

We didn't say a lot to each other that night. We didn't have to. We just held on to each other. Neither one of us wanted to let go. Sometimes you really do say it best when you say nothing at all.

Things began to change.

Every now and then that A-Personality side of me would exert itself and push right past that easy going B-side of me. The night I poured out all of the alcohol in our house was one of those times.

When J.E. and I first got married, his family owned a liquor store that stood right in front of The Trio Club. J.E. confided that there was a time in his life when he tried to drink that liquor store dry.

I couldn't imagine that. The man I knew could never have done that. I knew J.E. drank. I knew he often went out and had drinks with his father before coming home at night, but I never saw him in a state that some would call "wasted."

When I was growing up, alcohol was seldom in our home. My parents just weren't drinkers. I didn't grow up surrounded by alcohol, and I had decided I didn't want to be surrounded by alcohol now—especially with a baby on the way.

I understood that a lot of his "music crowd" liked to party. All three of The Browns— Jim Ed, Maxine and Bonnie—learned to drink adult beverages to fit in with that crowd; and The Browns were fast learners.

For several months, I had a promise that I made to God years earlier, swirling in my heart. Back when I was baptized in the sixth grade, I promised that I was going to be the person who would glorify HIS name. I didn't think getting tipsy glorified God.

As a teenager, if my date took me to a party where kids were drinking, I'd ask him to drive me home. Several times when J.E. and I were dating, he'd ask if I wanted to take a sip of his drink and honestly, I did take a sip or two. Every time I did, I'd find myself in the bathroom throwing up. If drinking was an acquired taste, then I was fine without any taste.

I never said a word to him about his after-work-time with his father, but I became leery when J.E. began to bring bottles of Crown Royal into the house. He never drank beer. He never liked the taste of it, but he enjoyed his drink of Canadian Whiskey and Coke in the evening.

I thought, I can't control what goes out of this house, but I can sure control what goes in it. I opened the kitchen cabinet and pulled down the bottle of Crown. There wasn't much alcohol in the bottle, but I seem to remember a surge of empowerment as I began to pour that whiskey down the drain. Every last drop gone. Then I tossed the empty bottle into the trash.

When J.E. came home, I told him what I had done. I explained my promise to God to glorify HIS name, and I came forward with my confession that I did not want alcohol in our home. I had been quiet for far too long about my feelings.

The timing couldn't have been more perfect. J.E. put one bottle down just in time to pick up another. Delivery time for our baby was two months away, but I was beginning to have contractions.

God, please don't let this baby come now! This baby still has some growing to do!

I don't remember who rushed me to the hospital when I went into premature labor. I know J.E. was deep in the woods logging with his dad. This was before the age of cell phones, and I had no way to reach him. Even if I could have called him on a cell, I don't think there would have been reception in the remote locations he and his dad ventured. I'm thinking now I might have driven myself to the hospital the first time. I say the first time, because there were many times that I visited St. Vincent's thinking "This is it!"

This scene played out several times over the next several weeks with J.E. and Momma Brown by my side every time thereafter. This pattern was kind of like the instructions on the back of a shampoo bottle: Apply. Rinse. Repeat. Only my instructions read: Labor pains. Hospital. Go home.

On September 13, 1962, I felt those same rapid labor pains. They weren't excruciating, but they sure got my attention. I started not to say anything. But I told J.E., and he and Momma Brown insisted we go to the hospital—just in case. It's a good thing we did, because on this September day, we were going to have a baby.

I wasn't frightened. I was ready to meet this child who had tried for weeks to kick his or her way out of solitude.

Mrs Brown was by my side saying, "Breathe, Becky. Just breathe." J.E. made phone calls to my family in Pine Bluff informing them that the stork was about to make a landing.

I remember him holding my hand and saying, "Rebecca Sue, we're going to have a baby today!" Then it becomes a blur.

Back in 1962 hospitals didn't have the elaborate birthing suites that they do now, and husbands weren't invited to participate in delivery or even watch from the wings in the delivery room. J.E. was relegated to the waiting room with the rest of the family while the doctor lulled me into a *twilight sleep,* a state of consciousness in which I was sleepy yet responsive.

When I "woke up," I was a mother!

Dr. McClintock walked into the waiting room and made the big announcement. "IT'S A BOY!"

Because he was premature, the nurses placed our son immediately into an incubator and wheeled him down to the nursery. I was awake now, and couldn't stand it. I knew I had to see our baby.

As soon as the nurses left my room, I got out of bed, slipped out the door, and began to make my way down a long hallway to the nursery. When the nurses saw me in the hall, they started to panic. "Mrs. Brown, what are you doing? You can't walk around like that. You just had a baby! Please stop. Let us get you a wheel chair !"

I wasn't having it. I told them I was just fine, and I was. I honestly didn't feel any pain. There was only one thing I was feeling at that moment, and that was the need to see my baby. A Grizzly Bear in my path would not have stopped me.

I had a dream weeks before he was born, and I knew he was going to be a boy and what he was going to look like. And there he was. My dream was right. The card placed in front of the incubator read Baby Brown, but I would have known him without that identification card.

He was such a little thing. He still had some growing to do. But he was absolutely perfect, and my goodness, he had a head full of dark hair, just like J.E. Of course, you know I'm going to say it: he was the most beautiful baby in the world!

We named him after J.E.—James Edward Brown, Jr.

Jim Ed was so proud!

On the way back to my room, hospital attendants once again began to squawk. I continued to tell them that I didn't need a wheel chair. I was fine! I wasn't walking down the hallway. It was more like I was floating down the hallway on cloud nine.

When the nurse walked into our room, she walked over to J.E. and said, "Here you go, Dad. Your baby wants to say hello."

It was an emotional moment for me, watching him cradle our newborn son so tenderly in his arms. Momma Brown was the second person to hold him. My heart was full of love watching her look down at her newborn grandson with such adoration. Then she turned to me and ever so gently transferred my baby boy into my own arms. He was home. It felt so right. This was all part of God's plan. I felt complete.

My eyes filled with tears. I felt so much JOY.

I felt so many emotions all at once. This sweet baby boy was a part of me and J.E. No matter what I would ever do from this day forward, I knew in my heart, that I could do no greater thing with my life than to give life to our child and raise him to be the best person he could be. This was my purpose. Those first few moments in that hospital room were life changing.

Dr. McClintock told me that when I left the hospital, our son would have to stay. Because he was premature, he needed to gain his strength. J.E. and I were looking at weeks of being apart from our son.

When he drove me home, it was a bittersweet moment for us. We were thankful we had a baby who was healthy, but disappointed that we were going home without him. Until the day we brought our son home, I drove back and forth to the hospital every day just to see him. If I could have rented a room there I would have.

I just can't begin to explain the pride and joy J.E. and I felt when we walked out of those hospital doors with our baby boy. Thinking back now, it was almost like a dream. He drove home slowly with our precious cargo in the car. We laughed about it later. Everything was the same, but nothing was the same. Two young, first-time parents finding their way!

That first night at home, I carefully laid our beautiful baby boy in his cradle next to our bedside. He was in peaceful slumber. I walked back into the nursery to turn off the light, and there I saw it: the mural I painted of the two little children praying to Jesus. I stopped in my tracks and said a prayer.

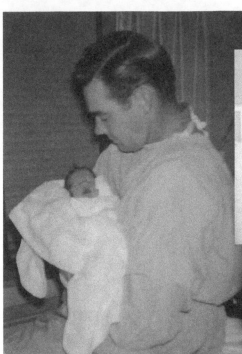

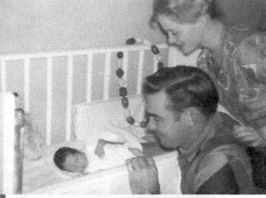

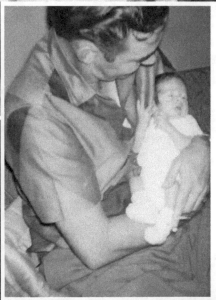

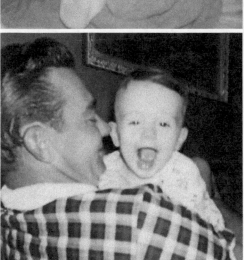

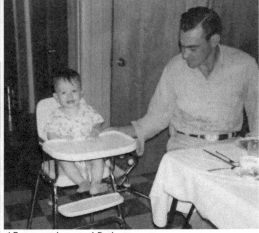

J.E. was such a good Dad.

75

Quiet moment with Buster and Becky

Our home on Williamsburg Road, Brentwood, TN.
Maryland Farms indoor horse track was behind our
house. The bus in the driveway we called Big Red.

J.E. holding Buster, leans on his '56 Chevy

Chapter Nine

Life was good.

Jim Ed, Maxine and Bonnie all had families now, but with those families came obligations. The Browns all had ties to Arkansas, but they continued to perform big shows miles away from their home base. They were traveling more and more by chartered plane during this time in their careers.

Because The Browns had achieved success in a variety of musical genres, they could perform on country, pop or rock shows. They were accepted everywhere. One night they could play a country music venue. The next night—a grand concert hall. The next night—a night club. Because the venues were different and the crowds were different at each venue, The Browns would change their set list accordingly to accommodate those different kinds of music lovers. Versatility equaled workability.

Bonnie and Maxine had nannies and house keepers to help them while they were on the road. My help came in the form of J.E.'s Aunt Maggie who resembled my beloved Aunt Florence from my childhood—in both looks and sweet temperament.

When our son was little, Aunt Maggie came to live with us for a while to help me with everyday household chores while I found my footing as a new mother. Aunt Maggie also helped me take care of our baby while I worked, and she taught me how to make her famous cornbread. Good cooks just ran in the Brown family.

The first time I heard Aunt Maggie call our son "Buster Brown," I thought to myself, "Oh No!" Buster Brown was an iconic comic strip character created sixty years earlier and had been adopted by the Brown Shoe Company as their mascot. Buster Brown was a mischievous pretty boy who dressed in what became known as a Buster Brown suit— a little suit jacket with dress shorts.

I'd hear Aunt Maggie say, "Come here you little Buster! Come here, Buster Brown!"

J.E. and I would say, "Oh, no Aunt Maggie! You can't call him that. You can't call him Buster Brown!" But the name stuck.

From that time forward, James Edward Brown, Jr. became Buster Brown.

Today our son is in his fifties, and we still call him Buster. I can't imagine calling him anything else.

While we were in Little Rock, we had an unexpected visit from Jim and Mary Reeves. I loved them from the first time I met them at The Trio Club back when J.E. and I were dating. It was apparent to me then how much they thought of J.E.

J.E. met Jim Reeves the first day he and Maxine ever stepped foot in a studio to record their first song *Looking Back To See* in 1954 in Shreveport, Louisiana—home of *The Louisiana Hayride*. J.E. was shocked to discover that Jim would be playing guitar on his session that day, along with piano great Floyd Cramer.

Jim was a *Hayride* regular and already had two #1 hits under his belt on Abbott Records, *Mexican Joe*[16] and *Bimbo*.[17] J.E. was a fan of Jim's music, and to think that Jim was playing on HIS record, just amazed him.

J.E. and Jim became fast friends. In those early days of J.E.'s career, he and Maxine, and eventually Bonnie, toured with Jim Reeves.

Many a time Jim, who was eleven years older than J.E. and had more experience on the road, helped The Browns out of quite a few predicaments that could have been disastrous for them. This group of country music crusaders had traveled more than a few miles together and had hundreds of road stories to prove it.

Jim and Mary were just passing through town, on their way to another show, when they arrived at our home for lunch. We had a nice visit, but it almost seemed as if their visit was a mission of sorts.

Jim and Mary wanted us to move to Nashville.

Jim laid it all out for us. J.E.'s record label, RCA, was in Nashville. The Grand Ole Opry was in Nashville. WSM Radio was in Nashville. The Disc Jockey Convention was in Nashville. All of the best studios and studio musicians were in Nashville. Most of J.E.'s fellow artist friends were in Nashville.

Jim reminded him that he would soon be thirty. Jim thought if J.E. wanted to continue a career in music, he needed to establish himself in Nashville too. We needed Nashville roots in order to grow.

There is an abundance of truth in the old saying *out of sight, out of mind*. J.E. knew that only too well. He promised Jim he would give his advice some deep thought and come to a decision.

Coming to that decision was a struggle for us.

For one thing J.E. didn't want to leave his dad in a bind. For years he had pulled double duty without complaint—helping his dad with the logging business while continuing to perform and tour with The Browns. J.E. was burning the candle at both ends.

Then there were those ego-deflating seeds planted by his dad. I don't think things were said to intentionally hurt J.E. I think Mr. Brown just didn't want to lose his best friend and partner.

He would often say things like, "J.E., when are you going to give this music thing up? You'll never be able to make it in the music business. You need a real job!"

That's funny. I thought The Browns were making it in the music business. They had placed twelve singles securely on the Billboard charts. Their crossover hit *The Three Bells* topped the country charts for two and a half months. They took Europe by storm, played the Grand Ole Opry regularly, and performed with music greats of all genres including Ricky Nelson and Bill Haley & The Comets.

In the end, J.E. had to follow his heart. Buster was almost a year old. The time was as right as it was ever going to be. He knew his sisters would probably remain in Arkansas with their families, but it was time to have a presence closer to the music epicenter.

We were moving to Nashville.

The 1960s were an era of change, and with our move to Nashville, J.E., Buster and I were swirling in change. Society as a whole was finding its way amidst the assassination of President John F. Kennedy, the escalation of U.S. troops in Vietnam, civil unrest, and revolutions against social norms that included the way we dressed, the music we listened to and our stance on drugs, sexuality, race and sexism. Yet the popular shows on television during that 1963-64 season rarely addressed the rising issues of the day.

Even as the winds of change were beginning to blow, most Americans still gathered around the TV set at night—resistant to the change they felt coming their way—and watched light-hearted programming that reflected family values from years past: *The Lucy Show, The Andy Griffith Show, Petticoat Junction* and *Bonanza*. The #1 rated TV program the year we moved to Nashville was *The Beverly Hillbillies*, and in some ways I saw parallels between our own situation and the show.

We were established in the music business and moving to an area of the country where we already had friends; however, like the Clampetts, we were making that move to better our lives.

Geographically we were also in for a change. Unlike the Clampetts stomping ground of Bugtussle, Pine Bluff and Little Rock were thriving cities. Nashville, however, was in a league all its own. We didn't know it at the time, but we were moving to Music City in its heyday.

In 1960 the population of Nashville was almost 171,000 people. By 1970, the population of Nashville soared to 448,000 residents. In one decade the city saw a growth spurt of 162%, and we were a part of that big boom.

Back when we moved to Nashville, it was a large city with a hometown feel that was known by several nicknames. WSM radio announcer David Cobb once used the title

"Music City USA" while referring to Nashville in a 1950s broadcast, and the moniker stuck. Because the city had hundreds and hundreds of churches throughout the downtown area and surrounding neighborhoods, Nashville became known as the "Buckle of the Bible Belt," and once the Parthenon was built for the World's Fair in 1897, many people referred to Nashville as "The Athens of The South."

Nashville's first skyscraper, The Life & Casualty Tower, punctured Music City's skyline just five years before we moved to town. The 55-acre Cheek estate built in 1929—home to prominent Nashville citizens Leslie & Mabel Cheek—opened its doors to the city as a botanical gardens and museum known as Cheekwood just three years before our arrival.

Nashville was dotted with majestic movie theaters like the Belle Meade Theatre, The Crescent, The Knickerbocker and the Paramount. Each of those beautiful buildings sported huge banners across their fronts that read AIR CONDITIONED. Times were changing in the 60's.

Downtown was home to all of the plush hotels of the day like the Andrew Jackson, the Maxwell House and the Hermitage. It was also home to some of our finer shopping establishments.

Cain Sloan was located on Church Street. It had fabulous store front window displays— especially during the holidays. If you had lunch in the Steeple Chase Room Monday-Friday on the 3rd floor of Cain Sloan, young ladies would stroll by while you ate, modeling outfits available in the store and giving you the prices if you were interested in making a purchase.

If you wanted a bowl of 3-way chili to eat for lunch in the 60's, you could buy yourself one at Varallo's downtown for a mere ten-cents. The best cheeseburger in town belonged to Rotiers on Elliston Place, while locals made the drive down Hwy 100 for fried chicken and biscuits from The Loveless Cafe. When we moved to Nashville, all three of these establishments had been in operation for years. Somehow, good food and good people survive the test of time, because fifty-five years later and they are still palate pleasing favorites in Nashville.

In 1963 Acme Farm Supply at the corner of First Avenue and Broadway really was a farm supply and fresh produce market; and where the Hard Rock Cafe now stands across the street, there stood an actual hardware store.

Vanderbilt University had quite the basketball team back then too. In 1965, Vandy took the SEC title in college basketball.

But first and foremost, Nashville was known for its country music. In the 1960s, Twang Town was the second largest music production center in the United States—second only to New York City. Anyone who loved country music, knew Nashville, Tennessee was operation central, and Music Row was the grand dame of that operation. Studios, publishing companies, record labels, media, writing rooms, management teams, artists, fan clubs—everybody who was anybody had an office or a presence on Music Row.

Tourists frequented Nashville just to get a glimpse of a bona fide country star, and now J.E. and I found ourselves in the middle of this Country Music Milky Way.

When we first moved to town, we looked at property in Hendersonville—a community north of Nashville. Jim and Mary Reeves lived in Hendersonville, and they were the ones who spurred on our move to the Volunteer State.

Hendersonville is bordered on one side by beautiful Old Hickory Lake. We talked about how nice it would be to have Jim and Mary as neighbors and have a home on the lake with a boat slip.

We had a beauty of a wooden boat back then—a Chris Craft—with a motor powerful enough to pull two skiers. J.E. was an excellent skier, and he taught me how to slalom.

We didn't get to the lake as often as we would have liked in those days because of professional demands and the responsibilities of raising a small child, but when we did manage to put our boat in the water and cut across the lake full throttle, it was sheer exhilaration.

I wish every one could have seen J.E. back then. He was something else on those skis. He was an athlete in high school and a former college basketball player at Arkansas State. Sports came easily to us, and we loved our time together as husband and wife enjoying the outdoors and sunshine; but in the end, we gave up the idea of moving to Hendersonville out of convenience. We settled on, what was then, a small country community eleven miles south of Nashville in Williamson County—Brentwood, Tennessee.

Back when we moved to Brentwood in 1963, it was a quiet community centered in the Tennessee rolling hillside with only a thousand or so people in residence. With the construction of I-65 in the 1960s, the community began to grow.

When Brentwood incorporated in 1969, six years after we began to call it home, the population of Brentwood had doubled to 3,378. Today this attractive business center and family-friendly community continues to thrive with over 42,000 residents, and J.E. and I witnessed most of that growth together.

We made Brentwood our home in 1963 mostly because the community provided the country style living we sought to raise a family. Also, many of our music friends lived nearby; so we had nearby extended family. Add the fact that Brentwood was convenient to downtown, and we knew we had made a wise choice. The airport, Music Row and the Grand Ole Opry were short drives for us.

Looking back, all I can say is God must have had a hand in our decision. As it turned out, J.E. would make that drive to the Opry thousands of times throughout his career.

On July 3, 1963 The Browns' dream of becoming members of the most venerable institution in country music history came true. The Browns became members of the Grand Ole Opry. Talk about a welcome to Nashville gift!

J.E. was so proud that night; he was bustin' buttons, and I was proud of him. I was proud of all The Browns. They had sacrificed so much to get to this moment. Yet I don't think they ever saw those all-nighters, and days away from their home and families, as sacrifice. It was what they had to do to make it to the top, and the Grand Ole Opry was the pinnacle for any performer.

That July night was hot as blue blazes in Nashville, Tennessee. The Ryman Auditorium was built through the efforts of steamboat shipping magnet Thomas G. Ryman and was originally known as The Union Gospel Tabernacle. The Ryman had no real dressing rooms to speak of, and it wasn't air conditioned. But I don't think any of us were feeling the heat that night as The Browns took their bow on the Grand Ole Opry stage to a standing ovation as its newest members. The only thing they felt that July night in 1963 was the love from the audience.

I remember on the ride home reminiscing with J.E. about the night's events. He had traveled quite the journey from that first night on the *Barnyard Frolic* in Arkansas to Nashville's Grand Ole Opry stage. You couldn't have wiped the smiles from our faces if you tried.

Jim Ed wasn't even thirty years old yet. At the age of twenty-nine, he was now one of country music's elite...a member of the Grand Ole Opry alongside the very heroes he used to listen to on the radio as a young boy: Roy Acuff, Minnie Pearl, Little Jimmy Dickens and Bill Monroe. He was also part of a new crop of Opry entertainers that included Loretta Lynn, Hank Locklin, Archie Campbell, Skeeter Davis, Billy Walker, Bobby Lord, Bill Anderson and George Hamilton IV. Life was good. It was after midnight as we traveled back to our home in Brentwood, but you would have thought the sun was shining in our car.

The only thing that put a cloud on the horizon that night was the absence of Patsy Cline, Hawkshaw Hawkins and Cowboy Copas from the Opry stage. Less than four months had past since their plane crashed, and all on board were killed outside of Camden, Tennessee along with pilot Randy Hughes. The group was on their way home after attending a benefit concert in Kansas City, Kansas for the family of recently departed disc jockey "Cactus" Jack Call.

I know J.E. missed seeing those great entertainers in the Opry wings that night. Thoughts of their deaths were still fresh on the minds of the country music community. Their passing was a big loss for their fans...a huge loss for Jim Ed, Maxine and Bonnie. They lost their friends.

A few months earlier Patsy and her husband Charlie Dick invited us for a visit to their home. They knew we were considering a move to Nashville, and they wanted us to consider moving to their neighborhood. I was thinking to myself, "How nice! Every one wants us to be their neighbors." I couldn't wait to move to Nashville.

Patsy died in March. We moved to Tennessee in April. I can only imagine what it would have been like to live next door to Patsy Cline. I'm pretty sure it never would have been boring.

Patsy was, in many ways, like Maxine. She could be outspoken and brash, but underneath, she had a heart of gold.

I could almost hear Patsy congratulate Jim Ed as he came off the Opry stage that first night as a full fledged Opry member. I think she would have thrown back her head and grabbed him with a big bear hug as she barked, "Welcome to the family, Hoss!"

I have no idea where we were or what was going on.

Buster and I took J.E. to the airport. He was heading off to London.

Promotional photos for Jim Ed's hit song Pop a Top

Chapter Ten

Life was in constant motion. Sometimes it felt like we were flying by the seat of our pants. When we hit the ground in Nashville, we hit the ground running.

Jim Ed was playing the Opry, traveling on tour dates and working on new recordings in the studio with his sisters. I joined the Jo Coulter Modeling Agency and began doing print work and commercials while teaching self improvement classes and raising Buster. Maxine decided, like J.E., that she wanted to be closer to the action. So she began to look for a house in anticipation of moving her family to Nashville while Bonnie made the decision to stay in Arkansas with Brownie and be a full time mom. It was agreed that Bonnie would come to Nashville to record with The Browns, and The Browns would hire another vocalist to take Bonnie's place on the road.

Meanwhile, we needed a place to live ourselves. We rented a house on Forrest Lawn Drive while we waited for our home to be completed on Williamsburg Road. Our home was designed by architect Dan Mosley. Dan was the architect who designed Eddy Arnold's home.

Our home was a mirror image of Eddy's house; it had the same floor plan. A few months after we moved into our home on Williamsburg Road, Marty and Marizona Robbins came to visit us. They liked the floor plan so much, they decided to use it too.

Immediately we began to look for a new church home, and we quickly found one. J.E. and I both liked Forrest Hills Baptist Church. Bob Daugherty was the minister there. Brother Bob made you feel like you'd known him all of your life. He was a dapper man in his 40s who sported a freshly pressed three piece suit every Sunday. His smile reached his eyes, and he preached from a place of love. I enjoyed attending his Bible studies. Maybe, just maybe, I could find those Bible chapters quicker with Brother Bob's guidance.

If you spent any time at all in Nashville in the 1960s, you came to understand the layered effect the music business created in our city. Chances are you knew at least one singer, songwriter, musician, producer or engineer. If you didn't work directly with someone in the music industry, then you worked indirectly with someone in the business. Country music touched lives and made friends.

I mentioned our architect Dan built Eddy Arnold's house. Dan had a brother, Charley, who lived across the street from us who was Brenda Lee's financial adviser. Charley's wife, Helen, loved to throw parties, and it didn't have to be a major holiday or birthday for us to celebrate. If she got a new lamp, Helen would throw a party to show it off. If she got a new rug, then we'd celebrate "out with the old — in with the new." It was at one of those fun shindigs that I first met Little Miss Dynamite.

I loved Brenda Lee and her husband Ronnie from the first moment I set eyes on them. J.E. already knew Brenda, but with one encounter, I felt like I had known Brenda all of my life. Her mischievous smile, twinkling eyes and gift for gab made me feel that way. Brenda is unpretentious and unapologetic for it. She is so real.

Charley pulled me to the side during the party and asked me if I would sit down with Brenda and casually offer my assistance to teach her how to dress.

I looked at Charley like he had two heads. Whatever did he mean? You don't say something like that to any woman, much less to Brenda Lee who by this time in her life was already an international sensation, friends with Elvis Presley, Jimmy Durante and Ed Sullivan.

Apparently, Charley thought, from a financial adviser's stand point, Brenda dressed too casually when she wasn't on stage.

It tickled me when Charley confided in a disapproving tone that Brenda ran around barefooted every chance she got — even in public. He leaned in and whispered that when Brenda wasn't working, she even went to town barefooted.

Well I thought this was delightful. I loved it. I loved her!

Brenda Lee was a scream!

I told Charley I wasn't going to speak to Brenda about how she dressed. If she wanted advice from someone, she would ask for it. Brenda was perfect just the way she was, with or without shoes and she still is.

The reality of living in Brentwood placed household names just households away.

Skeeter Davis lived down the street from us, and in 1963, Skeeter was celebrating the biggest record of her career, *The End of The World.*[18] The single sold over a million copies, and chances were, her disc jockey husband at the time, Ralph Emery, gave that record a few spins on his all night show on WSM Radio.

Skeeter was another person who kept it real. She was a sweetheart who loved animals. I can remember going to her house to visit and sitting there petting lots of dogs, lots and lots of dogs.

Other animal lovers in town were Tom T. and Dixie Hall, who once lived on nearby Edmondson Pike. Tom was from Dry Ridge, Kentucky and was newly arrived in Nashville. Tom was dating the spirited Miss Dixie at the time. Tom, Dixie, Jim Ed and I became good friends.

I think Tom and Dixie were perhaps two of the smartest people I have ever met. They were quick witted and fun to be around.

Dixie was also quite the cook. Years later, she would support a passion project of hers called Animal Land through the proceeds from a cookbook she put together.

It always amazed me that someone from England could cook southern delicacies to perfection the way Dixie could. Dixie could cook anything—from homemade cookies to home fried chicken. I still have Dixie's cookbooks, and some of her recipes remain family favorites.

More and more people were moving to Nashville every day. The Grand Ole Opry broadcasting country music over 50,000-watt, clear channel WSM 650AM was like a beacon to every wanna-be, and soon-to-be, hillbilly hopeful within listening distance. Nashville was now home to every major recording company in the nation. Trade publications settled in for the long haul in Music City. RCA Victor and Columbia Records had just sunk millions of dollars into brand new recording studios. Song licensing agencies BMI, ASCAP and SESAC all set up shop on Music Row—a four block stretch of older, residential homes along Sixteenth and Seventeenth Avenues that became operation central for Nashville's music industry.

As country crusaders captured a snippet of success, they made the pilgrimage from downtown apartments and boarding houses to the Nashville fringe. I think those artists who chose to settle in Brentwood enjoyed the slower pace that country living afforded, the antithesis to bustling Nashville just ten minutes away. Back in the 1960s, Brentwood rolled up its sidewalks at sunset, and that was ok by us.

Honestly, Brentwood in the early Sixties consisted of a couple of hotels, one hardware store, one corner barber shop, a family owned restaurant called Nobles that specialized in home cooking, or what we in the south like to refer to as a "meat and three," and Huff's Grocery. Like Nobles, Huff's was also family owned. Mr. Huff allowed most of his patrons to run a tab at his grocery store. At the end of the month, we would settle our accounts and start anew. Who in the world does that today? It truly was a simpler time.

We knew the names of the people with whom we did business. We knew their children's names, and they knew ours. We greeted each other with a smile when we walked through the door, and we talked about God, our families, politics, professions, sports, recipes and fishing. Mostly we just talked about the weather. But we talked to each other.

Brentwood was a good place to live, full of good people.

The man who helped define Eddy Arnold's country sound with his ting-a-ling steel guitar stylings, Little Roy Wiggins, lived across the street from us; and gospel great Jake Hess who sang lead with The Statesman Quartet, along with comedian Archie Campbell, also lived in our neighborhood. Archie had just moved to Brentwood from Knoxvillle as a replacement for Rod Brasfield on the nationally syndicated Prince Albert segment of the Grand Ole Opry.

Living on a beautiful farm amongst those bucolic Brentwood hills was Carl Smith, who placed four songs in the country top twenty the year we moved to town. Divorced from June Carter, Carl was now married to the beautiful Goldie Hill. Their farm was on Berry's Chapel. I used to take friends and family on tours to see their breathtaking farm.

Sanford, Florida native Bobby Lord became a member of the Opry in 1960 and had moved to town to host *Opry Almanac* on WSM-TV, and just down the road a ways was twenty-five year old songwriter Bill Anderson and his wife Betty. By 1963, Bill had placed five of his own records in the top ten on the Billboard music charts, including his mega hit *Still*.[19]

Jim Ed and Bill were at the top of their games, and Betty and I spent some time together. We were probably drawn together as friends because we could relate to the odd set of circumstances that "celebrity" brings to a household. One day our husbands would be home with us; one day they would be gone. Sometimes they would be gone for a weekend; sometimes for a week. Even when they were in town, the phone would ring requesting a public appearance, a trip to the studio or an interview. So even when J.E. and Bill were home, they weren't home. Yet we found wonderful moments of sanity in the midst of the insanity. Family time. Husband and wife time. Date nights with our friends.

I enjoyed attending music events with J.E., Bill and Betty. At times it felt like we were riding this crazy roller coaster together. We understood the highs and lows because we were living them, and at this point in our lives, the highs far out numbered the lows.

I think almost every one in town dreamed of having a career like country legends Webb Pierce and Eddy Arnold.

Webb was from West Monroe, Louisiana but moved to south Nashville area several years back. He and his wife Audrey had an incredible home on Franklin Road near Brentwood.

In 1963, Webb was only forty-two years old, but when you're in your twenties like J.E. and I were, Webb seemed like the wise, old man on the mountain. In eleven years of chart success, Webb placed fifty songs in the country top ten. Thirteen of those songs skyrocketed to the #1 spot. It was unbelievable.

We became friends with Webb and Audrey, and it didn't take long for Audrey to ask me to join her ladies' bowling team. I had bowled in high school, and enjoyed the sport, but I enjoyed spending time with my new friend the most.

When Ralph Emery heard I was on Audrey's bowling team, he was amazed. He said there was never anyone who looked less like a bowler than I did. I'm not sure what he meant by that. I'm not sure what a bowler is suppose to look like. Are petite blondes not allowed on the lanes? If Ralph thought I was too ladylike to bowl, then Audrey shouldn't have been allowed to walk through the front door.

Audrey Pierce was drop dead gorgeous! I never liked the term "trophy wife," but if I were going to use it, I'd use it to describe Audrey. Webb Pierce was handsome, but he over married. Audrey was as beautiful on the inside as she was on the outside—so kind and gracious—a soft spoken woman with a bouffant hairdo.

We both had bouffant hair styles back then. I see girls who bowl today with their hair falling across their eyes, and I think back to that time in our lives when Audrey and I would use half a can of Spray Net to keep our perfectly coiffed hair in place.

We bowled in an alley on Nolensville Road, and if I remember correctly, the name of our team was *The High Rollers*. I used to think our team name reflected our high bowling scores. Now I think it could have had something to do with the height of those bouffants. No matter. We always had fun when we bowled. I had about a 155 average.

J.E. liked to bowl too. I remember one year he joined a league. Several times over the course of our lives he actually bowled perfect scores. The coveted 300. There are professional bowlers who have never attained that goal! J.E. did it, more than once. He was an exceptional athlete.

And I can't talk about Brentwood without talking about Eddy Arnold.

Eddy Arnold was "Mr. Brentwood!" During the time we moved to the community, he had more chart records than anyone in the music business. At the age of 45, Eddy had 73 top ten records to his credit that included twenty-one #1 hits!

Eddy had accumulated a fortune in the music industry, which he then invested in real estate. Brentwood real estate. At one time, I think Eddy owned most of the town, but he didn't stop at real estate.

Eddy's investments included Brentwood's utility companies. Eddy owned Brentwood's Watersworks.

Every time I washed a dish, Eddy made money. Every time I took a bath or flushed a toilet, I could hear an imaginary "cha-ching" in the Arnold household. Every time I watered the yard or boiled potatoes, I increased Eddy's net worth.

Eddy Arnold was a great singer, but he was also a great businessman. We paid attention to how Eddy conducted his business, and we learned. There were many times over the years as the face of the music changed, and the faces of those who made the music changed, that I was thankful we paid attention.

Brentwood was home and still is—after all these years..

Photo for Jim Ed's Angel's Sunday *album cover—1971*

Portfolio head shot

The Country Place TV show: Jim Ed, Dave Barton, Corky Tittle and Ray Wix

Country Music Wives Fashion Show: Barbara Davis (wife of Danny Davis), Ellen Reeves (wife of Del Reeves), Barbara Luman (wife of Bob Luman), Bill Williams (WSM announcer), Jeannie Bare (wife of Bobby Bare), Aldona Phillips (wife of Stu Phillips), Becky, Brenda Wright (wife of Bobby Wright) and Ann Stuckey (wife of Nat Stuckey)

Our house on Williamsburg Road. The trim was painted turquoise and at Christmas I had a white flocked tree with turquoise ornaments.

Becky and Dorothy Vanlandingham

Chapter Eleven

There are some days you just can't forget...even though you wish with all your might that you could.

It was the end of July 1964, and J.E. and I traveled to Little Rock so Buster and I could visit with family. He dropped us off at his parents' house, while he, Maxine and Bonnie drove on to Dallas to perform on the *Big D Jamboree*.

It was a busy weekend for me. Buster was almost two years old, and both sets of grandparents wanted to coddle their grandson. I was running back and forth between Little Rock and Pine Bluff visiting as many family members as I could. Time was a precious commodity to me these days, and I wanted to make the most of every minute with my family and friends. We didn't have time to listen to the radio or watch television. Our family was too busy talking about new projects, reminiscing about old times and watching Buster play.

It was Sunday afternoon when I heard J.E.'s car pull in the driveway. Even with all the commotion over the past several days, I missed him. When he walked through the door, I greeted him with a brilliant smile. Something was wrong. He wasn't smiling back.

On their drive down to Dallas, The Browns heard a radio report that the plane of Jim Reeves was missing. Jim was flying back from Arkansas where he and his manager Dean Manuel were looking at a possible real estate investment when Jim radioed the airport that he was flying into a severe thunderstorm around Brentwood, Tennessee. He was just minutes away from home. That was the last radio communication the tower received from Jim. Jim Reeves and Dean Manuel were missing. There was a massive search for the plane. Hundreds of people volunteered their time hoping to find Jim and Dean alive.

Just a few hours before J.E. pulled into the driveway, The Browns heard it on the radio. The plane was found. No survivors.

I sat there in utter disbelief. I was in shock. I couldn't believe it! Jim Reeves was gone. That just didn't seem possible. I could see the anguish on J.E.'s face. Jim Reeves was like a brother to him.

J.E. asked me to pack my things as quickly as I could. He wanted to get home and see if there was anything he could do to help the family.

As a wife of an entertainer I immediately thought of Jim's wife Mary. I couldn't imagine the sadness that must be enveloping her right now. I prayed Mary wasn't alone. Jim had so many friends. I'm sure she must be surrounded by people trying to bring her some kind of comfort. If I were home, I'd be by her side too. Yes. We needed to get home.

We headed back to Nashville caravan style with Maxine and Bonnie following close behind in another car. The Browns were scheduled to record some new sides in the RCA Studios that week. I wondered if the new songs were sad songs because I didn't think it would be possible for The Browns to sing a happy tune...not for a very long time.

All the way home J.E. and I talked about Jim Reeves and Mary. When we weren't sharing stories, we were listening to the radio. Back then WSM was truly a clear channel, and we could hear the comforting tones of Ralph Emery as he shared more and more details about the fatal crash and rescue efforts.

From Ralph's reports we learned that over seven-hundred volunteers searched a 20 square mile radius for Jim's plane. Our friends Marty Robbins, Stonewall Jackson, Ernest Tubb, Chet Atkins, Eddy Arnold and even Tom Perryman were part of that search party. When Tom heard the news of the missing plane, he hopped in his car and drove all night from Texas to Tennessee to help.

Finally, forty-two hours after Jim's last radio communication, Jim's plane was found. It crashed less than two miles from our home in Brentwood.

The plane was recovered in a thick wooded area in the backyard of a neighboring home— just one hundred feet from their house. The people who lived there were out of town when the crash occurred. Eddy Arnold was called to the scene to help identify the bodies.

We listened to the radio in complete sadness. Country music had suffered so many recent losses. It was just over a year since the deaths of Cowboy Copas, Hawkshaw Hawkins and Patsy Cline shattered the country community...and then there was the death of Jack Anglin, of Johnnie and Jack fame who lost his life in a car accident on his way to Patsy's funeral. We were still grieving those losses.

––––––––––––––––––

Somehow, The Browns made it through their performance on the *Big D Jamboree*. J.E. said he barely remembered being on stage. His mind was on Jim the entire time. It was still on Jim. Even now, knowing Jim's fate, he couldn't believe it was true.

Ralph was playing song after song in tribute to Jim over the WSM airwaves. J.E. and I listened to *The Big Blizzard*,[20] *Mexican Joe, Four Walls*,[21] *He'll Have to Go*[22] and *Welcome to My World*.[23] It was approaching midnight, and we were getting closer to the house. It had been an emotional journey back to Brentwood. Buster was asleep, and J.E. was behind the wheel when Ralph played a song that Jim had written called *The Night Watch*.[24]

Jim Reeves' rich baritone voice filled the car. The lyrics seemed prophetic. At last, we found some comfort in Jim's own words.

So sleep, sleep in peace and rest

Don't be afraid of the darkness

All's well for over the land and the sea

God's keeping the night watch for you and for me

So many goodbyes.

So many changes.

The Browns as we knew them were no longer the same. Robbie Hardin was hired to replace Bonnie on the road.

Bonnie made it clear that she wanted to stay home, support Brownie's growing practice as a doctor in Dardanelle, Arkansas, and raise their beautiful daughters, Kelly and Robin. The three siblings decided that Bonnie would remain an integral part of the recording process as The Browns, and she would venture to Nashville whenever possible to perform on the Grand Ole Opry.

Maxine moved her family to the Nashville area to be closer to the action. She enjoyed performing, but she too began to feel the strain and pull of being both a single mother to three small children and an entertainer to the world. She became increasingly frustrated.

Likewise, J.E. became increasingly frustrated with Maxine. He thought Maxine was drinking too much on the road. To him it appeared that the road was just one big party for Maxine. She began her partying on the way to the performance; by the time the show was over, she slept all the way home from her antics. Maybe she drank to alleviate some of the pain she experienced in her back that made traveling uncomfortable; regardless, it was becoming an issue.

At first J.E. kept his frustration to himself. It wasn't until some time had past that he shared his concerns with me.

Over the years I remained steadfast to my rule of no alcohol in the house. Maxine and Bonnie understood my resolve, but whenever they were in town to rehearse new arrangements for the studio, more often than not, alcohol won out over family. It came to the point where J.E. had to practice with his sisters in their hotel room.

But that was rehearsal. On the road he had no control over when and where the drinking would happen. He and Robbie didn't drink at all, and it frustrated him that in addition to leading The Browns, more and more, he found himself in the role of babysitter. When you drink, your tongue often becomes loose, and loud. Sometimes Maxine would quip inappropriate remarks to those who crossed her path. Over time J.E. grew embarrassed by the situations, and he got tired of putting out fires.

Jim Ed took the music business seriously. That's the reason we uprooted our family and moved to Nashville. He didn't think Maxine was as serious as he was about the business anymore. She seemed bitter.

Things weren't gelling the way they used to, and even though Robbie sang great harmony, without Bonnie on the road, were The Browns really The Browns? We talked about J.E. going solo. It was a hard decision to make, because even with all of the issues surrounding Maxine, he cherished his time singing with her. She was his sister, and he loved her.

In 1965, Jim Ed met with Chet Atkins, who agreed to produce him as a solo act. He and Chet met with Maxine and Bonnie over lunch and explained their plans. RCA had opened the door for Jim Ed to continue in the business as a solo artist. In a selfless act of sibling love, the sisters gave Jim Ed their blessing to walk through it. In a way, I think it was a relief for all three.

We weren't starting over exactly, but it would take some time for J.E. to find his footing out there, and he knew it. Jim Ed was excited, grateful, and to be truthful, he was a little scared.

He felt comfortable singing with his sisters. When he stepped up to a microphone, that beautiful blend of sibling harmony he had loved since childhood was there. Now he would be out on that stage alone. If he succeeded, it would be his success; but if he failed, it would be his failure.

I reminded him of a Bible scripture we had recently read from. *Casting all your care upon him; for he cares for you.* I Peter 5:7 KJV.

I told him it was understandable to be scared, but he could give his fear to the Lord. The Lord loved us and would see us through this new adventure. We just had to continue to love God and have faith.

Chet Atkins had to be one of the nicest men on the planet. He was a guitar player like no other, a record executive for RCA and a producer. He was also one of the best friends The Browns ever had. There were times he would stop by the house to give J.E. songs to listen to for his upcoming album. Chet went the extra mile for his RCA artists. He worked with them, but he also got to know them as people.

At the time you're working with someone like Chet, you don't stop to realize just how big they are to the country music community. It's hard to put into words, but you don't think of them as stars. Practically every one you know is a star. That's just the reality of it. The extraordinary was ordinary to us. It is only in hindsight that I sit back in total disbelief at the people who sat around my kitchen table.

I look back now, and I see a member of the Musicians, Rock & Roll and Country Music Halls of Fame with fourteen Grammy awards to his credit, but sitting across from us at our kitchen table in the mid-60s, I saw only Chet, a gifted friend who entertained me in my home by playing two totally different songs simultaneously on his guitar—a musician who was more comfortable being a guitar player than a record executive. He had always pulled for The Browns and now he was pulling for J.E.

Chet assigned Felton Jarvis to work with Jim Ed and produce his new sound. On July 19, 1965 a blip appeared in a music industry trade publication under a heading titled *Format Forecast*. It read:

> *Jim Ed Brown, whose recordings with The Brown Trio for years have sold in volume, now steps out as a solo with his first release for RCA Victor "I Heard From a Memory Last Night." The label is reportedly planning an extensive promo campaign soon with prospects of giving him star status.*

Jim Ed was on his way. Now the big task at hand would be conditioning an audience used to hearing three part sibling harmony to hearing J.E. by himself.

I Heard From a Memory Last Night[25] reached the Country top forty. It was a respectable first effort for a young man who was trying to redefine his music.

Eddy Arnold asked Jim Ed to tour with him. That was a blessing. It was an honor to get the stamp of approval from a country music legend, and easier on J.E. knowing a friend was supporting him from the wings.

A year later, Jim Ed performed a concert in Nashville's Centennial Park with Tex Ritter. He gathered together a stellar group of Nashville musicians to back him that day. Weldon Myrick was on steel guitar. Bob Eggers played guitar. Bass was played by Dave Barton, and Harold Weekly was on drums. Over 10,000 people attended the performance. The next day, the newspapers gave J.E. rave reviews. Not only did the audience accept him, they embraced him. His confidence in himself soared. He knew he could go it alone.

Jim Ed signed with the Hubert Long Agency. More bookings came his way. New singles were released to country radio. Then the single that would become a career maker made its radio debut. *Pop A Top*[26] began its climb up the country charts on May 20, 1967. His career exploded!

Pop A Top was written by a great songwriter from Atlanta, Texas by the name of Nat Stuckey. It became a huge hit, a signature song for Jim Ed for the rest of his career. It was also one of the most played juke box songs of all time. J.E. was on the map.

A few months later, J.E. was scheduled to fly to Europe for a week's worth of performances of US military bases in England and Germany. The soldiers connected with him and *Pop A Top*. The tour was extended for another five weeks.

Things were going well.

Maxine and Bonnie couldn't have been more thrilled. They knew their brother was going to be ok.

In October 1967, Jim Ed, Maxine and Bonnie said goodbye to their faithful fans on WSM Radio. The Browns made their final appearance together and took their final bows on the Grand Ole Opry stage—the country music pinnacle. It was the end of an era, but on the other side of endings are new beginnings.

I was reminded of another passage of scripture which I shared with him. This time it was *Delight yourself in the Lord and he will give you the desires of your heart*. Psalms 37:4 KJV.

The first National Academy of Recording Arts & Sciences dinner and awards show. Jim Ed was a nominee.

Ed Shea, Becky and Jim Ed

Good friends—Gloria Williams, Linda Adams, Carlana Harwell, and Becky on a girls trip to Florida

Debbie Lott, Carlana Moscheo Harwell, and Becky at Jean Dudley Smith fashion show

Modeling portfolio pictures

Chapter Twelve

Buster was growing like a weed, and he brought so much happiness into our lives. When you have a baby, you see the world through your child's eyes. Everything is new and wonderful, and I did my best as a parent to keep it that way. It was no longer all about me; it was about J.E., me and this precious life for which we were responsible.

I think one of the greatest gifts God can give us is the gift of a child. J.E. and I began to talk about having another baby. Buster was five years old, and we wanted him to have a sibling. Secretly I was hoping for a girl.

I continued to work for the Jo Coulter Modeling Agency—in front of the camera and behind it. I still modeled, but I became a professional make-up artist for the agency as well, specializing in make-up for television shows and album covers. Between caring for Buster and my work, I was constantly on the go, but I still found myself missing J.E.

He was away from home a lot during this time in our lives. It is the nature of the beast. The demands of the music industry are great on the artist and the artist's family; so when I did find myself in the dumps, I'd pick up the phone and call my girlfriends. Who better to understand the trials of holding down the home front while your husband is on the road than another artist's wife.

Sally Arnold was Eddy's other half, and she taught me so much about being the wife of a country music celebrity. Sally was a little older than I was, and she already had multiple years of living with "country music stardom" under her belt. She was attractive, confident and comfortable in her own skin, and she had this wonderful way of telling it like it was without making you feel like you'd been put in your place. Sally's matter-of-factness was sprinkled with humor.

We'd talk about the blessings and fantastic opportunities the music industry provided our families, but we also talked about the pitfalls. Women throwing themselves at our husbands on a nightly basis was one of those pitfalls.

These women saw the wedding rings, but they didn't care. They would stand at the front of the stage "making eyes" at our husbands. They would scream in delight at their songs trying their best to call attention to themselves, and they would con their way backstage—sometimes promising "favors" to the band if they could just have a moment alone with our husbands.

Sally had a unique way of looking at these "trophy hunters.""You have to understand something," she'd say. "These women are not after our husbands. It's the celebrity they're after. If it ever comes down to it, I'll tell the little Jezebel she can have Eddy, but his dirty laundry and all of his bills are going with him!"

I loved Sally's take on life.

I confided that J. E. had a bit of a jealous streak where I was concerned too, but I nipped it years ago.

It happened early on in our relationship during the Disc Jockey Convention. We were attending the RCA party and I was chatting with a handsome, young announcer from New York. Evidently J.E. didn't like that. With a he-man swagger, he walked over to us and told the man to leave me alone. He said I was his wife.

Let me tell you, at that very moment, I was mortified.

When we left the party, I turned to him and said, "J. E., never do that again! The young man and I were having a simple conversation. He wasn't coming on to me, and if he were, I'm perfectly capable of handling myself." I continued, "J. E. you can trust me, and I certainly hope I can trust you."

He said I could. I believed him.

I also remember the advice Sally gave me about egos. She wisely shared that sometimes husbands who happen to be in the public eye begin to buy all the hype that surrounds them. They see the adoring fans and they begin to believe their own press. When they begin to get above their raisin', you have to remind them who they really are, and who they always have been.

What a reality check. That advice was good advice. Our children didn't need celebrities to love them; they needed dads. So when they came home, we treated them like every other husband/father in America. At home standing ovations were replaced by standing on toilets to change out light bulbs. Catching a bus was replaced by catching a ball with their sons in their front yards.

Yet we understood home for a "celebrity" husband was also a sanctuary. Every move he made at home wasn't scrutinized by the public. At home he could relax, and he could be loved for who he was, not for who other people thought he was.

Yes. Sally Arnold was a wonderful friend. As the years went by I taught Sally's granddaughter Michelle in my dance class. We remained good friends with the Arnolds until their deaths in 2008. Sally passed away just two months before Eddy. They were married sixty-six years.

Mary Reeves was another friend who gave me advice about the road and the music industry. I remember Mary saying, "Don't worry about all those women chasing after J.E. on the road. Remember. You are his wife. You're the one he wants. You're Mrs. Jim Ed Brown."

Mary was the driving force behind Jim Reeves. She often went on tour with him and spent much of her time promoting Jim Reeves' music—before and after his death. She kept his name alive.

Mary and I played tennis together. We often found ourselves back at her house after an exhilarating match eating a bowl of her chili. We even hunted together—well kind of.

We went on several group hunting expeditions together. Mary hunted for game with the rest of the party; I drove into town and hunted for bargains at the nearest antique shop. I really didn't enjoy trudging out into the darkness, well before the sun even thought about shining, in freezing weather, bundled up like a snowman and waiting for an animal to run by.

I remember my first and last real hunting trip vividly. My mother-in-law talked me into it. J.E. had taken me on a practice session earlier. He wanted to make sure I knew how to shoot the gun. I can't tell you what gauge that shotgun was, I just know that it knocked me to the ground when I fired it.

We were up before the chickens sitting in the darkness waiting for the break of dawn. It was bitterly cold. We put hand warmers in every pocket and Momma Brown placed a bucket of coals at our feet so we wouldn't freeze to death. We sat and waited—watching our breath make tiny clouds in the cold air.

Finally around 10am, I gave up and went back to the camp. At least I'd have some hot chili ready when the rest of the gang returned with their bounty. I was all alone there when a momma Razorback hog and her babies strolled right through the middle of the camp. It was my first time to see a Razorback hog, and let me tell you, they are scary looking creatures. Nothing you would want to tangle with by yourself in the woods.

My most cherished times with Mary were the times we laughed together. Perhaps we never laughed more than on an RCA tour of Europe with Chet Atkins, Danny Davis & The Nashville Brass, Dottie West, Bobby Bare, Skeeter Davis and Jim Ed. I accompanied him as his wife on that tour and Mary was there promoting Jim Reeves' music. Jim Ed stayed in London to work a few dates for British promoter, Mervyn Conn, who staged shows for the Beatles in the early '60s, and I went on with the rest of the group to Norway.

I knew Norway would be beautiful, I didn't know the flight to get to Norway would be frightening. I know now why they say, "Buckle your seat belts!" We hit a patch of turbulence that jolted us to our cores. At one point, the air seemed to vanish from beneath the plane. We dropped so hard and fast that our snack trays hit the ceiling of the aircraft. I can still hear the gasps from the passengers on board.

I'm not sure who, but I heard someone say, "Don't worry. This plane won't crash. There are too many celebrities on board." I thought to myself, "Yeah, right." That sentiment was of little comfort. Not that long ago, in two separate incidents, six of our friends took flights and never made it home.

To say I was happy to make it safely to the ground was an understatement. The door to the plane opened and we waited impatiently for the stairs to roll up to make our exit on to the tarmac. As I began my descent down the stairs, the wind hit me in the chest. It was vicious. We had to lean our bodies into the wind to make any head way at all toward the terminal. Our hair was whipping frantically in our faces; our clothes were plastered against our bodies. This was crazy. Welcome to Norway!

Since I was now solo for this leg of the journey, and so was Mary, we decided to room together.

I can't remember the name of the hotel where we stayed the first night in Norway, but it had enormous rooms—so big that our beds weren't side by side. They were on opposite sides of the room.

We were exhausted from our travels and decided to put on our pajamas and go straight to sleep. We said goodnight and jumped into our beds. Little did we know our mattresses were made of down. When we hopped in bed, we sunk like two deflated soufflés. Mary and I couldn't see each other across the room; we couldn't see anything but mattress. We looked like two half cocooned caterpillars. We howled with laughter, and the more we laughed, the funnier it got. The funnier it got, the farther we'd sink. I thought we'd never stop laughing. Those were great times.

I needed those times. I needed joy in my life. I was happy being a wife; I was happy being a mother, but somewhere along the way, I was losing the joy in my salvation. I attended church every week to feed my spirit and I tried to lead a good life. I knew God loved me, and I loved God, yet I felt the light I exuded as a Christian was gradually beginning to dim. I began to pray to God to restore that light. I prayed every day for the joy in my salvation to be restored.

Joy is not a shallow emotion. It consumes your entire being. Joy is faith, hope and love in one big, bright, beautiful, all-inclusive ball. I was consumed with joy once. I wanted to be consumed with joy again.

I stated in the beginning of my book that I believe God hears our prayers, and he answers them. We need only to open our eyes to see his vision.

One day I was driving home. I was whizzing through Little Rock on my way to Pine Bluff when I topped a hill on the interstate. At the bottom of the hill, a truck had blown a tire. Every one behind the truck hit their breaks. At least ten cars slammed into each other with major force. The mangled wreckage was awful. It all happened so fast.

I wasn't tailgating, so I began to pump my breaks in order to slow the cars following me. It didn't work. At least another ten cars piled up behind me, and there I was in the middle—me and my car. I was shaken but completely unscathed.

Soon after, I was flying home from Arkansas and something went terribly wrong with the plane. We made an emergency landing in Memphis and were escorted to the terminal by firetrucks and rescue vehicles.

Then, two weeks later the room in our home that we used as J.E.'s office caught fire. No one was hurt and nothing of value was in the room at the time of the blaze. He had recently moved the contents of his office downtown and set up shop in the Faron Young Building. He wasn't at home at the time of the fire. I had just taken him to the airport to catch a plane to London. Tandy Rice, his booking agent at the time, rushed over to see if he could help me. He asked, "Becky, do you need me to get him back home?"

I said, "Absolutely not. I can handle this." And I did.

I met another neighbor because of that fire, Lucille Blasingame. Lucille was married to Buddy Blasingame. He worked for Shelby Singleton, with whom had success with in Jeannie C. Riley's hit *Harper Valley PTA*.[27] Lucille rushed over to help. After the fire we discovered we both liked to paint and we went to the same church. She was a really good artist. We were also on the same page when it came to our faith.

I could write another book about Lucille and our friendship. One of my favorite "Lucille Stories" is when she decide to make homemade root beer. She made 40 bottles up and they stayed in her garage "until they were ready"—whatever that means. Then she moved all 40 inside and put them on a shelf in her pantry. One day she heard an explosion. When she entered the kitchen, there was glass and root beer coming through the louvered doors of her pantry. She immediately called the fire department. I can just imagine their reactions: I think they knew Lucille only too well. They sent the bomb squad to her house.

A man goes to her front door, covered from head to toe in protective armor. He asks Lucille to leave the house. He proceeds to carry the bottles out one by one to explode them safely on her back patio. She must have had enough yeast to blow up Brentwood.

Oh, and there was the time she called a local nursery and asked them if they could move a tree from her yard to her neighbors. They said, "you will have to dig it up and ball it." When the nursery later went to pick it up, it was balled up, the root system was about the size of a Volkswagen car. They had to get a fork lift and maybe even a permit to move it around the corner. I think they told Lucille to never call them again.

Lucille loved to work in the yard, even my yard. She taught me a lot about gardening.

In hindsight, that fire made it possible for me to change that room into a dance studio. I told Jo Coulter I enjoyed working for her, teaching self improvement classes, but dance was a true passion.

It never ceases to amaze me how God works and how he knows the desires of our hearts. "I get it, Lord! I understand."

I gave thanks and praised his name for restoring the joy of my salvation.

Someone who shared my love in Christ was Cindy Walker from Mexia, Texas. She was such a precious person. Cindy was filled with the Holy Spirit. Cindy exuded joy.

Like me, Cindy was a dancer and a singer; we had a lot in common. She was also a songwriter. Bob Wills recorded over fifty of Cindy's songs. Many of our friends did too, including Eddy Arnold who once gave her the line *You don't know me* and told her to write him a hit. Cindy did. The song became a top ten hit for Eddy, and went on to become a country classic performed by many artists over the years. *You Don't Know Me*[28] remains one of my favorite songs to this day.

In her songwriting hey day, Cindy and her mother Oree—a fine pianist who helped Cindy with her melodies—spent seven months in Mexia writing her music and five months in Nashville pitching their compositions and marketing their songs.

Whenever Cindy was in town, she'd attend church with us. Every time she did, Brother Bob would ask Cindy to sing a song for our congregation. Without fail, Cindy happily obliged. Usually she'd sing a song she had written, although sometimes she'd sing a song written by her grandfather, who was a noted composer of hymns. Talent ran in that family. Cindy had such a lovely voice, and when she sang, you could feel her love for the Lord.

In 1997, Cindy Walker was inducted into the Country Music Hall of Fame. J.E. and I were thrilled for our friend. Her mother, who was a vital part of her life, had passed away several years earlier. I watched the show with tears in my eyes as Cindy walked out on stage that night to accept her honor in a long glimmering dress adorned with long white gloves. She honored Oree on the CMHF Awards with a poem she had written. It brought the house down.

> In the 1980s, my mother bought me a dress for a BMI affair, and she said, "When they put you in the Hall of Fame, that's the dress I want you to wear." And I said, "Oh Mama, the Hall of Fame? Why that will never be." And the years went by, but my mother's words remained in my memory. And I know tonight she'd be happy, though she's gone now to her rest. But I think of all that she did for me, and tonight I'm wearing this dress.

The standing ovation Cindy received that night from her peers seemed to go on forever; it was thunderous. We were so proud of our friend!

Many accomplished people were woven into the fabric of our lives. Cindy once shared with me that she appeared in a movie with silver screen legend Gene Autry in the 1940s. Time and time again, I'd shake my head in astonishment at the reality of how small the world actually is and how fascinating it is, that somehow, we become interconnected in this fabric of life.

I spent many a Saturday morning in the movie theatre as a child with Lynda and Reggie and later with our younger brother, Art, who came along ten years after Reggie and me.

Back then, Gene Autry was our favorite singing cowboy in the white hat. Never in a million years, as I watched him save the West, would I have imagined that I would one day hold a conversation or share a meal with my silver screen idol—much less call him my friend.

Although Gene didn't live in Nashville, he spent a lot of time here doing work for the CMA. We visited with him many times over those years, and every time we did, we couldn't forget the fact that he was GENE AUTRY. We tried not to let it show, but we remained in awe. It was always there, in the back of our minds, that we were talking to one of our childhood heroes.

I can still hear Gene's voice as he'd try to convince J.E. to move to California. He'd say, "Son, you need to move to Hollywood and join the ranks of the cowboys. You'd be a natural." He repeated his plea time and time again. J.E. never gave the notion serious consideration, but just the idea that Gene Autry thought he'd make a great singing cowboy was an honor J. E. never forgot.

Years later we ventured out to Hollywood as Gene's guests. The man who gave us the western classic, *Back in the Saddle Again*,[29] had other interests besides cowboys and horses. He also loved baseball. In the early 1960s, he sunk some of the money from his movie and singing careers into major league baseball and became the owner of a team he renamed the California Angels. Gene invited us to attend an Angels game with him.

We couldn't believe it! Could it get any better than sitting in the spacious owner's box with Gene Autry, eating great food, watching baseball, and talking about life? I didn't think so.

Gene was happy that J.E. and I were together. He told us it was important to find someone who would tell you the truth when you needed to hear it.

In between innings, Gene shared that he never wanted to record what became one of the most popular Christmas songs of all time, *Rudolph the Red-Nosed Reindeer*.[30] His first wife, Ina, insisted it was a great song; she talked him in to it. He said marriage was kind of like baseball in that the two of you form a team. I learned a lot from Gene Autry, and maybe he learned a thing or two about me—like what a great catcher I was.

I was sitting in the box that day in Angel Stadium watching the game, when a foul ball came soaring towards me. On reflex I caught that ball! At first, Gene and J. E. were speechless. OK... well maybe I didn't reach out and catch the ball, but the ball did fly into our box and roll to my feet. I was thrilled when (on reflex) I reached down, picked up the ball, and held it over my head in triumph. Every one cheered! Gene began to tease me saying the Angels needed to sign me up. It was truly a moment.

He autographed the baseball for me that afternoon. What a memory!

I still have that baseball too. Today it resides in a curio cabinet between two Dresden & Royal Dalton ballerinas.

Tex Ritter was another silver screen cowboy who became our friend. I don't know how many westerns Tex starred in, but I do know between 1938-1945 he starred in over 40 "singing cowboy" motion pictures. I loved those movies the most.

Tex also sang the opening theme song to one of the most iconic westerns of all time. The 1952 motion picture was *High Noon* starring Gary Cooper and Grace Kelly. The action begins with a lone cowboy sitting on a rock—his horse by his side. You hear the beating of a drum, loud and steady, as opening credits begin to scroll and another cowboy on horseback tears across the screen in a full run. Tex begins to sing. I could feel his deep, soulful, drawling vocals all the way down to my toes. *Do not forsake me, oh my darlin'. . . on this our wedding daaaa-yaaaaa...*[31]

Oh my goodness! It was incredible. Tex was a classic.

By the mid-60s, he became a regular on the Grand Ole Opry. He moved to Nashville with his talented wife Dorothy, an actress/singer/dancer who he met on a movie set back in the '30s. They had a beautiful home not far from us on Franklin Road.

Tex became one of the founding members of the Country Music Association and spearheaded the effort to build the Country Music Hall of Fame. So you can imagine my chagrin when we visited with him one night backstage at the Ryman and J.E. informed him that I didn't like country music.

My mouth flew open. My eyes looked like saucers. I couldn't believe J. E. was standing there face to face with one of my silver screen idols, in the house that country music built no less, telling him that I didn't like country music. What in the world was J. E. thinking? I knew J. E. was teasing, but did Tex know?

I gathered all of the composure I could muster and calmly said, "Tex, J.E. is kidding you. I assure you that I do love country music, and as a girl I collected all of your 45 records. My favorite was *I'll Be A Sunbeam For Jesus.*[32]"

Tex chuckled a deep, throaty rumble. From that day forward, whenever I saw him in the Opry hallway, he'd smile at me. Sometimes he'd give me a wink.

We were blessed to have such wonderful friends, and we knew it. I say that, not because of the celebrity attached to these people, but because of the people they were. Good people.

We were family. Especially on the road. So many wonderful moments take center stage in my mind as I think back to those glorious times with our friends—and when they do, those memories from the RCA European tour dance out and take a bow.

This was the first time I had ever flown on a Boeing 747 jetliner. I had never seen such a beautiful, sleek thing. It was massive, new and shiny. This was an era where passengers still dressed up for air travel, and all of us were dressed to the nines as we boarded the plane that day.

I was feeling good about myself. I was even feeling good about my hair. Six weeks before we departed for the tour, I decided to make a drastic change. I decided to cut my hair in a short cropped style resembling the hairstyle of Twiggy—a popular model from the '60s. Like Twiggy, I was petite and blonde, and I too modeled. I thought the super short hair cut would accentuate the fashion of the times.

I was cooking dinner when J. E. walked in after a day at the studio. He saw me at the stove and did a double take. It was the double take that got me. I wanted to surprise him, and surprise him I did.

He stood there in silence.

J.E. not saying a word spoke volumes.

For weeks I wore a wig.

Finally my hair grew back just long enough to roll and perm—just in time for our trip. So there I was on a brand new Jumbo Jet, smartly dressed with my curly, no-maintenance, super short hair.

When it was time for dinner, the stewardess escorted our group to the upper deck. We ascended a spiral staircase to a beautiful dining room in the sky. Everything was so elegant—white linen table cloths, plates made of china, actual silverware and glasses of crystal. We shared a table for four with Dottie West and her husband, Byron Metcalf. Byron was Dottie's drummer, and the two were newlyweds. We talked about Dottie's new single *Country Sunshine*.[33] She was so excited.

I couldn't believe we were having a gourmet meal on an airplane. Everything was great until the pâté arrived. For the life of me, I didn't know what it was, but I was pretty sure I didn't want to eat it, whatever it was.

I whispered in J. E.'s ear, "What is this?" He looked at me in astonishment. He couldn't believe I didn't know what pâté was. He explained to me that it was usually liver, probably from a goose, minced into a spreadable paste. He was a connoisseur of fine food. He really liked it. Me? Not so much.

London was spectacular. While our husbands spent their days on a press tour, RCA provided us with a limousine and driver. Jeannie Bare (Bobby's wife), Barbara Davis (Danny's wife), Mary Reeves and I toured the city together. We were in charge of our destiny, and we had the time of our lives.

There was so much to see and do. We spent some time in Trafalgar Square—the fountains, the pigeons, the architecture—it was as if we stepped into a painting. We shopped at Harrod's, Europe's biggest department store containing over a million square feet of selling space. I bought a denim, long sleeve shirt—studded on the back, ragged for wear—a sign of the times. I couldn't wait to wear it through London with my long, plaid skirt and beret. This was so much fun!

I remember how exhilarating it felt to carry our shopping bags down the street, meet our driver on the corner and hand him our finds for the day. He opened our car door and gently placed our purchases in the trunk.

One blustery afternoon as we were sliding back into the limo after a delectable lunch, Mary turned to us and exclaimed, "I am never going back home! This is the good life for sure!"

We laughed and glanced out the window. There was Buckingham Palace. England already had a queen, but everyone in that car felt like a princess.

I loved London, and my thoughts secretly strolled back to a time several years earlier when I toured Great Britain with J.E.—just the two of us. *Pop A Top* had just made it's chart debut and was heading for the #1 slot. RCA sent J.E. on a press junket of England to promote his new single overseas. Although our schedule was hectic, we made time between shows, show cases and interviews to enjoy some sight seeing and simply being together. London was beautiful. We were so happy.

I didn't share it with the ladies, but during that trip together, our second child was conceived. London would always have a special place in my heart. Of all the friends in my life, J. E. was my best friend, and in 1967, my best friend and I learned our family of three would become a family of four. I remember it like it was yesterday.

Jim Ed leaving for a tour of Germany with Eddy Arnold and Don Bowman

Jim Ed, Becky, Dorothy and Tandy celebrating Tandy's birthday—1979

Lindsey, Reggie, Becky and Susan

Sounds and Styles Fashion Show:
Becky, Jeannie Bare (Bobby Bare),
Brenda Wright (Johnny Wright),
Barbara Luman (wife of Bob Luman)

London—early '70s
Jeannie Barre, Mary Reeves, and Becky

Chapter Thirteen

July Fourth is Independence Day, but for the next eighteen years, July 4, 1968 would be Dependence Day for J. E. and me, and we couldn't have been happier. That's the day we brought our beautiful daughter Kim into the world.

I woke up that morning with my doctor's voice ringing in my ears. "Becky, I wouldn't be surprised if you had your baby on July 4th." I simply took him at his word.

There would be no back and forth to the hospital like last time. No more going to the hospital unprepared. I woke up, packed a bag, dressed in a nice outfit, applied full make-up and did my hair. This time when our baby was born, I was going to look good. I had this giving birth thing down.

I remember having breakfast with J. E. and Buster when I made my big announcement. "Today is the day!" I'm not sure if either of them had faith in my proclamation, but around mid morning, I made believers out of them.

The labor pains began. This was nothing like the short bursts of pain I had with Buster. These pains made themselves known. Wow! This child was ready to make her debut.

J. E. drove me to Baptist Hospital and spent most of the day waiting with the other expectant fathers in the waiting room—partly because that was still the thing to do back then—and partly because he didn't want to hear the screams of other expectant mothers on the ward. The labor pains were terrible.

I changed out of my pretty outfit into a hospital gown. My hair that I fixed so perfectly that morning was in complete disarray. With each pain more intense than the next, I'd hold on to the bed rails and raise up in the bed trying to get some relief. I caught a glimpse of myself in the mirror. My eye makeup was running down my face. So much for looking good. I looked awful!

I thought this was going to be a piece of cake. I was wrong.

After eight hours of labor, two nurses began to wheel me into the delivery room—one on either side of my bed. I was groggy, but I knew they were having a conversation about me. Listening to them was like listening to a tennis match.

The nurse on the right said, "I don't think her water broke."

The nurse on the left would respond with, "I think it has."

Right. Left. Right. Left. Right. Left.

I think I surprised them both when I sat up, opened my eyes and said, "I assure you it has." That's the last thing I remember.

The next thing I know I'm holding my precious baby girl, Kim. She didn't have the head full of black hair Buster had at birth, but she was absolutely beautiful. We were thrilled, proud, and in love from the moment we set eyes on her.

Nashville Banner Newspaper reporter Red O Donnell delivered her birth announcement to the city of Nashville. Her name is Kimberly Summer Brown. Tongue in cheek Red wrote, "Why didn't they name her Winter."

Buster was six years old at the time of Kim's birth. He confided that he was happy to have a sister, but what he really wanted was a monkey! Eventually, Buster realized that Kim was as close to a monkey as it gets.

The joy I felt with one child was compounded ten fold with two children. Stereotypically we were the perfect family — one husband, one wife, one boy and one girl.

Looking back at the pictures from that time in our lives, I can see the happiness. Here we are at the beach in Florida. There's Buster and Kim building a sandcastle. The sandcastle is bigger than she is.

Here we are visiting grandparents in Arkansas. Buster sure is cute in that outfit his aunt made for him.

Oh my! There's J.E. playing in the snow with the kids. They're building a snowman.

And here we are on those family ski trips to Aspen that we'd take at Christmas time. The kids are a little older here. Where in the world did the time go!?!

Yes, the memories come flooding back. Here's a picture of a gift J. E. gave me on a trip back to Little Rock. He surprised me with a 1965 Ford Fastback Mustang in baby blue. It was something else. We followed each other home to Nashville that day, talking on our CB radios. I can't remember our handles back then, but two years later he changed his handle to *Pop A Top*.

As I was driving my new car home, I remember J. E. keying in and telling me to stay in the right hand lane. A car was speeding down the wrong side of the interstate. Again, an angel must have been on our shoulders because we avoided a collision. All of these thoughts come rushing back with a glance at this one picture.

When Kim came along, the car wasn't practical anymore. We let that car go for a more family friendly vehicle — something roomier and safer for children. Things I never worried about before I had children, I worried about now. For the first time in my life fear crept into my psyche.

It started with little things like: Is my baby breathing alright when I place her in the crib at night? Is Buster getting enough to eat? Why are they crying? Are they staying in the yard to play? Please don't walk behind that car!

I'd think about a constant barrage of "mother things." All mothers experience these thoughts, and these thoughts never go away.

The needs of my children changed with time; their problems changed, but even when they got older, I still felt responsible. To this very day I want to wipe away their tears and ensure all is right in their worlds.

After Kim was born, I began to teach dance. I still worked with the Jo Coulter Agency, but dance was such a part of me. It was my passion, and I was good at it. Teaching allowed me the luxury of fulfilling my personal life by staying home with my children, and yet it gave me a professional outlet of creative expression.

One night I was backstage at the Ryman with Jim Ed, and I asked Opry dancer, Margaret Smathers, to show me a few clogging steps that I might teach my students. Margaret was the wife of Ben Smathers, who headed the family dance troop, the Stoney Mountain Cloggers. The group danced regularly on the Grand Ole Opry stage for what became thirty-two years.

I'd never seen clogging until I started to accompany Jim Ed backstage. I was fascinated by it. I loved the high energy performances, and I appreciated the synchronicity of the dancers' moves coupled with the ability to showcase fancy, free-style footwork.

Margaret showed me some basic clogging steps. She was surprised at my ability to duplicate the moves so quickly. She began to show me more complicated steps. Again, I was able to parrot her motions. She said, "Becky, you won't believe this, but we've run into professional dancers who can't do these steps. Would you like to sub for us on the Opry if one of us gets sick or takes a leave of absence?"

I couldn't say yes fast enough. I absolutely loved it. I loved the Smathers family. I still do.

Some nights J. E. and I actually shared the Opry stage. He would be on stage singing, and I would be on stage dancing.

Ben Smathers was the Fred Astaire of the clogging world. Before a performance, Ben would wish us luck with that classic entertainer's creed, "Break a leg." When he danced you'd have thought both of his legs were broken or better yet you would have thought he didn't have a bone in his body. Ben could move in ways you wouldn't think possible. He was an amazing dancer.

I can't begin to tell you what a thrill it was to dance at the Ryman to the lively sounds of The Fruit Jar Drinkers or the Crook Brothers as the fiddler sawed down on *Black Mountain Rag*,[34] *Alabama Jubilee*[35] or *Orange Blossom Special*.[36] Every performance was a work out, and the crowd roared with appreciation.

In 1969, Jim Ed raised the bar just a little higher. That was the year he made himself at home in America's living room every week with a half hour syndicated television show of his own. Show Biz Productions produced *Jim Ed Brown's Country Place*.

The show revealed Jim Ed's tour bus slowly making its way up a mountain road in the Smokies. At the top of the mountain, he stops the bus and invites the audience to join him and his friends inside a chalet known as the Country Place.

Friends like Bobby Bare, Jerry Reed, Connie Smith, Jean Shepard, George Morgan and Bill Monroe joined Jim Ed in a Smoky Mountain home setting sharing songs and stories. The goal was to make the television viewer feel like he or she was part of a down-home, family visit loaded with great music.

Jim Ed persuaded Crystal Gayle to join the show. It launched her music career and she became a regular on *Jim Ed Brown's Country Place* while she was still a teenager. Crystal had long hair then too, but it only came down to her shoulder blades. It was six years before her first #1 record, but I would listen to her sing on the show, and I just knew she was destined for stardom.

The power of television was life changing. We all knew it. In one night, Jim Ed could reach as many people on television as he could touring the country with live performances for an entire year. His popularity was continuing to grow, and with that popularity came the daily buses of fans.

We found ourselves on Nashville's Country Music Celebrity Tour of Homes. Buses filled with tourists hoping to snag a priceless, keepsake photo of their favorite country star would pay money to hop a tour bus and ride around town while the driver stopped in front of our homes. The guide informed the fans who owned the home and shared a little bit about the star who lived there.

It's an odd thing to realize that, over the years, thousands of strangers knew where we lived. Odder yet when you think those strangers paid money to discover where we lived. Eventually, those daily bus stops in front of our home became routine. So routine, that at times, I'd forget they were there—usually to my dismay.

The way our home on Williamsburg Road was positioned made it difficult to see those tour buses coming. One day I was sitting on my front porch in my blue pajamas. I had huge rollers in my hair, and I was reading the paper. I heard the bus before I saw it. I never looked up, but when I cut my eyes over the top of the paper, I could see the tour bus was parked right in front of our home. I could almost hear the pop of flash bulbs and camera clicks as I gave a little wave and went inside.

Another time, I was running after Buster with a switch. I turned the corner of the house, and there stood the tour bus. I thought to myself what do I do now? Without missing a beat, I just kept on running—straight to the neighbor's yard like I lived next door.

Then there was the time Buster decided to get in on the act and cash in on some of the action. Even as a boy he showed signs of real entrepreneurship when he opened a lemonade stand for the sightseers on those buses. Bonnie and Maxine were at the house visiting that day, and the three of us had more fun running to the store, buying cups, ice and other supplies for Buster's "business." As I recall, he made out like a bandit from his efforts that afternoon.

Fans couldn't get enough of their favorite country music celebrities back then—that included knowing details about their families and their wives. Meeting the wife of an entertainer was one degree closer to the entertainer.

For three years in the late sixties and early seventies, I volunteered as a model for the Sounds and Styles Fashion Show, co-sponsored by American Business Women and ASCAP. As Jim Ed's wife, I was proud to represent my husband in the show. I enjoyed wearing the fashionable styles provided by Castnor Knots, a Nashville based department store chain, and I enjoyed sharing the stage with other celebrity wives and friends.

Everyone was so beautiful. Jeannie Bare (wife of Bobby Bare) walked the show along with Ellen Reeves (Del's wife), Tinkie Hamilton (George IV), Aldonna Phillips (Stu), Ann Stuckey (Nat), Kathleen George (wife of Lonzo and Oscar Fame) and Brenda Wright (wife of Bobby Wright—son of Johnny Wright and Kitty Wells). We raised a lot of money for charity doing that show. It was a fun way we could give back to an industry that had given us so much.

I enjoyed modeling, but I wanted more. In between raising children and teaching dance, I utilized my skills as a professional makeup artist and joined Jo Coulter on the productions of various television programs she contracted.

It was an exciting time for country music on TV. Our music was expanding its boundaries, changing its face and appealing to a new audience of country music fans. Never was that so evident than on *The Johnny Cash Show*.

I was a makeup artist on Johnny's show for most of its fifty-eight episodes. Taped at the Ryman Auditorium from June 1969-March 1971, the country music variety show aired on ABC. I worked with program regulars June Carter, The Carter Family, The Statler Brothers and Carl Perkins.

Proving that country music has universal appeal, I also met and worked with artists outside the typical country box. Over that two year period, Joni Mitchell, Bob Dylan,

Neil Young, James Taylor, Gordon Lightfoot and Louie Armstrong joined Johnny on stage. Of course the country heavyweights were there too—artists like Merle Haggard, George Jones and Marty Robbins. The variety of artists I met working on that set was astounding.

For me, the encounter that stands out the most, is the time I worked with Audie Murphy. Audie was one of the most decorated combat soldiers of World War II; he received the coveted Medal of Honor at the age of nineteen.

He was also one of my favorite motion picture cowboys. So it was a secret thrill for me when the cast and crew broke for lunch, Audie and I sat together on the backstage steps of the Ryman, located in the alley facing the back door of Tootsie's. He confided to me that he made these television appearances to promote his movies. We basked in the sun and made small talk that afternoon like two old friends.

I never took for granted the opportunities that the music industry afforded me. Sometimes those opportunities occurred in the most ironic of ways.

One morning, the telephone rang at the house. It was Jo Coulter on the line wanting to know if I could make myself available for an album cover shoot later that afternoon. She explained that I only had a few hours to arrange for a sitter and get ready. I told Jo I could make it happen, and I asked who the album cover was for.

She said, "I received a call just a few moments ago from RCA. The model they hired for the shoot isn't working out. The production coordinator asked me if I have a model on my roster with a pretty profile. I said I do; her name is Becky. I asked who the album cover was for, and he replied Jim Ed Brown! What are the odds?"

Jo continued, "I told him that you were Jim Ed's wife! He couldn't believe it either. I assured him that you have the prettiest profile of anyone on our roster. On the spot he asked me to get a confirmation from you. So are we good? You need to be there at four o'clock."

When J. E. and I were sitting across the kitchen table from each other having coffee earlier that day, never in our wildest dreams did we think we would be working together that afternoon. Just like that, I was on the cover of his new album titled Morning.

The cover oozes intimacy with a close up of me reclining, staring into J.E.'s eyes as he leans in for a kiss. The agency that produced the cover went on to win an industry award for Best Artistic Design for an Album Cover; the single Morning[37] went on to become one of Jim Ed's greatest hits, and I went on to grace the cover of three more of his albums: Angel's Sunday,[38] Evening[39] and It's That Time of Night.[40]

It had been five years since Jim Ed began his solo career. He had proven that he could make it on his own. He had his own TV show, he had hit records; he had tour dates on the calendar, yet something was missing. He knew that "something" was harmony. If he were going to be happy with his show, he would need to introduce the harmonious blends learned in childhood into his music once again. Harmony was a part of Jim Ed.

By happenstance, my friend Mona Roark introduced me to a sister duo originally from Independence, Missouri at a church social. The Cates Sisters, Marcy and Margie, were dark haired, girl-next-door beauties who could play twin fiddles and sing the sweetest harmonies. I couldn't wait to tell J. E. about them. He only had to listen to them sing to know he loved them as much as I did.

The Cates joined his group in 1970. They didn't distract from the show; they enhanced the show. They were a good fit. He liked having his three part harmony back, and I liked knowing I discovered the Cates Sisters in church.

———————————

Church was important to us as a family, although we weren't able to attend Sunday service together as often as we hoped. On the weekends that J.E. didn't play the Opry, he played the road. Often he'd travel long distances to his shows. Usually he'd arrive home from a tour exhausted between 4-5am on Sunday morning. Sometimes it would be mid day. It was difficult for him to attend services with us.

So many times he'd say, "Becky, I am so glad you went to church today. Thank you for taking the kids."

After he rested a bit, we'd have Sunday dinner as a family, and I'd share the day's message with him. I looked forward to that time with my family.

Spiritually I was surrounded by great role models. Pat Anthony was my neighbor and my Sunday school teacher from whom I learned so much. In 1971, Pat invited me to her home to meet the best selling author of a new book we had just read, *The Hiding Place*.[41] I will never forget my time spent in the company of Corrie Ten Boom. She changed the way I saw the world.

Corrie was a simple Dutch watchmaker and Christian who became active in the Dutch underground hiding Jewish refugees after the Nazis invaded the Netherlands in 1940. At the risk of dire consequences if her actions were discovered, she helped many Jews escape the Nazi Holocaust. Eventually she was captured and imprisoned in a Nazi concentration camp. Almost a year after her hellish incarceration, Corrie was released. She later learned that her release was due to a clerical error. A week after she regained her freedom, all of the women in her age group were sent to the gas chamber.

Corrie made such an impact on my life. From the moment I said hello, I could feel God's grace emanating from within her. I knew she was filled with the Holy Spirit. She was a walking testament of how an average person can endure and conquer anything through God's extraordinary power. A scholar of the Bible, she freely shared her faith with us that day.

There were times over the years that Corrie's story helped shape my own story. Her book is filled with wisdom learned through heart wrenching experience. There is guidance there to many problems:

How to recover from shattered dreams. . .

Security in the midst of insecurity. . .

Getting along with less. . .

Handling separation. . .

What to do when evil wins. . .

How to forgive. . .

How God can use my weaknesses. . .

How to deal with difficult people. . .

How to love my enemies. . .

How to deal with death.

I remember the tribulations endured by Corrie and how she came out on the other side. Through the most grievous conditions, she held firm to her convictions and stood on the solid ground of her faith. If she did what she did, then I, too, can do all things through Christ who strengthens me.

Corrie passed away in 1983 at the age of eighty-nine. Her legacy remains a guiding force in my life.

———————————————————

J.E. and I were frugal with our money. We still had everything we needed and most of what we wanted. However, we knew the importance of saving our money and investing wisely. We had seen the heartaches a "living for today only" philosophy had brought to some of our family and friends.

I was visiting my friend, Ima, at her Brentwood farmhouse one afternoon when I looked out of her kitchen window. I exclaimed, "Oh my goodness, Ima! This property next door is absolutely beautiful. Who owns this property?" She told me the property belonged to Mr. Blackman.

As soon as J.E. came home from the road, I drove him over to Mr. Blackman's place on Cloverland Drive. With one glance, he felt the same way I did. This property would be a good investment.

He knocked on Mr. Blackman's door and asked him if we could buy some of his land. Mr. Blackman told him no, but J.E. made him an offer anyway. Six months later, Mr. Blackman called us back and said if our offer was still good, the property was ours.

J. E. and I began to build our dream home. This would be the place we would grow old together.

We chose our friends Cliff Parrish to build our house and Gil Carter, who designed our beautiful church, as our architect. Back in those building days, I believe I spent more time with Gil than I did with J.E..

Gil wanted to know everything about us: our likes and dislikes, our immediate needs, our future needs, our recreational needs, our business needs. Only then did he begin to draw up our plans.

We decided our home would sit back from the road with a long tree lined driveway. I chose traditional colonial as the style of the home, and once I did, he encouraged me to stay true to the integrity of the traditional grandeur. The widow's walk I wanted was vetoed by Gil, along with a few other modern ideas that he said didn't fit the traditional colonial vision.

He designed a large basement with plenty of space for band rehearsals and an office for J.E. There was also plenty of room for the kids to play downstairs. On one end of the house, Gil designed a space for my dance studio. This was absolutely wonderful. I could teach dance classes, J.E. could rehearse with his band, we didn't get in each other's way, and we didn't have to leave home.

With Gil as my guide, I spent hours and hours choosing the materials, colors, fixtures and floorings that formed the interior to our 10,000 square foot cocoon. I can still hear his voice as he gave me advice. "Now, Becky, make sure you really like everything you choose because when you move into a big home, you're not going to want to redecorate it every five or ten years." I took his advice to heart.

Almost forty-five years later and I still have the same muted orange colored walls in my dining and living rooms. They've been repainted and touched up a time or two, but they still sport the original color. I also have the same wall paper placed in my kitchen in 1974.

We knew our fifty-one acre estate gave us plenty of room to suit our lifestyle. Immediately, we built a barn on the property. It was large enough to house the tour bus on one side, while the other side consisted of horse stalls and a tack room. Eventually we built tennis courts; once the grandchildren were born, we added a swimming pool.

The home on Williamsburg Road had served us well. As I walked out the door there for the last time, I thought about all of the people who had walked into our lives through that same door since our move to Nashville. Our lives had changed so much since we took that leap of faith.

In a nostalgic moment, I remembered the time I answered a knock at this door and discovered a clean cut man in his early thirties who explained he was a songwriter who had a song he thought J.E. might want to record. I invited him in. J.E. met with him, though he passed on the song. That man was Willie Nelson. To this day, I wonder what the song was that Willie pitched to him. If it ended up being a big hit for someone else though, maybe I'd rather not know.

Then there was the time, a group of cute, young female fans came to this door asking, between giggles, if Jim Ed lived here. They looked me up and down and said, "Oh my goodness! Are you the wife?' I got a kick out of the whole thing and smiled. I thought about the conversation Sally Arnold and I had.

Yes. I am Jim Ed's wife. That's all I'll ever be. I might be in his shadow, but I'm happy there. I am content. That was a good thing.

After eleven years in Brentwood, I was closing an old door and about to open a new one. I didn't know what the future would hold as we made this move down the road, but I sensed a new chapter in our lives was about to begin.

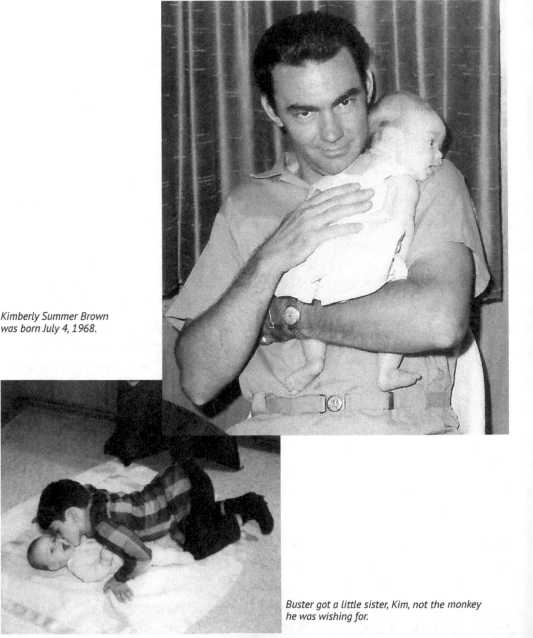

Kimberly Summer Brown was born July 4, 1968.

Buster got a little sister, Kim, not the monkey he was wishing for.

J.E., such a good Dad, but he didn't change diapers.

From a Christmas Special, Kim and Jim Ed

This was when Kim was really sweet.

Kim modeling for Castner Knott, Betty Borth was fashion director.

Kim was always content in her daddy's arms.

Buster - 1965

Buster, Becky, J.E. and Kim

The Murdocks, Jody, Perry and Hardy, Buster (in the middle) and Kim (far right) after a good time rolling around in the mud.

Kim and Buster

Chapter Fourteen

The 1970s are a decade I will never forget. It was a roller coaster ride like no other. Our highs were so high, and our lows—well let's just say, there were times that I didn't think we could fall any lower. In retrospect, I understand that it's the combination of those highs and lows and how we handled those experiences that make us who we are today— so I have found peace and gratitude in both the pinnacles and the depths. However, it is the good times where I continue to focus most of my reflections. In so many ways, the '70s were a glorious decade for J.E. and me. We were blessed.

In the early '70s, country music continued to gain acceptance by a broader audience all over the world. As Jim Ed's wife, I was part of the country music entourage who took a bite out of the Big Apple.

There are only a few institutions that can claim iconic status when it comes to musical performances. The Grand Ole Opry certainly earned that distinction, along with Carnegie Hall and the then new Kennedy Center. In 1972, large ads began to appear in the *New York Times, Post* and *Daily News,* promoting a huge country music package at one of America's oldest iconic entertainment complexes, Madison Square Garden. Excitement was in the air. Tickets were going fast.

I always enjoyed traveling with J.E., especially when we traveled to New York. New York City was one of my favorite places. I loved the kaleidoscope of colors, sounds, activities, food, people and cultures. I knew this trip would be extra special because the promoters were anticipating a sold out crowd. It had been a year since *Nashville At The Garden* brightened the spirits of Manhattanites.

New York City was ready for Music City, and Music City didn't disappoint. Jim Ed took center stage at Madison Square Garden that night along with Lynn Anderson, Jack Greene, Jeannie Seely, Sonny James, Loretta Lynn and Conway Twitty, and I was right there in the big middle of all those country greats. Radio personality T Tommy Cutrer was the master of ceremonies for this monumental show. I worked alongside Tommy on *The Johnny Cash Show,* where he served as our show announcer.

As a witness to the event, I knew my husband and all of our friends on the Garden stage knocked it out of the park. J.E. used to say it was always a thrill to see thousands of people in the crowd singing along to his songs. New Yorkers couldn't get enough of these country crusaders. They were singing, applauding and cheering like crazy. The night ended with multiple standing ovations and encores.

The next day the newspaper reviews were unbelievable. "*Nashville At The Garden performed to a record breaking crowd!*" Columnists wrote that each and every artist gave show stopping performances. I was so proud of J.E. I couldn't wipe the smile off my face. It was a night I will never forget.

March 3, 1973 was a big day for country music, and a big day for me too.

That was the only day in the history of the *Grammy Awards* that the Grammy's held their award show in Nashville, Tennessee. All other shows, before or since, have been held in either New York City or Los Angeles.

I remember arriving at The Tennessee Theatre by mid morning. Sadly, it no longer exists. It was a magnificent eleven story Art Deco style 2,000 seat theatre on Church Street with a huge lighted sign out front that stood nine stories high. In the 1980s, the theatre was demolished to make way for a high rise apartment building. Some people called that progress, but I wasn't one of them.

On this day the beautiful, old building was in her glory. I had all of my makeup set up for a 1pm call. The day was hectic. There were people everywhere. The CBS production crew were blocking shots for the show that night; musicians were hustling on and off stage for sound check; stagehands were checking props and set pieces; wardrobe consultants were tending to evening ware and stage costumes; publicists, managers, agents and artists were trying to locate dressing rooms and find a moment to talk to the room full of reporters down the hall. A steady line of the world's best of the best, from all genres of music, made their way to my chair.

I saw Roberta Flack, Aretha Franklin, Helen Reddy, Issac Hayes, Donna Fargo, Charley Pride, and show host Jonathan Winters. I enjoyed working television shows, but I enjoyed working these kinds of shows the most because of the variety of entertainers these shows brought their audiences.

I remember Ringo Starr took a turn in my chair. We chit chatted about the big night ahead as I applied some powder to his face. It's the strangest thing, but when I think about Ringo—even today—I can still see the top of his dark hair with that little gray cowlick that refused to be tamed.

As day turned into night, a constant stream of limousines pulled up to the theatre—depositing precious celebrity cargo helped from the confines of their regal rides to walk the royal red carpet. A massive crowd of onlookers gathered around makeshift barricades hoping for a glimpse of their favorite stars as they made their way to the theatre entrance, stopping every few feet to talk to various members of the press. Two huge searchlights waved back and forth in a rhythmic motion slicing the sky with an almost tangible beam of light. The entire scene was spectacular.

Since my day started early, I was able to leave the necessary show touch-ups to the other makeup artists who joined us later in the day. Right before show time, I slipped into evening clothes and took a seat beside J.E. in the audience. The show was absolutely amazing. On this night, I was able to have the best of both worlds.

―――――――――――――

Perhaps the highlight of my time as a professional makeup artist was the day I worked the NBC television special *Timex Presents Opryland USA* in October of '73. Opryland had only been in operation a year at that point, and along with the great entertainment, the show was an introduction of sorts to the wholesome variety of shows and rides the theme park afforded its visitors. The cast of park performers cherished the opportunity to work alongside entertainer heavyweights. It was a dream come true for most of those kids.

If you've ever been to a television taping, then you know everything on a set is hurry up and wait. So there was plenty of time between takes to engage an artist in conversation. I enjoyed meeting everyone on this set. By the end of the day, the entire cast felt like best friends. It just so happened that these best friends were Petula Clark, Tennessee Ernie Ford, Melba Moore, Wayne Newton and Carol Lawrence.

As a dancer myself, I especially enjoyed watching Carol Lawrence dance. I had followed her career on Broadway, and I thought she was amazing. Bob Wynn produced the show, Bill Walker was music director, and every scene was a spectacular production.

A wonderful twist to my day was my encounter with actor/comedian, Danny Thomas. He unexpectedly popped by the set to visit with his good friend Tennessee Ernie Ford. Danny confided that it was difficult to have both a well known TV family and a real life family. He said he made sure his real life family knew they were loved.

I understood what he meant. As a spouse of an entertainer, I had to share Jim Ed with fans, colleagues, news media, disc jockeys and the band. That can be hard to do at times. I would watch him lose track of time when he talked to his fans after a show. I was satisfied to wait in the wings while he chatted. I hoped he would finish quickly, but he seldom did. The fans were special to him and I understood that.

―――――――――――――

The '70s was the decade I discovered tennis—a sport I've been playing for over 45 years now. I wish I could say. I was initially attracted to the game because of the athleticism and skill involved. Truth is, I thought the tennis outfits most women wore to play the game were cute.

My first tennis friend was Jackie Peters, wife of Ben Peters, who later became a member of the Songwriters Hall of Fame. When Jackie and I began to play, Ben had just written a huge hit for Charley Pride, *Kiss An Angel Good Morning*,[43] so, as wives of husbands in the music business, Jackie and I were a support to each other on and off the court.

We bought our tennis rackets, we bought those cute outfits, and we headed for the YMCA for our first lesson. We learned how to serve, hit a forehand ground stroke, a backhand ground stroke and how to score a game. Thinking we knew it all, we scheduled a singles match. Very quickly it became obvious that we didn't even know what we didn't know—but there was something about the game that felt right to me.

Jackie and I took lessons at the Dolphin Club, and I began to get serious about the game. Tennis appealed to my competitive nature, and it made me feel better. Sweating it out on the court chasing those fuzzy tennis balls and strategically hitting them over a net to my opponent—sometimes with such force and might—was a wonderful way to release pent up energy. In addition to the physical challenge, the game required as much mental thought as it did technical expertise. I liked this game!

I joined a tennis team and was paired with Donna Rolin. I discovered she was a Jim Reeves fan. She also loved J.E.'s music. How cool was that?

I have to say I have never met a tennis player I didn't like. It is not all about winning. It's about building friendships with players who share the love of the game.

I took a leave of absence from the game for a few years. The first day I picked up my racket again, I thought I would surely die it was so hot. It felt like an oven, but eventually I built up my resistance to the heat

I was working so hard to up the level of my game,. My coach told me I needed to hit the ball 500 times, and that was just the forehand volley. He suggested I watch and emulate Betty Jones play. Betty was a top player at the Dolphin Club. She had great strokes, knew where to be on the court, and displayed excellent sportsmanship. The next thing I know Betty is moving to Birmingham, but she was back after 4 years.

In those early years of tennis, I could hang with the good players. I believe that being a dancer helped me get to the ball. I used to say, "If I could just hit the ball when I got to it." After many lessons with my tennis teacher, Rick Grooms, I was beginning to improve my strokes and raise the level of my game.

By now I was enjoying the game so much that we added a tennis court to the grounds of our new home. When J.E. wasn't on the road, he would come out and hit with me. He was a good player; he would have been a great player if he had invested the time. There just wasn't a lot of extra time back then. His energy and efforts were invested in his music.

I've gone on to play quite a few tournaments since I began playing tennis, and I suppose, I've won my fair share. Even today I am a member of the Nashville Area Ladies' Tennis Association and the United States Tennis Association. I continue to play 4-5 times a week.

Looking back, some of those quiet, everyday moments with J.E. are the moments I cherish the most. Both of us enjoyed working side by side in the kitchen. J.E. absolutely loved those times.

Fig, cherry, crab apples, plum and pear trees adorned our yard. We had fun picking the fruit and making jams and jellies together. Not only did we fill enough mason jars to see us through the winter, but we were able to share our homemade spreads with family and friends.

Then there was the garden. There's something extremely satisfying about slicing a tomato or a cucumber that you grew yourself, or shelling a bushel of peas that you picked on your own, knowing the meal you are about to eat is there because you tended to the soil and helped those vegetables grow.

About the only thing we didn't grow ourselves was corn, so we went to the Farmer's Market just north of downtown Nashville for that. I always liked the sights and smells of the fresh produce grown by our locals. The vegetables were piled on tables in adjacent booths under a large covered shed.

Pops of yellows, browns, reds, greens, purples and oranges were everywhere. It was a feast for the senses. I could tarry there all day, but I was on a mission.

J.E. had to have field corn; he didn't care for sweet corn. So I went to the market one day, and I asked a farmer if he had field corn for sale. He looked at me like I was crazy and said, "All corn is grown in a field!"

Trying to explain to him what I wanted was exasperating. I never did figure out if he was pulling my leg. I was able to leave the market with field corn that day, but it wasn't from that character.

We usually bought a hundred ears of corn at a time from the Farmer's Market, and it was J.E.'s job to cut the corn off the cob. It was an all day affair, but he didn't mind. After we'd cut the corn, we'd scrape those cobs—not leaving anything edible behind. Then we'd put the corn in bags and freeze it.

Field corn made the best cream style corn. We'd put it in a skillet and fry it up. It was absolutely delicious, and one of his favorites.

Maintaining fifty-one acres in Brentwood was a lot of upkeep, but it meant there was room for the kids to play and explore. J.E. and I bought Buster and Kim motor bikes and go-carts. They finally had a place to safely ride them. Then we decided to spoil Kim with a pony. My goodness, she was one happy girl. She called her pony Lady, and I do believe, if I would have allowed it, she would have slept with Lady at night.

Kim's love for horses continued to grow, and as only a daughter who has her dad wrapped around her little finger can, she talked J.E. into buying her a show horse. Jimmy's Red Bomber was the name of the quarter horse that won her heart. She spent hours with Jimmy cleaning his stall, brushing his beautiful red coat and training to ride him in competition.

Kim was quite the equestrian. She showed hunt seat and western pleasure and even went to the Quarter Horse Congress in Ohio. Of course all the ribbons and accolades lead to us adopting yet another horse into the family—Truck On A Long. Kim called him Trucker.

Showing horses is the gift that keeps on giving. Between boarding, maintaining, riding lessons, paying entrance fees, purchasing adornment for both horse and rider, and travel expenses, this avocation was very costly; but she loved it, and we loved her. My family had encouraged me from a young age to discover my talents and passions, and I wanted to give my children that same opportunity.

Our family of horses continued to grow when Kim made friends with the two little girls across the street. Amber and Courtney were the daughters of our friends Lee and Karen Gillock, and Lee told us his girls wanted horses of their own, too. He asked if we would board them. Of course we said yes.

No one could have prepared me for the knock on my door at four o'clock in the morning. I was sound asleep and startled awake by the explosive Tap. Tap. Tap. Tap. Tap. I jumped up, grabbed my robe and flew down the hall. There it was again. Tap. Tap. Tap. Tap. Tap. I heard the faint cry of someone calling a name from outside. As I got closer, I was able to make out the muffled sounds. "Police! Mrs. Brown are you there?"

My heart was racing as I opened the door to discover four police cars in my driveway. Their sirens weren't on, but their blue lights were blinking in the darkness, casting eerie, intermittent shadows against the house.

An officer identified himself and asked, "Mrs. Brown, do you own any horses?"

"Yes I do," I replied. I wondered what in the world this was all about. Was I dreaming?

"Mrs. Brown we have reports that several horses are running free down Edmondson Pike. Is there any chance they belong to you?"

There I stood in my pajamas slowing shaking my head up and down.

I couldn't believe it. Things like this never happened when J.E. was in town. These kinds of crazy things only seemed to happen to us when he was on the road.

Luckily, one of the officers knew how to handle horses, because I sure didn't. A group of Brentwood's finest wrangled those horses from the streets of Brentwood back to the Brown's fenced in pasture.

Maybe I should mention here that in addition to the four horses in our stable, J.E. decided cattle would be a good investment, so he purchased fifteen cows. It sounded good in theory, but he was on the road too much to take care of them. That job fell to the rest of us. Many a time, those cows decided that they wanted to visit our neighbors. Thank goodness we had understanding neighbors with good senses of humor. Between the horse and cow wrangling, our homestead was sounding more and more like the Old West.

After all this time, I will confess that I never was much of a horse person. I tolerated the horses because of Kim's love for them, but I'm REALLY not a cow person. The day J.E. sold those cows was a happy day for Becky Brown.

I was teaching dance in my new home studio, and I loved it! I felt as though I'm was sitting on top of the world.

In addition to J.E.'s comings and goings with his music, maintaining a tour bus parked in our barn, working professionally as a makeup artist and model, tending the garden, taking care of the grounds, taking the kids to and from their after school activities and wrangling horses and cattle when needed, I now had mothers pulling in and out of my driveway almost daily—depositing their children at my studio threshold. It was organized chaos, and I couldn't have been happier.

Though Kim's primary passion was still on her horses at this point in her life, she was beginning to take an interest in dance as well. I was eager to share my love for dance with her—as a teacher and a mother. Even Buster at the age of twelve expressed a desire to take tap dancing classes with me. I could tell from the first lesson that he showed promise, but the first lesson was all there ever was. After that first day, he broke his leg while playing basketball. That was the end of that.

In the meantime we enrolled Kim in gymnastic classes where she attended with her friend, Debbie Miller. With permission, I utilized the facility to brush up on my own gymnastic skills while I waited for the girls to finish their lesson. I practiced moves used in floor routines that I still remembered from past lessons of my youth and competitions of my own. I even practiced a few skills on the trampoline, though it wasn't one of my favorites—not since that accident years ago.

Now here I was, jumping on the trampoline again while Kim took her gymnastic lessons. There were no mishaps on the trampoline this time, so I decided to try my hand at the uneven bars. I should have stopped at the trampoline. When I whipped myself to the floor from the uneven bars, I ripped most of the skin right off my palms.

A few days later, I took Kim to the doctor for a checkup when the doctor noticed the bandages on both of my hands. He said, "Becky, what in the world did you do?"

I smiled and said, "I was practicing for the Senior Olympics."

1975 was one of the best years of Jim Ed's career. In the early '70s, he began to appear in commercials for the Dollar General Stores. Based on the popularity of those commercials and the relatability of Jim Ed to Dollar General's family friendly market, in 1975, Dollar General founder Cal Turner asked him to be their national spokesperson. That was a huge boost for Jim Ed.

The corporate office was only a short drive away in Scottsville, Kentucky, and Cal wanted to ensure Dollar General stayed true to its small town roots. The majority of Dollar General Stores were located in rural communities with populations of 20,000 people or less. It seemed the majority of their patrons liked Jim Ed and his music.

Cal made sure an autographed picture of Jim Ed hung beside every Dollar General cash register. Down home media campaigns placed him in America's homes, cars and businesses via television and radio spots. Many times I'd open a newspaper to see J.E. staring back at me in a printed Dollar General ad.

A year after he became national spokesperson, Dollar General exceeded annual sales of 100 million dollars. In 1977, Cal Sr. passed the torch to his son Cal Turner Jr., who asked Jim Ed to stay on board as the face of Dollar General. The company continued to see unprecedented growth.

Cal Jr. was quoted as saying, "It's not a family business anymore, but our business is a family." That's the way the Turner family made us feel. We felt like we were apart of their family—and in a way, our family became America's family too. Often Buster, Kim and I would appear in those commercials with Jim Ed—especially at Christmas time. I can still hear him say "Every day is dollar day at the Dollar General Store."

Just when we thought it couldn't get any better, Bill Graham with Show Biz Productions asked Jim Ed to host a new syndicated television show called *Nashville On The Road*, a country music variety series taped in various amusement and theme parks throughout the United States. Country music fans ate it up!

Season One, which aired in 1975, found the loud and lovable Jerry Clower, a country humorist from Liberty, Mississippi, as Jim Ed's co-host. Wendy Holcombe, an adorable blonde haired, blue-eyed banjo player from Alabaster, Alabama became a semi-regular that first season, and of course, he was joined each week by the Cates Sisters and his band the Gems.

The best and brightest in the business would fly in for a day of taping. It was always somewhere different—from the top deck of the *USS Alabama* battleship in Mobile, to Cypress Gardens in Winter Haven, Florida, to the Stanley Hotel in Estes Park, Colorado.

The Kendalls, Billy Crash Craddock, Dottsy, Jacky Ward, Dave & Sugar, Sonny James, Billy Walker, Sammi Smith, Ed Bruce, Margo Smith, Mickey Gilley, B.J. Thomas, Jeannie Seely, Jack Greene, Carl Perkins, and other country notables performed their songs and visited with Jim Ed on camera.

J.E. also sang several songs during the course of each show. I enjoyed hearing him sing material that he made famous, but I also enjoyed hearing him sing those great American standards on the show.

The show ran for six years with Jim Ed as host. Today, *Nashville On The Road* is considered a classic among country music programming.

We always managed to have the most fun with all our dance students over the years.

The Becky Brown Dance Machine opened the Italian Street Festival for about five years in a row.

Jim Ed helping Kim on her pony, Lady.

Kim and Jimmy's Red Bomber

Kim on Trucker

Timex presents Opryland USA Special 1973 with Ernie Ford, Bill Hinson (choreographer), Carol Lawrence, and Petula Clark

Jim Ed with Marcie and Margie Cates on the Jimmy Dean Show, early '70s

Becky practicing her serve, always working on her game

Becky Jones, Donna Rolin, Vickie Weatherly, and Becky

Linda Carpenter and I, we won the Lawrence Invitational Tournament.

Vintage. I hope he is not carrying a wooden racket.

One of Becky's paintings of their home in Brentwood—with historic elements—the '56 T-bird, Kim with Trucker, and the triplets building a snowman

Our home in Brentwood. I think I see 3 horses in the field.

137

Wendy Holcomb (from Nashville on the Road), my Dad (our bookkeeper) and Tandy Rice

Gabriella Hoffman, Linda Adams (my tennis partner), Becky, J.E., Patsy Bradley at the reception before the Music City Tennis Tour. Do I dare say Linda and I kicked rear that year.

Chapter Fifteen

I prayed about this next chapter of my life. I wondered if I should include it. I also sought guidance from my pastor and close friends. All agreed that I should share my story because on the other side of the pain, there is forgiveness. In the end, the decision to relive these memories is mine alone. It is time to tell my truth, the way I lived it.

Years ago, my husband had an affair. The tryst became a front page headline in the *Nashville Banner*. Magazines and country radio fueled the flames of gossip. Untruths were publicly told; they were shared and believed. Sadly, no one in the media ever came to me and asked me how I felt—what I was going through.

Yet, even now as I write, I worry about the feelings of the other woman. By the grace of God and with the distance of time, she and I became friends. I worry that ripping off the band-aid will hurt that friendship; however, I remind myself that my intention isn't to cause her pain. This story is about me. It is about my hurt and my healing. Forty years later, I can still walk in a room and hear whispers. The rumor mill continues to churn.

I believe that when we are thrown into the fire, we will either parish or we will come out on the other side as a beautiful sculpture. It is the hard times in life that reveal and build strength in character. In hindsight, I am thankful for those lessons in forgiveness that J.E. and I learned.

None of us are perfect. I once told my daughter you have to see the worst in someone to know who they really are. Only then can you decide if you should leave them or love them.

I believed in my vows. Marriage to me was for better or worse, richer or poorer, in sickness and in health. I was committed to my marriage.

I knew J.E. was a heartthrob. I knew there were women. His record label encouraged it. Wives, on the other hand, were discouraged from traveling with their husbands. Record execs said it was better for record sales if we didn't. I won't say I was happy about it.

Honestly, I tried not to think about it at all. In retrospect, it was like an ostrich sticking its head in the sand—that's the way you got through it. I was told this was all part of the business.

I knew what I was getting into. I also knew Jim Ed loved me, and he loved his children—however, we all have weaknesses. This one particular woman was a weakness for him, and even though, she too was married at the time, she had her sights on J.E. Although she tried and almost succeeded, I couldn't and wouldn't allow her to destroy the life we built together.

I would like this part of my story to be about survival.

We survived.

It wasn't easy, but we did it—by faith and with trust in God.

So, I share the details now, only to prove to the world that it doesn't matter how bad it gets. With prayer, belief, love and forgiveness, there is no obstacle that can not be overcome.

———————————————————

In 1976, RCA producer Bob Ferguson found a new song he wanted Jim Ed to record, *I Don't Want To Have To Marry You*.[43] Bob wanted him to cut the song as a duet, and he found a partner to sing it with him.

J.E. didn't know what to do. He was less than thrilled with the idea because he wasn't looking for a duet partner. Begrudgingly, he agreed to the session.

The first time he met her was in the studio, as they were about to record the tracks. He wasn't very personable that night because he thought Bob was tying his hands, but by the end of the evening, he had to admit that their voices blended well, and the song was good.

It all happened so fast. There were talks of her joining J.E. on the road. It was important to him that I meet her right away, so I did.

Like Jim Ed, she and I met in the studio. We discussed the difficulty of road life, and we laughed about traveling the highway on a bus full of guys. She confided that she had a husband and three children. When she told me she was a Christian, I was relieved. She appeared to be level headed. I liked her.

As luck would have it, *I Don't Want To Have To Marry You* soared to #1. We were all shocked at the way the song climbed. The RCA publicity team worked its magic. The new duo was the talk of country music, and soon named *CMA Duo of the Year*.

J.E. and I were elated and celebrated the success. The award meant more money, more road dates and more interviews to keep the wheel in motion.

I thought J.E. was grounded, but I watched the transformation as he saddled up his high horse. He and I had talked about stuff like this—how you can't believe everything that's said about you. You have to let some of those affirmations go in one ear and out the other; otherwise, you'll get too big for your britches. I think he fell into the trap. For the first time in his life, he began to believe the hype.

She soon joined the cast of *Nashville On The Road*. I attended a show meeting in which producer Bill Graham suggested that they create more chemistry on camera when they sang their songs together. He encouraged smoldering gazes and flirtatious glances. Bill said it made for a better show.

It didn't take long for the whispers to begin.

My friends said, "Becky, the way they look at each other on that TV show—how do you deal with that?" I explained it the way it was explained to me. "Oh I don't think anything about that. They look at each other that way to increase the ratings."

Then my mom attended a show in Hot Springs. She couldn't believe what she saw. Mom called me and said Jim Ed's duet partner was looking at him as if she were the one married to him. Mom suggested that I become more aware. I did just that.

That summer my mom came to visit. J.E. insisted that we travel with the band to Richmond, Virginia for a show date.

From the moment we boarded the bus, I knew something wasn't right. The laughter on the bus stopped once the band saw we were settling in for the trip. There was a feeling of uneasiness. One of the guys questioned, "Are you sure it's ok for you to go? Does she know you're going?"

Oh my! This was an eye opener, I felt like the other woman on my own bus. When she saw that I was there, she went back to her stateroom and slammed the door. She remained there for most of the trip.

J.E. spent most of his time behind the wheel of the bus. Eventually, one of the band members yelled, "Jim Ed wants coffee!" Before I could get off of the sofa, she flew out of her room to make the coffee. It was obvious to me that she considered him to be hers, and I was invading her turf. I was totally blindsided.

Still, J.E. convinced me that nothing was going on.

He told me she had shared a lot with him about her unhappy marriage. Let me tell you, a married woman frequently sharing intimate stories about her unhappy married life with a married man who is not her husband can be a recipe for disaster.

In 1978, as I was cleaning the bus in preparation for an upcoming tour, I found a letter in his stateroom. My heart sank. It was to J.E. from her. It read:

> *We have been together for two years, and I know I told you my love for you could see me through anything, but it seems the pain is too much. You are happy in your home life, and you need to nurture that. I think we need to end our relationship professionally and personally.*

There it was.

It was out in the open.

I confronted J.E. He told me he made the biggest mistake of his life. He apologized over and over again, and he assured me that the affair was over before I read that letter. He wasn't in love with her, but he didn't want to lose what the two of them had professionally, either. Contractually, they had obligations to RCA, concert venues and television shows. Professionally, they were tied together for the next several years. Quitting now could ruin them both.

This was a lot to process. Upon hearing what he had to say, I didn't see her letter as a farewell letter at all. In my opinion, she liked the fame and fortune more than he did. I saw the letter as an ultimatum note. Choose Becky and your family, or choose me and your career—but choose.

Over and over J.E. said, "It's you I love, Becky!" Though my heart was badly bruised, I still loved him. He was my husband and the father of my children.

Those who yield to temptation may say they're not hurting anyone else, but they are so wrong. The ripple affects are endless.

I remember coming in from the garden when I saw her standing at my kitchen sink. She stopped by the house to pick up a paycheck. Of all days, my hair was braided in tiny braids all over my head. I said, "I'm so sorry you've been hurt. I would love to sit down and quietly talk with you about it."

She huffed, "What are you talking about?"

I said, "I know you're in love with my husband."

"I'm not in love with him," she sputtered. "Why would you think that?"

"Because," I replied. "I have the letter you wrote him."

She wheeled around and flew down the steps to the office in our basement. I was right on her heels. She was standing in front of my dad's desk when I slapped the hell out of her. I slapped her right to the floor. The fall broke her glasses and caused a little cut right above the bridge of her nose.

J.E. heard the commotion and ran into the office. He grabbed me. I screamed, "You think you can hold me? No way!"

She was standing again and had a smirk on her face. J.E. yelled for her to get out. "You need to leave—NOW!" He said it 3-4 times before she moved, and when she did begin to move she moved slowly—taking her time walking through my house.

I broke free from his hold, and raced after her. When she heard me coming, she began to walk faster. She got in her car and locked the doors, but she didn't drive away. She just sat there.

My '56 T-Bird was parked close by, and the top was down. I ran over and grabbed my tennis racket from the backseat. I drew back my racket to smash her windshield when I stopped myself. I hissed, " I'm not going to destroy my good racket on you and your car. You're not worthy! You'd be wise to never step foot on my property again. Never again!"

She drove away slowly.

I was engulfed by emotion. Momentarily void of reason. How could I have lost it like that? I hated that my children witnessed my rage. It is a huge regret of mine. Buster thought I was hyperventilating, and he tried to place a brown bag on my head. No child should ever have to do that for a parent. The next day I went to the doctor. I thought I had experienced a nervous breakdown. He said what I experienced was anger—pure and simple.

For the first time in my life, I felt real hate. My life was spiraling out of control. Every day J.E. told me he loved me, but he continued to work with her. Every time the bus pulled out of the driveway, I knew they were together. I waited for things to change, but they didn't.

Three or four months went by, and I placed a copy of that letter in her husband's mailbox. He called me and told me the letter was his first indicator of a deception. He confided that for the past two years she had instructed him to stay away from me—that I was a jealous person. In hindsight, I think we came to understand that she didn't want us to get together and compare notes.

He gave up his job to be with their kids so she could live her dream. He soon filed for divorce.

I fell into a deep depression. I wanted her gone. I didn't like what I was reading in interviews, and I didn't like the love songs they were singing on stage.

I didn't know who I was anymore.

I slapped someone to the ground.

I wished someone dead.

I was upset with God.

My prayers were full of questions. "God, how could you let this happen? How could this happen to me?"

I was hurting. My children were hurting, and I couldn't fix it. My church prayed for me, and although I was frustrated and filled with sadness, I continued to pray through the turmoil.

As I look back, I appreciate my dear friends who listened to my tale of woe. I remember telling a group of friends, "I learned to fix biscuits, pinto beans and cornbread, and now he's going to ride off into the sunset singing duets and living happily ever after."

143

Things were bad at home. When the new show program came out that J.E. sold to audiences on the road, and our family wasn't included in it, things got worse. I had enough. Our arguments at home intensified. In retrospect, all I did was give her ammunition to use against me. I didn't have to worry about her taking J.E. away; I was driving him away.

J.E. asked me to go on the road with him, but every time I did, she threw a fit. On one particular show date, she didn't show up at all.

J.E. was getting it from both sides. He was miserable, and he decided to rent an apartment so he could get away from us both. I made it clear that if he moved out, I would file for divorce. I watched him leave, then I picked up the phone and called the lawyer.

The Bible says in Proverbs 25:24 KJV *It is better to dwell in the corner of a housetop, than in a house with a contentious woman.* That contentious woman was me.

Even while we lived apart, J.E. called me every day. He begged me not to go through with the divorce.

Then on June 11, 1980, I opened the morning newspaper, and the bold headline splashed across the front page of the *Nashville Banner* hit me squarely between the eyes. *Singing Duo's Friends Say; Jim Ed and his singing partner may tie the knot.*

J.E. was as blindsided as I was. He was devastated. He drove to the newspaper to confront writer Bill Hance. He demanded to know where Bill got his information.

I wanted to die.

All kinds of thoughts were whirling around in my head. J.E. said he was hoping for a reconciliation, but the newspaper insinuated that he was about to wed her. How many people had played me for a fool? How many people knew about this affair from the beginning, but never told me—people who looked me in the eye every day and said good morning? What did I do to cause this? What didn't I do that I could have done? Humiliation was pressing down on my chest like a boulder. My will was gone. I felt like I had no value. I couldn't bring myself to get out of bed.

My sister-in-law Susan saw the newspaper, and she rushed right over. I told her I wanted to die. Instead of trying to talk me out of it, Susan pulled out a notebook and a pen and sat down on the edge of my bed. She began to make a list. She said, "Ok when you do die, I would like to have your gold necklace...and that fox coat in your closet is nice...and I'd also like dibs on your '56 T-Bird."

I looked at her in astonishment. Then we both started to laugh. Susan snapped me out of feeling sorry for myself. She was wise beyond her years.

I am so over it. I knew I was at a crossroads in my life.

J.E. had disappointed me. By not standing up TO her, he didn't stand up FOR me.

A few weeks after the newspaper article came out, Susan and I went over to Jim Ed's house early one evening to have some papers signed that Buster needed for school. She was there, and there we all stood—the four of us in one room.

I asked her if she was aware that J.E. didn't want a divorce. She accused me of lying; then she turned to J.E. and said maybe you need to tell us the truth.

He looked at her and said, "I LOVE BECKY, and I DO NOT WANT A DIVORCE...but I love singing with you."

Susan and I made a hasty exit. All hell broke loose in that apartment. He asked her to leave and locked the door behind her, but she continued to cause a disturbance outside.

I don't know the details of what went on after that, and I don't care to know, but I did receive a phone call at home around midnight. It was her. She wanted me to know I could have my husband. She didn't want him anymore.

If there is any humor to be found in this story, I found it in that conversation. What did she mean, I could have my husband? I already had him. We were not divorced yet. The papers weren't signed. He was still my husband.

It was over for Jim Ed. His desire to sing with her ended that night. He dismissed his singing partner of four and a-half years. Their up and down relationship came to a dead stop.

A week later, on October 1, 1980, in the same newspaper that caused me such pain with their sensational stories and blurbs about our lives, I read an interview with Jim Ed and the *Nashville Banner's* Entertainment Editor, Red O'Donnell. So many things had been said—true and untrue—that J.E. wanted to set the record straight. In the story he was quoted as saying:

> ...I have never asked her to marry me. (Her) dismissal was not a spur of the moment decision. It has been a long time coming.

> ...If Becky and I get back together, my whole world will look wonderful. I'm just hoping—and praying—Becky will relent and give our marriage of (18 years) a chance to survive.

> ...What with my TV show, recording, stage shows and commercials, I've been living in a dream world. Success has come my way—but without Becky success doesn't mean a thing. I'm not self-pitying myself. I'm just repenting publicly. Work is not enough. I've learned a good wife is necessary. I hope I haven't learned too late. My advice to men, especially married men, is to hold on to what you got.

> ...My main concern at this time is to regain the respect and love of my wife Becky.

As beautiful as his words were to me, they were too little, too late. Those years of fighting for my marriage had taken a toll on me and our children.

It was one of the hardest things I ever did, but I divorced J.E.

J.E. and I attending a party - 1979

Diana Luster

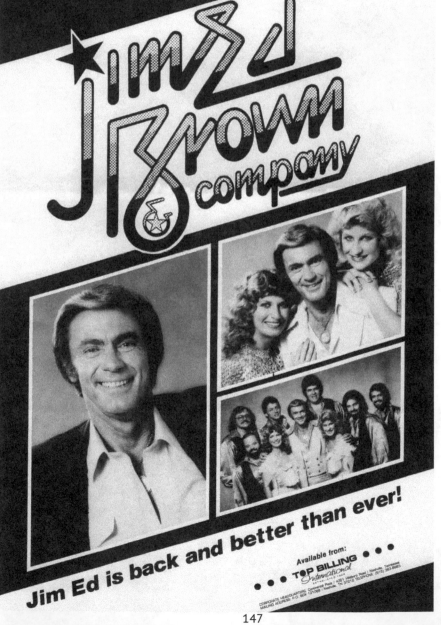

1979 or 80

DONREY

ᗷ CHAMBER OF COMMERCE
Welcomes Home
JIM ED BROWN
SPECIAL APPEARANCE
1981 Miss Arkansas USA Pageant
MARCH 23-24

A pageant where Becky was a judge

Chapter Sixteen

I never imagined myself as a divorced woman. I had spent half of my life building us up; and now, with the stroke of a pen, everything we built together was torn apart.

J.E. and I continued to speak to each other throughout the divorce. We would always be a part of each other's lives because of the kids, but it was something more for him. J.E. was on a mission to get me back. He couldn't believe he allowed the situation to get so out of control.

Less than a month after the divorce, I allowed J.E. to move back home so he could be close to the children, but he stayed in an apartment we had in the basement. He entered through the back entrance, and the door between the upstairs and downstairs remained locked.

Everyday he told me he loved me. Everyday he asked for my forgiveness. We began to see each other on small dates, and I even flew to a couple of road dates with him. We kept an open dialog.

J.E. began going to church regularly. When he rededicated his life to Christ, I was overjoyed. He was baptized anew.

We attended couple's counseling at church under the guidance of our pastor. I'll never forget one day Brother Lawrence looked at J.E. and asked, "J.E., how long did it take you to get yourself in this mess?"

J.E. replied, "2½ years."

Brother Lawrence put his hand on J.E.'s shoulder and said, "Well, it just might take you 2½ years to dig yourself out!"

Counseling made me examine my own thoughts and my fears—they were all over the map.

I remembered what it felt like to be together yet feel alone.

I was afraid, perhaps, that if I forgave him too quickly, history would repeat itself. I knew I didn't have another fight in me.

Someone I loved betrayed my trust, and my entire family suffered the consequences.

I knew our children were disappointed and bewildered.

I knew my reputation had suffered. I heard the talk. People whispered that I must have a man on the side; that's why I allowed J.E. to stray.

I tortured myself by going back to the day I first found that letter from her. In the letter, she wrote they needed to end their relationship of two years. What if I had turned a blind eye to the affair? What if I hadn't said a thing? Was it really over then, or was it truly a ploy to tighten her hold on J.E. as I suspected? If I had just kept my mouth shut, would we be divorced now? And if I did hold my tongue, could I have lived with the knowledge of betrayal festering inside me?

Every nagging doubt and negative thought crept into my head. But then, something amazing began to happen.

I began to understand that the countless hours of replaying the mistakes, along with the could-haves and should-haves, were wasted energy. I needed to stop thinking about the problem and start thinking about the solution. If J.E. and I were to have a future, I needed to think forward.

I prayed for hours and hours every day asking God for guidance—asking HIM for answers. I prayed my heart out. Over and over I'd ask, "God why do you want me to take this man back? He disappointed me."

And then I was still.

I was quiet.

I waited, and I heard HIS voice.

HIS message was always the same. "Because he loves you."

There were times I'd hear God ask me a question. "How can I forgive you, if you won't forgive him?"

The verse raced through my mind. *But if you do not forgive men their sins, Your Father will not forgive your sins.* Mathew 6:15 NIV.

I was harboring such anger and malice. I needed forgiveness.

Even as a newly single woman, as I began to look at other single men, I knew in my heart it was not right for me.

My emotional pain was still fresh. He couldn't say anything right. I would strike back at the most innocuous comment creating a hostile home environment at times. I couldn't help myself. Maybe on some deep-seeded, subconscious level, I needed him to feel the hurt that I felt.

The bitterness and dissension had taken a tole on us physically, too. J.E. looked weary. He lost weight, and he appeared to age. I myself was down to a hundred pounds sopping wet.

It was all so wrong. No longer could I continue to throw stones.

I prayed more. "God why should I take him back?"

Again and again he would answer. "Because he loves you"

J.E. and I began to talk in earnest about getting back together, but before I could commit to him again, he needed to clean the slate. I needed to know about those years with her. I wanted him to share everything, and he did. We had many conversations about those years because I wanted to know every detail. I never wanted to be in the dark again. Some of the things he said were difficult for him to share because he never wanted me to know. He didn't want to hurt me, but in the end, I think we both felt cleansed. We had to grieve the loss of trust and innocence, to feel whole again.

J.E. wrote me a seven page letter saying he was going to be a better husband and father. He took full responsibility for his actions stating he had placed his career before me and the kids. He would never do that again. And he said he never loved her—he never even thought he loved her—he only loved me. He said all the fame and money in the world wasn't worth losing me. Over and over he asked for my forgiveness.

There were those who tried to get in my ear and said don't take him back. Once a cheater, always a cheater. He only wants you back because you're a trophy wife. I had to laugh. I'm not sure I knew what a trophy wife was, but I'm pretty sure they didn't clean toilets or mop floors.

Then there were people like Tom and Billie Perryman who told me J.E. loved me; he always loved me and always would. We belonged together.

Again I prayed. Again I heard God's voice. "Forgive him. He loves you." And just like that, I let go of my ill feelings. I gave it to God, and HE removed the anger and hate that was eating me alive. The love I had for J.E. was beneath that anger, and it was unscathed.

We were only divorced for five months.

It was with a renewed heart that I remarried J.E. on October 11, 1981 at Forest Hills Baptist Church. Rev. Lloyd Lawrence performed the ceremony before a small group of family and friends.

I knew I could trust J.E. again because God said I could. HE was in control. Our marriage was on track; there would be no train wrecks for us.

A few days later we attended the CMA Awards together as husband and wife. Jim Ed told reporters our remarriage was the happiest event of his life. I had to agree.

As He always has, God amazed me. J.E. and I could forgive and love again and pick up where we left off before the turmoil happened—like it never happened. That is how God works. HE blessed us beyond measure.

At our first major appearance as a newly remarried couple during the 1981 CMA Awards, there were two other estranged country music couples who reunited in time for the event: Lynn Anderson reunited with her husband Harold "Spook" Stream, and Faron Young announced that he had ended a five year separation from his longtime wife, Hilda. One reporter called the event "reconciliation night" at the Grand Ole Opry House.

As fate would have it, J.E. and I would be the only couple of the three to withstand the pressures and strains of stardom. We not only survived, we thrived. To God we gave the glory.

J.E. said, "Becky, you've always been there for me. You stayed home to raise the kids. You stood by my side at music functions and parties. While I entertained in the spotlight, you never once complained about standing in the wings, and not once did I hear a word of complaint from you when I shared my time with the fans. You're my rock, Rebecca Sue."

Hearing him say those things was music to my ears. I believe when two people marry, they come together as one; however, there are still two sets of dreams to be fulfilled. I believe as married partners, we support each other.

I was proud of Jim Ed and all that he had accomplished, and he was proud of me, but I think when we remarried, he saw our lives through clearer eyes. He acknowledged the sacrifices we all made so he could live his dream—even though I never considered my decisions to be sacrifices.

I was involved in church, I painted and played tennis, and I continued to teach dance. I did what I could within the confines of our schedules and J.E.'s work demands. Any decisions to put my own career on hold, and not step it up to the next level, were not made from a place of sacrifice; they were made from a place of love for J.E. and our family.

J.E. told me, "I got too busy for us, Becky. I'm going to fix that."

He set out to make some of my own dreams come true. Once again, he turned to our friend, architect Gil Carter, to design a dance studio. We found the land and built on Franklin Pike Circle. The building was beautiful, and the studio was state of the art with wall to wall mirrors and floating dance floors. It was wonderful to have my own studio away from the house.

Just a few years earlier, I had worked out of my home on a major project for Jane Alsup, an alumni of the Opryland Entertainment division. I choreographed two shows for

Jane titled *Lullaby of Broadway* and *Raise-A-Ruckus Tonight,* which were sold in Texas, Tennessee and Kentucky specifically for convention and industrial audiences. Working on those shows gave me the idea to organize my own company of dancers. As nice as my home studio was, the new studio with its space and technological advancements heightened my excitement at the possibility of forming my own group.

Meanwhile, Jim Ed's career didn't miss a beat. He hired two of the sweetest and most talented young ladies to join his show—Diane Morgan and Christy Russell. Like before, I met with these vocalists before any final decisions were made. This time, however, my radar was up. Since my private life had been mocked by the media, I explained to these girls some of what I had been through, adding I never wanted my family to face a situation like that again. I sensed that Diane and Christy were genuine. I felt at peace knowing that they were part of J.E's show. I knew we had chosen wisely.

Diane stayed with J.E. for a few years before leaving to take a job with Reba McEntire. Christy met the love of her life while touring with J.E.—she married his steel player Daryl Hornberger. Both Daryl and Christy stayed with J.E's show until the day he died in 2015. Christy was with us for thirty-four years.

March 3, 1983 was a game changer for country music. That was the day that WSM launched a new country music cable network that operated out of the Opryland complex called TNN (*The Nashville Network*). A few months later, Gaylord Entertainment purchased the network.

Television played an important role once again in Jim Ed's career. He was into America's living room daily as the host for the TNN amateur talent show, *You Can Be a Star.* The exposure he received on TNN—including his frequent appearances on flagship show *Nashville Now*—were invaluable for renewed interest in his music by fan faithfuls, as well as introducing him to a whole new audience of country music converts.

Produced by Allen Reid and Mady Land, Jim Ed loved working with the cast and crew of *You Can Be A Star.* Back then, the show announcer was Larry Black, who went on to build his own country music empire with the productions of *Country's Family Reunion* and *Larry's Country Diner.*

Jim Ed hosted the show for six years, and many of the artists who filed through the show's ranks became superstars and friends. Lang Scott was the winner of Season One. Lang would go on to become a successful business mogul; he married country starlet Linda Davis and the two became parents of Hillary Scott who grew up to be the driving force behind country super group Lady Antebellum.

Trisha Yearwood, a then receptionist for MTM Records, came in second overall in the Season Five competition. (I'd like to know what ever happened to the Season Five winner.) Alan Jackson, who was working in the TNN mail room at the time, made his national TV debut on the show. He sang us all to break with a verse of George Jones' *He Stopped Loving Her Today.*[44]

I am amazed to say that Randy Travis was one of those artists who was rejected by the show. His audition tape didn't make the cut. A few years later, Randy was burning up the charts with his own #1 hits! I'd say that was a big swing and a miss for *You Can Be a Star.*

This show, and the opportunities it afforded J.E., were a blessing to our family—just as the friendships we made through the making of this show continue to be a blessing to me today.

1983 was also the year I made my own dream come true of starting my own dance troop. I made several trips to New York City. As I've already stated in this book, I love the energy of this city—home to some of the best theatrical productions in the world. It was here I studied the choreography of Joe Layton, Agnes DeMille, Michael Kidd and Bob Fosse.

With each journey to the Big Apple, I'd try my best to see the group *The American Dance Machine* perform. Their interpretation of famous Broadway selections was electrifying. I wanted to start a similar dance company in which I could give young dancers back home a platform from which to express their creativity while honing and perfecting the fundamental skills of dance.

I watched with pride as Kim continued to improve her own dancing techniques. She really was quite good. I was hoping this would be a venture we could experience together.

I called my company the Becky Brown Dance Machine, and I started with twenty students. Together Kim and I selected the music for our performances. We also created the choreography for both national and regional dance competitions, as well as, dates at fairs and festivals in Brentwood and Nashville. My friend, Ardie Lawrence, designed the costumes for our productions—reminiscent to the costumes worn in blockbuster Broadway productions.

We held our recitals at TPAC, Nashville's beautiful performing arts center. Whenever J.E. attended a show, he marveled at the skills displayed by these young dancers and the intricate details in the show's production. It takes a lot of effort to make a show look effortless. He was blown away every time!

One of our students, twelve year old Samantha Reynolds, secured a dance audition in Atlanta for Disney. Kim choreographed a powerful 90-second dance routine for Samantha filled with difficult moves. Samantha nailed it. She impressed the judges so much that after she finished, they asked her to stay so they could record it and have her read for them. Samantha declined the reading because she had to get back to Nashville for her confirmation into the Catholic church that night. One of the judges chased her out the door and gave her his card—stating that he would contact her parents about working with Disney.

Kim was so proud of her! In the end, however, her parents declined the offer. Even though Disney would have overseen Samantha's education, her parents did not want Samantha to leave home at such a young age. That year, the group of chosen *Disney Kids* included Christina Aguilera, Justin Timberlake, Britney Spears and Jessica Simpson.

God was in charge of our lives. We held fast to our resolve and trust in God's love. That didn't mean that we would never have to tread through the valleys of life; but when we did, we knew God would show us the way to higher ground if we simply stood firm on our faith.

In 1983, my twin brother Reggie had twins of his own. Reggie and his wife, Susan, gave birth to Beth and Wes. Multiple births run in our family—and just like Reggie and me, this set of twins was a boy and a girl. It wasn't long after delivery that Wes was diagnosed with Cystic Fibrosis—a genetic disorder that affects mostly the lungs, but can also affect the pancreas and the liver. Only 1,000 new cases of CF are diagnosed each year in the United States. The news was devastating.

God's timing of the diagnosis was amazing. During this time in our lives, J.E. was spokesperson for Children's Hospital in Little Rock, Arkansas—one of the largest pediatric medical centers in the United States. It is the goal of Children's Hospital to provide world-class medical care to children and their families.

For ten years, J.E. and Hillary Rodham Clinton spearheaded a telethon to raise funds for the hospital and pediatric medical research. In a snap decision, J.E. brought Susan and Wes to Little Rock. He called the very doctors he met while working those telethons and asked them if they would examine Wes and give Susan some answers.

Because of his work with Children's Hospital, he knew right where to go, and he knew whom to ask for help.

Today Wes is in his thirties. He is a good looking young man and a true miracle.

Tandy Rice was the president of *Top Billing International*, a talent agency that propelled the careers of Jim Ed, Porter Wagoner and Tom T. Hall. In 2014, Tandy became the first inductee into the Nashville Association of Talent Directors Hall of Fame. Back in the 1980s, Tandy had a 100-watt smile and a wide open personality to go with it. He also had a heart of gold when it came to helping us with our every day needs. Tandy was more than our agent, he was our friend.

It was Tandy who gave us Diana Luster—well kind of. Diana worked for Tandy in his office, but when we needed help, he loaned her to us to help run our office. We never gave her back. Instead, we made her an honorary member of the family.

Diana helped us out in ways that were beyond any job description for office manager. In addition to caring for our financial books and bookings, road trips and engagements, she also took care of Buster and Kim when J.E. and I were out of town.

One weekend, Diana stayed at the house to babysit the kids. On this particular night, we told Kim she could invite a girlfriend to the house for a sleepover. While Diana was downstairs taking care of some business, Kim and her friend decided to have an icing fight in my studio. They mixed up some homemade icing like you would put on a cake, and they began to sling it at each other.

Icing was everywhere—on the walls—on the mirrors—on the floor. Once it dried, it adhered to the surfaces of my studio like concrete. Diana said it took her hours to clean that mess up.

Kim was always getting into mischief. Once when she was very young, she crawled in bed with us in the middle of the night. The room was dark, but I felt her wiggle under the covers. I patted her head and told her to go to sleep. Little did I know that before she so innocently crawled under the sheets, she had foraged through my makeup kit. Kim applied my red lipstick all over her body.

The next morning when I threw back the covers, I inhaled a sharp breath. It looked like a homicide had taken place in our bed. Red lipstick was smeared everywhere. Kim sat up with a big smile on her very red cheeks—grinning from ear to ear.

Diana was indeed special to us. Not just anyone can survive Kim AND Truman. Truman was a gold and blue McCaw . I remember someone we knew had some baby McCaws, and I happened to say, "Oh, that would be so cool."

Be careful what you say, folks. My friend gave me one of those birds as a gift. The lifespan of a McCaw is one hundred years.

Truman was a handful to say the least. For some reason he really attached himself to me. I'd open his cage, and he'd follow me into the kitchen to hang out. McCaws are very loving creatures, but they can also bite your finger off.

Because a bird like Truman requires a lot of attention, we often passed him around amongst the Brown family for care. When Truman stayed with us, I would yell at Kim to get ready for school in the morning. I'd say, "Kim, get up! It's time for you to go to school!" Pretty soon Truman was squawking the same thing. "Kim, get up! Kim, get up!" We didn't need an alarm clock in our family. We had Truman.

Bonnie and Brownie enjoyed having Truman the longest, but whenever Maxine went over to their house to visit them, she'd walk past Truman and whisper, "You shit ass." Maxine was a good teacher.

It wasn't long before that little vulgarity became Truman's favorite phrase.

Eventually, Truman made it back to us, and invariably someone would walk in a room, and Truman would whisper, "You shit ass." He sounded just like Maxine.

We tried to be good pet parents and not laugh at Truman's choice of words when the kids were around—but we couldn't help ourselves. Of course we'd admonish Truman, telling him "Bad bird". He'd just look at us, cock his head and let another "You shit ass" quietly fly on by.

Today Truman resides in a bird sanctuary in Pigeon Forge, Tennessee. I think I might try to find him one day. They say McCaw's never forget. I just hope that if I do find him and walk up to him to say hello, he responds with "Kim, wake up!" For the record, I have my doubts.

Robbi Nash is another angel who looked after us. Robbi was, and continues to be, a wonderful family friend who we met through our friendship with Diana. Robbi helped us with computer work and Kim with her homework. Many a time, she'd heat up that iron and press J.E.'s clothes for *You Can Be A Star,* and she sometimes answered the phone at my new studio while I was teaching a class. I'm not sure what we would do if we didn't have friends like Diana and Robbi.

At one time, paper jewelery was the rage in fashion. As a hobby, I made a variety of paper pins and earrings for my friends to wear—mostly harlequins, little bears and fish.

My dear friend Terry Tomlinson thought she could sell my jewelry, and before I knew it, she marched into the office of McClures Department store in her long mink coat, with my jewelry case in hand, and asked to see the buyer. Terry walked out with a contract.

Oh my goodness! We had to mass produce! There was only one problem: We weren't ready to mass produce.

Almost overnight my office turned into operation central. Terry got me into this so she helped in the assembly line process. Kim got in on the act and made tiny fish scales for those fish pins, and Diana became a painter. I can still hear her exclaim, "But, Becky, I don't know how to paint!"

At times we resembled Lucille Ball working in that chocolate factory, but in the end we made the deadline. The jewelry line was a success. I can't begin to tell you what a thrill it was to walk down the street and see someone wearing one of my designs. Great things can be accomplished when you have great people by your side.

Our family is growing. We have a daughter-in-law now!

In 1984, Buster married Leigh Biggs, an attractive blonde from McGehee, Arkansas. They met in college at the University of Arkansas where Buster studied chemical engineering and Leigh studied fashion design. We traveled to McGehee for the ceremony, and I remember being excited for Buster on the drive over.

The wedding was beautiful—and big. So many family members and friends came to share in their happiness. Leigh's sister, Shannon, was her maid of honor and Kim was one of the bride's maids.

As a mother, a thousand different memories raced through my mind as they said their "I dos." I remembered the day Buster was born and the day we took him home.

I remembered the day he took his first steps and the day he said his first word. Trips to see his grand-parents, getting ready for church, ballgames, broken bones, broken hearts, birthdays, Christmases, graduations and family vacations—all of those times brought us to this day.

I was pleased and proud that Buster found the right hand to hold as he began to maneuver through life with his new bride. I prayed his foundation was solid. I knew in my heart that it was.

Looking back at the '80s, some of my favorite times were those family trips. I remember shortly before Buster married, Buster, Kim, Jim Ed and I took a vacation together to Aspen, Colorado.

The first day out we decided to take a ski lesson to brush up on our skills. We took a chairlift to the top of Buttermilk Mountain and were separated into small groups according to our skill level.

I was placed in an advanced group consisting of seven guys in what the instructor called a "kick butt" class. He held no punches when he said if we didn't think we could cut this class, we were welcome to ski on down the mountain and get some hot chocolate. Never in my life have I shied away from a challenge.

At first we skied in a single line—staying in control of our skis. Then we took turns being the leader—executing thrilling jumps. It was the perfect workout. I loved it.

At lunch we stopped at a quaint restaurant on the side of the mountain. We were sitting there eating, when the guys from my lesson asked how Buster and I had met. I laughed and said, "I met Buster at the hospital when I gave birth to him."

They actually thought we were a couple. I do believe Buster was mortified, and if he could have, he would have crawled under the table.

I stayed with that class all day, and met Kim at the bottom afterward. We drove into Aspen and had a lovely dinner with J.E.

Another ski trip that stands out in my memory was the time J.E., Kim, Buster, Leigh and I drove up to Sugar Mountain in North Carolina with our neighbors Bill and Carla Benefield and our church friends Norbert and Betty Borth, who I first met at the *Sounds and Styles Fashion Show*. Betty was a fashion director at Castner Knot, and I ended up modeling for her for the next twenty-five years.

Since we all wanted to ride over to North Carolina together, J.E. decided to drive the bus. Driving a top heavy, 40 feet long vehicle around extremely steep, hairpin turns in the dead of winter can be a harrowing experience, but J.E. was an good driver, and we made it to our destination late in the day. Only problem was our condos were on top of a steep mountain. He drove that bus straight up that mountain effortlessly. The next morning, people walked out of their condos in shock. Everyone wanted to know how in the world we got a big bus like that to the top of the mountain.

From the start of my first day on the slopes, I saw red flags. I was a little concerned when I discovered that we'd be skiing on artificial snow. When it gets too cold, artificial snow turns to ice. I prefer powder. Then as I hopped on the chairlift to take me to the top of the run, I could hear snippets of conversation from a group of boys riding in front of me. I could tell they didn't have a clue what they were doing. I was a little nervous with them on the ski run, so waited for them to ski down in front of me.

When I did embark on my journey to the bottom of the mountain, a young skier who I was told held the record as the fastest skier in North Carolina, pushed off behind me. On his way down, he took his eyes off of the slope to look at a couple of downed skiers to the side. That's when he plowed into me. He hit me so hard that we actually flew through the air. I landed to the side of the mountain with such force that the fall broke my ski boot. Kim and Buster witnessed the entire thing.

The next thing I knew the ski patrol skied me down the mountain on a stretcher. Upon examination, they sent me home with instructions to keep my foot elevated as much as I could. They said I was lucky it was just a sprain.

I hobbled back to the condo and fried a skillet full of chicken for the gang. I wanted them to have something good to eat when they came in from their day in the snow.

Around 5a.m. the next morning, I woke up with the dry heaves. I gently shook J.E. awake and told him I needed to go to the hospital. He told me to try not to think about it, get back in bed and try to get some rest. We'd go to the hospital when the sun was up. So, that's what I did.

Later that morning the doctor at the hospital couldn't believe it. For the better part of an entire day, I had been walking around on a broken leg. He asked everyone in the room to leave. He reset me leg without giving me anything for the pain. I just had to soldier up. Next to having a baby, that was probably the most intense pain I ever experienced. Thank goodness it was quick.

The remainder of my vacation was spent nursing that leg. Then when it was time to go home, it took a police escort to clear the way in order for us to get our bus to the bottom of the mountain. That was a memorable vacation for sure.

You meet some very interesting people in the entertainment industry. One of the most fascinating couples we ever met were Ed and Vonna Jo Gregory. Ed ran a thriving carnival business known as *United Shows of America*. He set up the amusements for the Florida State Fair, in addition to thirty other fairs and festivals across the United States. He even staged shows at the White House.

Our friend Dave Barton introduced us to the Gregory's one night over dinner at O'Charley's. It wasn't long before we all became friends.

If you knew Ed for any length of time, you knew their was an interesting dichotomy to his character. Ed could be as down home as apple pie—All-American red, white and blue; but when it came to business, Ed could tow a hard line—he could be tough.

One of the things Nashville seemed to love the most about Ed were his Christmas parties. They were extravagant. The talk of the town!

For several years, J.E. and I co-hosted those parties with Ed and Jo. Artists, musicians, music business associates, TNN casts and crews, Grand Ole Opry members, United Shows executives, politicians and friends all gathered at the Gregory home dressed in their holiday finest. Valets parked cars, bartenders poured good cheer, and waiters offered guests the best in Christmas delectables from silver trays. Outside, a large white tent enclosed a full buffet and a dance floor where party goers could dance the night away to a full band. Those were great days!

Today, Ed and Jo's son and daughter-in-law, Donnie and Jackie, are the godparents to our grandchildren.

———————————————

Times with friends were important to us. J.E. saw his music friends regularly at the Opry and on road dates, but he wanted a chance to sit down and really visit with his friends away from work. He wanted the spouses to get to know one another too, and he wanted husbands and wives to gather in a familiar place outside of the public eye—where they could exhale and simply be themselves. That's why we started a gathering called EATIN' MEETIN'S.

We took turns hosting these events. On Sunday afternoons, we'd bring a pot luck dish, and we'd eat and fellowship together. Bill Carlisle used to say, "I'm not coming if Becky doesn't fix her banana pudding!"

It was a lot of work setting up those tables and chairs, but it was worth it. Long before the TV series *Country Family Reunion*, we'd sit around and tell stories about the early days in the business. J.E. loved hearing all of those wonderful tales, and he told a few himself.

We hosted many of those Eatin' Meetin's at our home. Billy and Bettie Walker hosted a few, along with Tom T. and Dixie Hall and Opry dancer Melvin and Beverly Sloan.

When I think back now to all of the famous folks gathered around those tables, I just shake my head in wonder. However, at an Eatin' Meetin' there was no such thing as celebrity—only friends seated around tables enjoying each other's company.

I can see it now: Stu and Aldonna Phillips, Ernie and Betty Ashworth, Jack and June Greene, Jeanne Pruett and Eddie Fulton, Hairl and Paula Hensley, Brother Oswald and Eunita Kirby, Carl and Goldie Smith, John and Marie Hartford, Tom and Billie Perryman, Bill and Becky Anderson, Dickey and Katie Lee, Stonewall and Juanita Jackson, Grandpa and Ramona Jones, Brenda Lee and Ronnie Shacklett, Ray and Jeanne Pillow, Jessie Coulter and Waylon Jennings, Sam and Robin Wellington, Porter Wagoner, John Conlee, Jim Glaser, Jean Shepard and Bennie Burchfield, Johnny Russell, George Riddle, Norma Jean, Margie Bowes, Mac Wiseman, Woody Paul and Charlie Walker.

There would be 50-60 of us gathered together at those Eatin Meetin's. I look back at the list now, and it makes me sad to see how many of these great people are no longer with us—but then I think of a quote from an old Dr. Seuss book.

Don't cry because it's over; smile because it happened.[45]

I was all smiles.

Nashville Banner

Nashville, Tennessee □ Tuesday afternoon, October 13, 1981 □ Vol 105, No. 160 □ Mu

Banner photo by Don Fost

Jim Ed Brown and wife Becky, recently remarried, beam during the awards show.

Trophies or not, 3 stars hail 'reconciliation night' wins

By Red O'Donnell
Banner Entertainment Editor

Country music has its share of "heartbreak" songs, and the pressures and strains of stardom have taken their toll on many singers' romances and marriages.

But true love still wins now and then, and it was "reconciliation night" Monday at the Grand Ole Opry House at the Country Music Association

CMA Week

Awards show for three country music stars — Jim Ed Brown, Lynn Anderson, and Faron Young — whose marriages had been on the rocks.

Jim Ed and his wife Becky were beaming like newlyweds because they are newlyweds. After 17 years of being man

and wife and a divorce more than a year ago, they were remarried Sunday night at Forest Hills Baptist Church, with Rev. Lloyd Lawrence performing the ceremony.

The two had called it quits following Brown's controversial and well-publicized romance with singer partner, Helen Cornelius.

But Jim Ed and Becky re-

Please see BROWN, page A-6

161

Ground breaking for my new studio

Nearly done

162

Jackie Bell, me, Susan and Reggie Perry at my studio opening

Kim, J.E. and Becky

J.E. and I walking into my studio for the first time

Jim Ed and Christy Russell (later married Daryl Hornburger)

*Mike Baker, Christy Hornburger, Jim Ed, Daryl Hornburger,
Terry Duncan, Kim, Bonnie, and Maxine*

*Dina Johnson, Joey Giovannetti, Kim, Daryl Hornburger,
Becky, Christy Hornburger, Terry Duncan and Mike Baker*

Have I told you that J.E. was always singing.

Kim - 1985

I remember this well. We had just finished a great meal at Ed and Jo Gregory's.

Leigh and Buster's wedding - July 27, 1985

Kim, Becky, Buster and J.E. at Leigh and Buster's wedding

Buster, Becky, J.E. and Kim on ski trip to Aspen, Colorado - 1976

Chapter Seventeen

Although the dance studio J.E. built for me on Franklin Pike Circle was glorious, after five years of working outside of the home, we had an amazing offer from someone who wanted to buy the building. In order to simplify our lives, I moved my dance classes back to my home studio.

Kim, who had spent a year studying dance at Gus Giordano's studio in Evanston, Illinois, also moved back to Brentwood. To accommodate the new circumstances, we made new additions to our home and built Kim her own apartment and dance studio. My studio was growing by leaps and bounds, so having her teach in a studio adjacent to mine was a blessing. She brought fresh ideas to the table; her choreography was amazing, and under our combined tutelage, our dancers exceeded all expectations--plus, I enjoyed having my daughter close by. Kim and I had been through a lot together.

It's always fascinating to me how God places certain people in our lives for a purpose we may not fully comprehend at the time. We think we know why we are connected, but true understanding only becomes apparent with time. Tom Goddard was one of those people.

Tom was our reflexologist and a very dear friend who once helped Kim overcome some painful knee problems when she was younger. Before seeing Tom, I had taken Kim to an orthopedic doctor who performed arthroscopic surgery to determine the cause of her pain. I was a little upset when the doctor called me back to his office with no clear cut answers. Instead, he asked me if I MADE her dance. I looked him squarely in the eyes, and I said, "Absolutely not. I have never made Kim do anything she didn't want to do."

We left the doctor's office that day feeling defeated, but an internal voice urged me to call Tom. He had cured me of tennis elbow when I couldn't even lift my arm to brush my hair—maybe he could help Kim. He began to work with her and discovered that she had loose elasticity in her joints. Tom directed her toward a strength building mission. By following his instructions, the pain went away.

In 1989, Kim and I convinced J.E. to go to Tom for a general check up. While a reflexologist isn't an M.D., by applying pressure to specific points to the feet, hands and face, he can ascertain much about the body as a whole. The theory behind the hands on practice of reflexology is that these pressure points correspond to specific organs and systems in the body. Upon examination, Tom said, "Jim Ed, you need to go to a heart doctor as soon as possible. Something isn't right."

J.E. left Tom's office, called our brother-in-law Brownie, who he trusted completely, and made the six-hour drive to Brownie's office in Dardanelle, Arkansas the next day. After a series of tests, Brownie determined that there was indeed blockage to the heart. He immediately sent J.E. back to Nashville to see a heart specialist.

Just like that—in a matter of days—J.E. was having open heart surgery. Once again, life turned on a dime. It seemed one day he was singing his heart out on the Grand Ole Opry stage, and the next day he was having open heart surgery—a quadruple bypass.

I remember this time vividly. For one thing I was in the big middle of putting in a new kitchen floor, and the kitchen was a wreck. It was a total nightmare. For another thing, it was Thanksgiving time. Suddenly nothing was important to me except J.E.

I remember a phone call from Maxine. She said, "Becky, you must be worried sick." I replied, "Maxine, I don't worry about things I don't have control over. This is in God's hands."

I found myself on my knees praying that J.E. would make it through the surgery. I asked God to lift him up in the palm of His hand—to guide the hands of the surgeon—and oversee his recovery. I had faith that He would.

We were thankful that open heart surgery had come along way over the years with medical advancements. Yet the thought of the surgery itself was still a scary thing to us.

My prayers were answered. J.E. overcame the trauma of the surgery and the recuperation afterward like a trooper.

Together, J.E. and I attended classes at the hospital on how to cook for a healthier heart. No more cooking like Momma Brown for us. Both Mr. and Mrs. Brown died at relatively young ages: J.E.'s father was 62 when he passed away; his mother was only 58. Both suffered from heart conditions.

It wasn't easy to change old habits, but J.E. did it. He gave up many of the things he really liked to eat, and for a long time stayed true to a heart healthy diet. He also started each new day with a walk. He couldn't believe how much better he felt. He was back to work in no time.

We often wondered if he hadn't seen Tom Goddard when he did, what would have happened? I believe the reason for God's placement of Tom in our lives was abundantly clear.

For the most part, I was very fortunate where my own health was concerned in the '80s and '90s. I had no ailments. I give all the credit to glucosamine chrondroitin/MSM. I do remember my back pain was so bad, I taught a dance class once with an ice pack on my back. It was on that occasion that I broke down and went to the doctor.

Years earlier, my doctor informed me that he had two patients by the name of Becky

Brown who frequented his practice. I wasn't the only one. He always had to make sure he had the right Becky Brown's chart before entering the examination room.

I booked an appointment to discuss my back pain, but my regular doctor was on vacation. The receptionist scheduled me with the other doctor in the clinic.

I was escorted to the examination room by a nurse and told to lie down.

A few minutes later the new doctor walked in and asked me to lift my leg as high as I could. I took my leg and touched my nose.

The doctor looked very shocked. He picked up my chart, and as he walked out the door he mumbled, "It's very clear, you are not THIS Becky Brown."

As it turned out, my back pain went away.

―――――――――――――――

J.E. asked me to go to lunch with him. In a very nonchalant manner, he explained that we would be dining with a small group of people who were interested in casting a host for a new television travel show.

I liked the group instantly. Mike Runnels would be one of the producers of the show. We also met with show directors Bill Landers and Robin Creasman. I had no idea at the time, but the luncheon was actually an audition of sorts for us both. The group was looking for a set of co-hosts for the show—specifically a husband and wife team.

I listened intently as they explained that the show would entail a lot of travel throughout the continental United States sharing adventures of the RV lifestyle as the hosts toured some of the most popular and scenic tourists destinations in America.

Did I hear that right? Hosts? Who was the other host?

It didn't take me long to realize that the other host for consideration was me. I remember hearing them say, "Becky, you'll be good at this because you're believable."

Believable? I didn't know how to be anything but believable, whatever that meant. I've always been just me. Good, bad, or otherwise that's all I've ever been.

By the time the luncheon was over, I knew they liked us. The job was ours if we wanted it.

Poor J.E. I bet I exclaimed, "They want me to be co-host!" at least one hundred times on the drive home. He got such a kick out of me. I was excited—and I think I was in shock. Never in a million years did I think I would be traveling the country, working alongside Jim Ed Brown. We were so happy!

The show was called *Going Our Way,* and things were indeed going our way for J.E. and me. Ever since we both placed God at the center of our marriage, our cup overflowed with blessings.

Going Our Way aired for five seasons on The Nashville Network from 1990-1995. For 60 minutes each week we'd take armchair travelers to vacation destinations that they might want to experience for themselves one day—from the rugged majesty of our national parks, to the sandy surf of Hilton Head Island, South Carolina. With each landmark location we'd sample the traditions, culture, food and music that made that area of the country unique. Jim Ed and I skied down snowy mountains, rafted down raging rivers, hiked some of the most beautiful trails in the world, and hopped aboard jeeps, scooters and horses. We even rode those pack mules at the Grand Canyon on those narrow trails as they made their descent to the canyon floor below. I believe my prayer that day was, "Lord, please don't let this mule stumble."

One of the most daunting adventures we experienced was when the producers asked us to take a hot air balloon ride in Arizona. For someone who rarely gets frightened, I admit I was a little scared that day. The afternoon was not conducive for a balloon ride; the winds were way too erratic and gusty. However, in the world of production, you often have only a small window of time to grab a necessary shot before moving on to the next location--such was the case on that particular day. As soon as the crew got what they needed, and the ground crew brought us down to earth, I finally exhaled.

One of the most memorable tape days for me was the day we witnessed the young athletes practice for the Winter Olympics at Lake Placid, New York. The kids perfected their flips and aerial tricks by skiing off of a large man-made slope. Since there was no snow to be found in the heat of summer, they landed in a pool of water.

I can't begin to describe all of the wonderful things I was able to see and do with Jim Ed by my side because of this great opportunity. I was lucky to be associated with such a talented crew. Charley Wilsey was the camera operator for the show, and he traveled with his wife, Becky, as his assistant.

Our directors, Bill and Robin, were both good singers and musicians, and there were several episodes in which we concluded the show by singing around a campfire, enjoying the camaraderie amongst neighbors for which RV travel is known. The best part of the entire experience was working with matter-of-fact Christians.

From the very beginning, however, the crew had their work cut out for them when it came to working with me. I had a hard time walking and talking at the same time.

We were in Tahlequah, Oklahoma, and I couldn't pronounce "Tahlequah" to save my life. I don't know how many takes it took me to get it right. Truthfully, I don't want to know.

Then there was Kissimmee, Florida. Again, I couldn't say the name of the city correctly. To add to my frustration, every time the camera began to roll, J.E. would softly sing in my ear, "Kiss sem me once, and Kiss sem me twice, and Kiss sem me once again..." Finally I told Bill to just give J.E. my lines.

And then there were the jokes and pranks. One night we arrived in South Carolina a little later than expected for a taping the next day. We were trying to hurry and take our bags to the room when Bill and Robin offered to do it for us. They knew that Buster and Leigh had driven in from Atlanta to have dinner with us. They told us to enjoy the time with our kids, and the bags would be in the room upon our return. We thanked them for their generosity and hurried out the lobby entrance.

After dinner, we picked up our key from the front desk and walked to our room. J.E. unlocked the door.

Unbelievable! There was a man in our bed. He appeared to be asleep and snoring loud enough to wake the dead.

I tugged on J.E.'s sleeve and whispered, "Shut the door, J.E. We have the wrong room! Don't wake him up. Let's go."

He just stood there. Again I whispered, "Come on! He's asleep. I don't like this. We have the wrong room!"

Suddenly we heard laughter coming from the bushes outside of our window. It was Bill and Robin with their walkie talkie. The other walkie talkie was in our bed next to a cigar shaped lump of pillows under the covers.

J.E. was suspicious from the beginning, but I fell for their gag hook, line and sinker. Incidents like that were always happening with this bunch of people. I like to say we laughed our way across the United States. It was so much fun.

Throughout our five years of being on the road with *Going Our Way*, I gained a new respect for J.E.'s talents. No matter the situation, He never got his feathers ruffled. If he made a mistake, he'd just fix it and move on. I knew he was good in front of the camera; this show simply reminded me just how good he really was.

In 1992, *Going Our Way* received a *National Service Award* from the Recreational Vehicle Association. I was proud of that honor. It meant we were doing a good job. Not only were we showcasing the RV industry, but we were also promoting family-friendly activities— encouraging others to slow down and savor life.

One of the nicest compliments I think we ever received came from Bill during the taping of this show. After several years of being on the road together, he turned to us one day and said, "You know, I don't believe I've ever heard a single cross word from either of you toward the other. I've only seen two kind-hearted people when it comes to how you treat each other. I see the love."

I wouldn't give anything for my time with J.E. on that show. It will always be very special to me.

December 5, 1994: I remember it like it was yesterday. J.E. and I were in Las Vegas with Ed and Jo Gregory when we received a phone call with news that nearly every mother and father with grown children longs to hear. We were first time grandparents! Not once. Not twice. But three times over! Buster and Leigh had just delivered triplets, two boys and a girl!

We didn't know exactly when our grand babies would be born. From the beginning, it was doubtful Leigh would carry the babies to term. The pregnancy had been difficult for her. She was actually admitted to the hospital weeks earlier on complete bed rest and monitoring. She did everything she could to give those three tiny lives inside her time to gain the strength they needed to enter this world. As predicted, they made their debut early. They were little, but strong.

At just over a pound and a half, our beautiful Isabella Victoria was the smallest of the three. We knew it would be a while before she could join her brothers at home. She was so, so tiny—but we knew right away, she was also a fighter. Oliver Hudson and Hampton Arthur rounded out the trio at approximately three pounds a piece.

Buster and Leigh were beside themselves with happiness! They had waited for ten years to hold a baby in their arms. Now God had blessed them with three miracles at once.

We caught a flight home from Vegas as quickly as we could, then made the drive over to Atlanta to see these little cherubs. We couldn't wait to hold them either.

Laying eyes on those children for the first time, we were consumed with adoration. No words could ever adequately express the instantaneous love we felt. We prayed that God would allow us to live long enough to see this next generation of Brown children grow up. We were two proud grandparents—Becky and Poppy.

It wasn't long before Buster, Leigh, Isabella, Oliver and Hampton were coming to visit us in Brentwood. Even though we only lived a few hours away, that was quite the trip for the Fab Five. Three car seats, three babies to oversee, and a car packed to the gills with all of the things you need, or might need, to take care of three little ones.

I'd rent baby beds and have them set up by the time the kids arrived. Leigh would bring their high chairs from home, and we took them for afternoon walks in the sweetest stroller designed specifically for triplets. No matter where we went, when those children were together, they drew a crowd—especially when Leigh was pushing that stroller seven months pregnant.

That's right! Less than a year after the triplets were born, Buster and Leigh were pregnant again. Becky and Poppy welcomed their fourth grand baby Genevieve Elise into the world on May 10, 1996—another precious baby girl. Then there were four!

I remember one very special night at The Grand Ole Opry, our entire family was standing together in the Opry wings. Bonnie and Maxine were in town, and Opry President Bob Whittaker invited them to join Jim Ed on stage for a reunion of The Browns. The crowd roared when they heard The Browns were taking the stage, but the big show-stealers that night weren't Jim Ed, Maxine and Bonnie. They were Isabella, Hampton and Oliver.

Before Jim Ed introduced the song they were going to sing, he stepped up to the microphone with an energetic Isabella in his arms. She must have been about two years old, and she looked so cute in her pink and white dress with a big girlie bow in her hair.

Jim Ed said, " I've got a little tiger here. You've had The Browns all these years; I'd like to introduce you to the new generation of Browns. My son and his wife had triplets a while back, and these are our grandchildren."

The crowd began a collective, "Awwwwww...." that quickly changed to delighted laughter. It wasn't easy to wrangle three two-year-olds loose to their own devices on the Opry stage.

Just like at home, they took off in every direction when Jim Ed called them by name. Maxine chased after Hampton who sprinted toward stage left. Aunt Kim scooped up Oliver who quickly toddled toward stage right, and once Jim Ed put Isabella down, she headed straight to center stage—right toward the footlights. Bonnie chased after her, and like a championship cutting horse shooooed her to the Opry wings where she escaped not once, but twice—both times scurrying back to the spotlight. Finally, Bob Whittaker himself chased Isabella down and carried her back to mom and dad, who were proudly standing in the wings holding Genevieve who was just a tiny baby at the time. It was a true Opry moment—a shining example of the heart of the Grand Ole Opry: FAMILY.

I guess we should have known by her actions that night, that when she grew up, Isabella would choose a career in music just like Poppy. I believe all of our grandchildren harbor a deep affection for the arts, How could they not? Their grandfather was an Opry legend, and their grandmother and aunt are professional dancers. Instead of talking about nightlights in their rooms, they grew up with talk of spotlights on stages.

When they were six years old (Genevieve was four and a-half), J.E. took the grandchildren into the studio and recorded a fun Christmas song *Big Foot Rides With Santa*.[46] A few weeks later they willingly performed that song on the Grand Ole Opry stage with their Poppy. We called it their official Grand Ole Opry debut!

The next year, Kim and I convinced Buster and Leigh to give us permission to take the children to a performance by the Rockettes at the Opry House. I say "convince" because Buster and Leigh warned us multiple times that we were wasting our money. They said their children wouldn't sit still for a three hour show. They predicted a disastrous end to our evening.

As we were taking our seats, Kim and I explained to the kids that Samantha Reynolds— the young dancer who turned down the offer to be a Disney kid when she was 12—used to be a student of ours and was now a member of this famous dance troop. This made the night extra special for us all. We told the children to watch for her on stage.

From the snappy opening number, to the finale that included the majestic splendor of the Christmas story with its living nativity scene, the children were spellbound—all four of them. We couldn't wait to get home and gloat to Buster and Leigh.

Then when Genevieve turned seven, she informed her Poppy that she would perform his #1 hit *Pop A Top* with him on the Grand Ole Opry stage. It was her idea. She said she'd been practicing, and she wasn't taking no for an answer. So like any grandfather in

J.E.'s position would do, he introduced Genevieve to the Opry audience that night, and *Pop A Top* became a duet.

I don't think you've ever really heard that song, until you've heard a seven-year -old sing:

> *Pop A Top Again*
>
> *I just got time for one more round*
>
> *Set 'em up my friend*
>
> *Then I'll be gone*
>
> *Then you can let some other fool sit down*

Yes, I think from a young age, we discovered each grandchild was 75% "All-American kid" and 25% "ham!"

GOING OUR
WAY

JIM ED & BECKY BROWN

Going Our Way - Here we go!

Going Our Way - Skiing Big Bear

Going Our Way - Grand Canyon

Going Our Way - Yellow Stone

Going Our Way - Maybe Jim Ed should have taken Gene Autrey's offer to be in Western movies.

Going Our Way Monterey, California

Going Our Way - The best crew ever—Robin Creasman, Becky and Charley Wilsey, an RV representative, Jim Ed, Me and Bill Landers

Leigh with Genevieve, Buster holding Isabella, Kim with Hampton, me, Jim Ed holding Oliver backstage at the Opry

All the grandchildren singing a Christmas song with Jim Ed on the Opry

Chapter Eighteen

By the mid '90s, it was time to try something new. For forty years, Jim Ed had traveled up and down America's highways taking his music to the fans. Now it was time for the fans to come to him. Like so many other country stars in Nashville, Jim Ed made the pilgrimage to Branson, Missouri.

He headlined at the Ozark Theatre on Hwy 76. He had Branson's #1 Morning Show, which featured the talents of The Branson Brothers, Fiddlin' Nancy Hensen, Debby Campbell—daughter of Glen Campbell—and our very own Kim (billed as Kim Ed) who joined her father's show as both a singer and a dancer.

Jim Ed enjoyed the advantages of staying in one place. It afforded him time to relax after a show instead of contending with the hundred and one little things you have to do when you travel to your next concert. However, it didn't take him long to realize that he wanted to perform a little closer to home—closer to his beloved Grand Ole Opry. He decided to buck the trend of putting down roots in Branson, and he began to headline a show at a theatre in Pigeon Forge, Tennessee.

We loved the Smoky Mountains, so much so, that we decided to buy a second home in Pigeon Forge. I still taught my dance classes at my home studio in Brentwood, but on weekends I'd drive over to Pigeon Forge and join J.E. and Kim, who once again performed with her dad on stage. She even opened her own dance studio in Pigeon Forge. She is so talented. She scheduled her students around her show times at the theatre.

It was here that God took me by the hand and showed me how to love like I never thought possible. Just a few miles away, J.E.'s one time duet partner was performing in a supper club she opened in Gatlinburg. The burdens and demands of operating that venue were staggering. After many conversations with me, seeking my blessing, J.E. decided to ask her if she wanted to sing with him again on his show. At one time they created some memorable music. As singing partners they were good together.

After all those years apart, she accepted his invitation on one condition: she would only work with J.E. if it were ok with me.

Some of my friends were astounded that I would allow him and her to perform on stage together again. They wanted to know how in the world I could sit there and watch them sing love songs to each other knowing their history.

I guess my best answer is, that's exactly what it was—history. Believe it or not, I found myself taking up for her and defending her.

When J.E. and I remarried in 1981, I wiped the slate clean. We really did start anew. I trusted him.

It's a difficult thing to explain because I'm not sure I could have forgiven without God's presence in my life. I'm not sure it's humanly possible. When you give a heavy burden to God, he makes mashed potatoes out of it. He helps you see the big picture, and the grievances of the past are just not important.

Before Jesus died on the cross, he spoke to his Father and said, "Forgive them, for they know not what they do." Neither J.E. nor she knew the full extent of the repercussions their actions would cause.

People make mistakes. People absolutely make mistakes. The thing that was so unfortunate in our case was that those mistakes were played out and judged in the public eye. Everyone knew, or thought they knew, what we were going through. Our lives were an open book.

Many times when I'd drive over to spend a weekend with J.E. in Pigeon Forge, the three of us would go out to dinner. I began to enjoy her company. In the late '70s when they were riding the wave of success as a singing duo, she and I were merely business acquaintances. With time shared in the Smokies, we began to really talk. We laughed together, and we even shopped together. We became friends.

It was years before we actually apologized to each other. We both had done some things we regretted, and eventually we both said, "I'm sorry for the pain I caused you." We had to find our footing first—our rhythm. Sometimes it is better to move forward without words. Sometimes actions speak louder than words. I believed she was sincere in her actions. It was something I sensed. I could feel it in my bones. Without being fully aware that it was happening, it just happened. We forged a strange, new friendship—a friendship we've nurtured for the past 20+ years.

I remember J.E. said to me once that he believed if she had the chance to do it all over again, she would have handled things very differently. In hindsight, I have to admit, I would have too.

Once every one thousand years, the world is witness to the changing of a millennium. Jim Ed ushered in 2000 with a performance at the Grand Ole Opry the night of

December 31, 1999. He wouldn't have dreamed of being anywhere else. With a jovial, "I will return!" he left the house, only to arrive back home around 10pm to a party in full swing. We were surrounded by those we loved as we counted down to a new century—a new millennium--together. It was such a great night. We were so happy!

A few days later, J.E. was even happier. He pulled out his boots and camouflage, double checked his rifles and scopes, gassed up the truck and headed out to Stuttgart, Arkansas, Duck Capital of The World, for the annual Opry Duck Hunt. At least I think it was Stuttgart. The location occasionally changed, but the purpose of those outings never did.

The Opry men and male management weathered freezing temperatures, early mornings and gusty winds to sit in a spartan-like, makeshift blind hidden in the reeds just above the waterline. An old stove gave them what little warmth they had as they dined on beef jerky and cold sandwiches, and waited for the opportunity to bring down some web-footed fowl. Upon command, one of the locals would send prized dogs to swim out and retrieve the downed ducks. The trained canines would paddle them back to the blind. It was quite an experience. J.E. considered the tradition of the Opry Duck Hunt to be a highlight of his year.

Over time, the players of this "All Boys" Club changed, but I think in 2000 J.E. was joined by Opry managers Bob Whittaker and Jerry Strobel, along with Little Jimmy Dickens, Jimmy C. Newman, Billy Walker, Charlie Walker, John Conlee and Mike Snider. No women were allowed on these expeditions. These men really roughed it. This was their chance to get back to basics, reconnect with nature and each other, and just be. They took inventory of years past, and they set their course for the upcoming year. Sharing that duck blind was metaphoric in a way, because over the years, most of these men had been through the trenches together many times over.

August 29, 2001 we set sail on the Grand Ole Opry Cruise to Alaska. Jim Ed was booked as one of the entertainers on board, and we had so much fun. Bonnie and Brownie decided to join us, and we extended our vacation with a family tour of Alaska's interior by way of Alaska Railroad.

We boarded the train in Anchorage and stopped for a few days in Talkeetna for some sightseeing. That's when Bonnie and I got adventurous.

We booked ourselves a bus trip to Denali National Park and Preserve. I'm not sure what we were expecting, but it wasn't a yellow school bus with bench seats and windows that slid up and down. We traveled toward the mountaintop on dirt roads with hair pin curves, and when the driver finally made a pit stop, we stood in line in the middle of no where to take our turn at a port-a-potty. When we made it to our destination, we couldn't see much of Mt. McKinley, the tallest mountain in North America, because of poor weather conditions, but it was an experience Bonnie and I would never forget.

We reunited with our husbands and boarded the train once again. This time we were headed to the North Pole, a small Alaskan city near Fairbanks known for its year-round

Christmas decorations—including candy cane striped street lights. The North Pole had a Christmas store called Santa Claus House with walls covered in letters to Santa written by children. We enjoyed this fairyland. There was an innocence to the area—an innocence that was shattered the very next day.

We were in Fairbanks, Alaska—September 11, 2001. It was early morning, and I was the only one up. I was watching TV when the network abruptly switched to breaking news. I couldn't believe what I was seeing. One of the Twin Towers in New York City had been hit by a plane.

J.E. and I had an adjoining room with Bonnie and Brownie. I woke everyone up, and we watched the horrific events of the day unfold together. We watched the towers fall, we heard that the Pentagon was hit, and we learned of a plane crash in a field in Pennsylvania. What was the world coming to? We tried to make sense of it all, but we couldn't. We prayed for the families, and we prayed for our country. Nearly 3,000 people had lost their lives; over 6,000 people were injured.

My mind wandered back to a time the year before when Kim and I took a girl's trip to New York. We had dinner in a restaurant on top of one of those towers. How many people were innocently grabbing a bite of breakfast in one of those restaurants planning a day of vacation that morning when the first plane hit? Did they make it safely outside?

Civilian airspace in the United States and Canada was immediately closed.

Planes in the air at the time of the insanity were instructed to land at nearby airports—escorted in with military supervision. Planes remained grounded the next day. We could not fly out. We had to sit, and wait and wonder.

When the airports re-opened on the 13th, it was chaos. We stayed in Alaska for several more days, but our patience was wearing thin. We wanted to go home. We wanted to hug our kids and grand kids.

We took a chance and drove to the airport. When we got to the ticket counter, we crossed our fingers behind our backs and told the attendant that J.E. had a heart condition and needed to get home for care; Brownie was his doctor. Miraculously we made a flight to Chicago O'Hare. At least we'd be closer to Nashville. Once we boarded, however, we were shocked at what we saw. The plane was packed with people. Everyone was grumpy and anxious. Security was heightened. Nerves were frayed.

If we thought the flight was bad, the airport was worse—wall to wall people everywhere we looked. Like us, everyone was trying their best to get home. There was no one to help any of us with our luggage. We were responsible for getting our bags to the next leg of the journey. Suitcases that ordinarily would have been sent on to a conveyor belt were individually opened by security guards and checked for anything out of the ordinary. After all, something as simple as a box cutter had destroyed thousands of lives.

We had a tough time getting back to Nashville, but when we did, I wanted to kiss the ground. I was so relieved—so thankful.

As parents, you pray your children will find that special someone with whom they will share the rest of their lives. Buster found his special someone in Leigh, and now Kim had found her special someone in Mike Corwin. They married in 2002 in a small ceremony with family and friends at a little wedding chapel near the Opry. Kim was a beautiful bride. In one of his proudest fatherly moments, J.E. walked Kim down the aisle. She was beaming with joy.

Mike is a Doctor of Veterinary Medicine, and their love story began when Kim took her white Samoyed dog, Navarre, to see Mike for a checkup. I believe these two were meant for one another. Mike is handsome, but he's also kind. He's good to Kim, and he's good to me too. I know he loves me, and I love him. I also love my fifth grandchild Catherine who we inherited the day they said I do. Catherine was just a small child when Kim and Mike married. Today she is studying international law at a college in South Carolina. My goodness! Where does the time go?

Mike specializes in the health care of exotic animals. A love for exotics is a passion they share. When they first got married, they owned a Monitor Lizard named Drako as a pet. No watch dog was necessary when Drako was around.

One night, Kim and Mike were out of town, and someone broke into their home to rob them. Evidently the thief climbed the back steps to the second floor. Unbeknownst to the robber, Mike always let Drako out of his cage at night to roam free. He kept the door to the downstairs shut, but the upstairs belonged to Drako when they were gone.

Well, the thief helped himself to some of Mike's most cherished possessions. Then as the police later learned, he sat at Mike's desk in his office, and helped himself to one of Mike's beers. It was about this time that Drako decided to walk out of the bathroom. He saw the stranger sitting there, and charged him.

What I would have given to have seen this guy's face. Can you imagine being charged by a prehistoric looking Monitor Lizard? Drako's body was over a foot and a half long, which didn't include his extremely long and powerful tail. He had a thick neck and sharp claws, and could really move when he wanted to.

The thief freaked out, I'm sure. He fled the scene. It wasn't long before the police caught him, and when they did, they noticed one big bite mark on his ankle—mysteriously belonging to one Monitor Lizard.

As J.E. and I began to slow down a bit, I accompanied him to more and more of his out of town shows. I joined him on many of his country cruises, we flew to Sweden together with a group of Elvis fans for a concert, and I remember a trip to St. Lucia with Ray Pillow and Connie Smith. I was amazed at how much the locals loved traditional country music there. I even flew with J.E. and Charlie McCoy to Japan for Kenji Nagatomi's *Country*

Dream Festival. Kenji has performed and promoted country music for decades in Japan, and Jim Ed was well received in his country. Years ago, RCA released many of Jim Ed's records in Japan, and he even recorded one of his songs phonetically in Japanese.

But perhaps the most memorable trip for me was the trip we took with Bonnie and Brownie out west. There was no work involved in this trip. We were simply tourists enjoying the sights. It's hard to believe, but when artists are on the road, they usually only see the back of a bus and the concert venue. They pass through a lot of country, but experience very little of it. We wanted to do and see it all.

Ben Lampley came along and took us in his RV.

First stop was Dardanelle, Arkansas to pick up Bonnie and Brownie. Then we seemed to eat our way across the United States. It was pizza in Henrietta, Oklahoma, then Mexican food in Amarillo, Texas. More Mexican food in Santa Fe, New Mexico. Followed by a tequila tasting. That was a first for Bonnie and me. We decided we liked the expensive tequila the best, of course.

In Santa Fe, we took in the Georgia O'Keefe Museum, lunched at La Fonda Hotel, found a community of hippies at an old "Ghost Town," shopped for Indian jewelry and took in a Flamingo dance show. Then it was on to Vegas. We were told since 9-11, no one was allowed to drive across Hoover Dam in an RV, so we found an alternative route. Nothing was going to stop us from seeing Celine Dion. On to Salt Lake City, Utah where we marveled at the amazing acoustics of the Mormon Tabernacle, over to Wyoming to take in the beautiful scenery and some shopping in Jackson Hole, and a sprint to Yellowstone National Park to see Old Faithful do her thing. Back around to Deadwood, South Dakota for a tour of the Buffalo Bill Historical Museum and finally a stop in Rapid City, South Dakota to see the magnificent sight of Mt. Rushmore.

I don't think I have ever enjoyed a vacation more. I loved all of the wonderful things J.E. and I were able to experience together. It's not just where you go, it's who you're with when you get there that counts.

At home in Nashville snow with Navarre

Music Mountain Theater in Pigeon Forge, TN (Back Row) Brent Burkett, Sam Wellington, Berl Lyons and Richard Garratt (Front Row) Alex and Elmer, Johnny Russell and Jim Ed

Celebrating Christmas with my cat, Bob Burns

"Kim Ed" promo photo—1990

Kim and Mike's wedding—2002
J.E., Kim, Mike, Rachel (cousin) and Catherine

Kim sang with Jim Ed on the Opry—1995

Family photo—It is never easy to get this group together.
Leigh, Buster, Genevieve, Becky, Mike, Catherine
Kim, J.E., Hampton, Isabella, Oliver—2005

Easter Morning—Hampton, Isabella, Genevieve and Oliver

Genevieve, Oliver, Hampton,
Isabella and J.E.

Genevieve, Leigh, Hampton, Buster, Mike, Kim, Catherine
J.E., Oliver, Isabella and Becky

189

Alaska Grand Ole Opry Cruise—2001 Brownie, Becky, Jim Ed and Bonnie

Becky and Bonnie making friends in Cody, Wyoming

Talkeetna, Alaska
Jim Ed, Bonnie and Becky taking in the sights

Chapter Nineteen

I have cancer.

I never questioned, "Why me?"

I never questioned, "Why not me?"

I never questioned.

Feeling sorry for myself never entered my mind. I was too busy planning my course of action.

I discovered the lump by accident and went straight to my doctor, Dr. Sharon Wright, who sent me to Dr Laura Lawson for a biopsy.

I remember sitting there in the examination room when Dr. Lawson entered carrying a folder with my charts inside. From the very first time I met her, I knew she was the doctor for me. She entered my examination room wearing turquoise sandals with yellow toenail polish. The turquoise and yellow scarf she wore around her neck accented both beautifully. I'd been told by my friends she was a good doctor; now I knew she was stylish as well. I knew we'd hit it off.

On this day, however, before she had spoken a single word, I could tell by the look on her face that the news wasn't good. In a calm voice she said, "Becky, you have breast cancer."

In an equally calm voice I replied, "Ok...Alright...Well, I guess you'll just have to perform a mastectomy. Let's hit this head on."

I think Dr. Lawson thought I was the one who would be shocked by the news. Instead, she stood there with a surprised look on her face. She said in all of her years of practicing medicine, she never had a patient with my attitude.

I explained to her that I had a lot to be thankful for. For whatever reason, this was a piece of my puzzle. It was a journey I must go on. And while I didn't understand it, I would deal with it. I would be a brave warrior. The hardest part would be telling my family.

I drove myself home, mentally preparing my thoughts. When I got to the house I asked J.E. and Kim to join me at the kitchen table. It was there that I broke the news.

"I don't want any cry babies," I lectured. "I want you to be concerned, but I also want you to know that I will hit this head on. I know I'm going to be ok. I have already turned this over to God. I have breast cancer. However, I will be fine."

I know I jerked the rug right out from under them, but I also got a real sense that they had peace because I had such peace with my circumstances. I saw the tears begin to well in their eyes—even after my declaration that I didn't want to see any tears. I knew it wasn't right of me to tell them how to feel. I certainly didn't want anyone telling me how to feel. Sometimes it's perfectly ok to cry. Sometimes our tears cleanse away our fears.

My dear sister-in-law, Susan, volunteered to be my chemo partner. I believe that I had the best. She picked me up at the house, sat with me through each and every treatment and brought me home when it was over.

I didn't quite know what to expect from the first treatment. The nurse escorted us to my infusion room, made sure I was comfortable in a beige recliner with a little table attached, and began to hang my chemo-cocktail to the IV stand next to me. I said, "Bring it on! Let's go!" Then we waited for this concoction to surge through my veins. How odd to think it was both a poison and a cure.

I was happy to have Susan with me. The two to three hours it took for each round of chemo gave us a chance to visit. We spent such-quality time together. I remember thinking *How am I supposed to feel? I don't feel bad. What's happening?*

I think I'd heard every horror story imaginable about the side effects of chemo, but I never got sick. My appetite remained normal. I was even given four rounds of the heavy hitter known as "Red Devil" Chemo—a concoction that earned its name because of its red color and side effects: low blood cell counts, low platelets, loss of hair and mouth sores. No matter how much research you do on a medication, you don't know how your body will react to it until the medicine is actually making its way through your circulatory system.

After each round of Red Devil, I'd have to go back to the hospital the next day to get a shot to counter the side effects. The day after that, I'd have a hard time getting out of bed.

Susan would walk into my room and say, "Ok, Becky, sit up! It's time to walk down the hall." I'd say, "That's wonderful. I feel great. Let's do this!" As hard as I tried, the truth was that I couldn't do it. I could barely move at all.

Upon hearing my story at a later treatment, a nurse confided that she once had the same experience after a Red Devil treatment. She explained that she was sitting on the couch, just a few feet from the refrigerator, yet she couldn't get up to get a glass of water. She told me it would get better, and it did.

Many times during my treatments I would think about my good friend Marion Clark. Marion shared so many of her close friends with me over the years. It was through her that I met Tom Goddard, advertising exec Lee Choate and Dolly's sister Willadeene Parton. These friendships gave me strength in my times of need.

Marion was such a free spirit. When she was younger, she hiked all over Europe in the '60s. Thirty-five years ago she battled breast cancer—back when the treatment was brutal. After five years of remission, the cancer returned. It was her decision to forgo additional treatments. She didn't live very long after that decision, but her spirit lives on in the hearts of all who knew her. I'd sit in my chair with the new and improved chemo drugs racing through my body, and I'd think, "Marion, I'm fighting this fight for both of us."

I was told from the very first treatment that I would lose my hair. The nurses said I should be prepared, so I decided to nip that in the bud too. I went to my beautician Darlene and I asked her to shave my head—all of it. I wanted my hair gone.

Trying to spare me any embarrassment, she asked if I wanted her to shave my head in the back room. I told her no. I wanted her to work from her usual chair in the center of the salon.

You know how people say you'll still look beautiful with no hair. Well, I wanted to see the reaction of the other people in the salon to my new look. I heard the low hum of the shears as it glided methodically over my head. My hair began to form a blonde puddle at our feet. I saw the stolen glances from both male and female customers in the mirror as Darlene worked, and I heard the whispers: *What is she doing? Oh my gosh! What is she doing?*

I turned to Darlene and I said, "Their reactions spoke volumes."

She placed a wig on my head that I had purchased days earlier. It was the same color that my hair was, and she trimmed it to look like my old hairstyle. I took a long look at my new self in the mirror, thanked Darlene for her help; then I left the salon and drove myself home.

Opry legend Jeannie Seely helped me keep a positive attitude. She told me I should use this time to experiment with different wigs and hairstyles. Until my own hair grew back, that's exactly what I did. I also loved wearing baseball caps, and Jeannie gave me a cap that I still cherish. On the front, in bold letters, it reads "Fight like a girl." Today I am eight years cancer free.

I think, perhaps, I am one of the most vain people in the world. Susan laughs at how many mirrors I have in my house, and she often jokes that I have never met a mirror I didn't like. Through three months of chemo treatments, a double mastectomy, six weeks of daily radiation and numerous reconstructive surgeries, I got out of bed every day that I could, got dressed, fixed my hair, and applied my makeup. After every reconstruction surgery, I would ask my doctor, "When can I play tennis?" He would tell me at least 3 months, but I was back on the court in a few weeks.

Of course I don't wear make-up or fix my hair when I play tennis, but this journey of mine reaffirmed what I knew all along. What other people think of me doesn't define me. My makeup, hair, or my breasts certainly don't define who I am. The only thing that defines me as a person is that inner voice that controls my thoughts, my words and actions.

From 2003-2015, Jim Ed hosted a syndicated radio show called *Country Music Greats Radio Hour*. The program was recorded in two one-hour segments at a studio in Nashville and spanned the years of country music from the 1940s to present day. As the host, he helped the show grow from a few stations to nearly two hundred affiliates. What made the show special was his insider knowledge and first hand accounts of the legends of country music.

On August 10, 2013, Jim Ed officially became one of those legends he so often talked about on his show. He became a member of a very small club—one of the few to join the ranks of a handful of men and women to claim a 50 year membership on the Grand Ole Opry.

He was so excited. We were excited for him. Maxine and Bonnie stood by their brother's side that night, along with our entire family—our children and our grandchildren. We all took pictures together at a special party held in Jim Ed's honor backstage in Studio A where they used to tape the TV show *Hee Haw*. There were so many people in those photos. Had our family really grown that much over the years? We looked like a dynasty. The music was one thing, but the people in those photos were our legacy—these people who we loved so much.

Friends and fellow Opry members crowded the Opry hallways to help Jim Ed celebrate his Opry Golden Anniversary, and our dear friends Bobby and Jeannie Bare joined us in the Opry wings. It was only fitting to have Bobby there. He and J.E. had weathered the past fifty years in the music business together.

Jim Ed took center stage to debut his new single. The song, *In Style Again*,[47] was written by Lance Miller and Austin Cunningham. Bobby produced Jim Ed's new single, and we were anxious to gauge the audience reaction. When he began to sing in his velvet-smooth baritone voice, you could have heard a pin drop in the Opry House. The crowd was hanging on to every note...every word.

> *Like an old sharecropper's shack in need of paint,*
>
> *I can't pretend to be somethin' that I ain't.*
>
> *I'd give my right arm if I could see,*
>
> *That look in your eyes when you still believed in me.*
>
> *I'd like to be in style again some day.*
>
> *No one wants to feel like they've been thrown away.*
>
> *Yes nothin' lasts forever, but it hurts to be replaced*
>
> *By a younger, fresher, pretty face.*
>
> *So if only for a while*
>
> *I'd like to be in style again some day.*

Who gave the world the right to turn the page

and leave me here feelin' twice my age.

There's nothin' quite as hard as the fall

And the changes are so cruel once you've had it all.

There were good times.

We had some good times.

We were flying high

There were no goodbyes

I had everything you wanted or needed

I was needed.

I'd like to be in style again some day.

No one wants to feel like they've been thrown away.

Yes nothin' lasts forever, but it hurts to be replaced

By a younger, fresher, pretty face.

So if only for a while

I'd like to be in style again some day.

Until the last note, there was silence. Even for a few seconds after the song, silence hung in the air. The audience was still absorbing the message, caught up in the moment. Then like a bolt of lightning, their flash of appreciation was electrifying. The crowd erupted in a long, thunderous applause. Fans hopped to their feet. They whistled, and they cheered. Jim Ed took a bow befitting his fifty year tenure on country music's most venerable stage. I could tell he was overcome with emotion.

Bobby Bare leaned down to me and whispered in my ear, "I have a new found respect for that man's voice."

I thought to myself, I don't think I've ever heard J.E. sing more beautifully than I did tonight.

Opry Vice President and General Manager Pete Fisher presented Jim Ed with an antique watch in honor of his fifty years of time making the Grand Ole Opry what it is today. Jim Ed then stepped up to the microphone, and with an emotion laced tremor in his voice said, "I want to thank the fans and the music industry for embracing me all these years and to the Opry for allowing me to call it home."

After J.E.'s open heart surgery in 1989, I thought there was nothing he couldn't overcome. I watched him tackle one obstacle after another with little or no complaint.

In 2002, he was bush hogging the back of our property. He hopped off the tractor to pick something up from the ground and jumped over a log. He didn't realize that on the other side of the log there was a deep hole. When his foot hit the ground, he crushed his heel and couldn't get up. Crippled by the pain, he realized no one knew where he was. Luckily, he remembered he had a cell phone, and he called Kim, who came to his rescue. She was always looking out for us.

The accident changed the way he did things. He gave up some of the outdoor chores he used to do around the property. Though he still bush hogged when needed, he only cut the front fields.

In 2007, he had a hip replacement. For a time, he walked with the help of a cane, but he didn't let his discomfort stop him from performing on the road or the Grand Ole Opry. I don't think he felt any pain when he was on stage but only the love from the audience. I think that most entertainers are that way.

Then in 2010, he went to the doctor because of a year long problem with his digestive system. Of all things, Jim Ed was diagnosed with Alpha-gal. Alpha-gal is also known as the "meat allergy." The doctor believed that Jim Ed had been bitten by a tick—specifically the lone star tick, which are very prevalent in the southern United States. These tick bites cause a delayed allergic reaction to meat from mammals, resulting in digestive issues and rashes.

No more hamburgers or barbecued ribs for J.E. For the rest of his life, he was allergic to any kind of meat with hooves. That meant no pork, beef, veal, lamb or deer.

Thank goodness there was no reaction to fish or poultry. From day one of his diagnosis, he ate chicken, fish, shrimp, crab legs, lobster and crappie. When Joe Stampley heard the news, he brought J.E. a big mess of fish from his freezer. He was one happy camper that day.

In 2013 the bombshell dropped.

J.E. was suffering from shortness of breath. A member of his band noticed a difference in the way he was singing on stage and begged him to go to a doctor and get a checkup. J.E. made an appointment with Dr. Barbara Brown, a very good friend of his. After a thorough examination accompanied by tests, Dr. Brown referred J.E. to a lung specialist.

He was driving to a show in Columbus, Georgia when he got a call from his doctor suggesting that he come in to the office to receive the news of his test results. She suggested he come as soon as possible. Kim and I were with him in her office the next day when the specialist delivered the news.

J.E. had small cell lung cancer.

Hearing the word "cancer" was a shock to the system. I think we were all stunned.

Tears began to flow when the doctor went on to explain that although small cell lung cancer usually responds well to chemo at first, when the cancer reappears in the body, chemotherapy doesn't help at all.

J.E. asked how much time she thought he had. It was explained that while each patient is different, with treatment, he was probably looking at a year.

Without hesitation, J.E. said he was ready to fight. He was determined to beat the odds.

On September 28, 2014, He posted the message below on his facebook page.

> *Some of you may have heard various rumors since I have had to cancel a few shows over the past weekend. To clarify and put those rumors to bed, I wanted to just come out and explain what is going on. Two weeks ago, I was diagnosed with lung cancer. At that time, I was in shock and scared as I really didn't know what that really meant. After testing, the doctors have asked me to take the next four months off from touring and to focus on chemotherapy and radiation treatments to shrink the cancer cells. I will keep you updated on the progress. I am forever grateful for the love, support and prayers during this time.*

Two days later on September 30, 2014, J.E. appeared in a video that he posted on his facebook page. He wanted to reassure his fans that he was doing everything he could to get better. Even though the news of his battle was only a few days old, the outpouring of love and support from his friends was phenomenal.

In the video, his voice was strong, and he was all smiles as he explained that he had his first treatment today, and he was going to beat this little thing called cancer, adding, "I'm going to be alright."

The next ten months are a blur. They were filled with trips to the hospital, visits to doctor's offices, good days, bad days, some wonderful surprises and long days of work in his home office. Jim Ed had a new album about to be released—his first solo project in thirty-five years. Not even cancer was going to stop him from meeting the target release date of January 2015. It was only three months away.

Jim Ed and The Browns celebrating 50 years on the Grand Ole Opry in 2013—Maxine, Eddie Stubbs, Jim Ed and Bonnie

Jim Ed and Becky celebrating 50 years on the Grand Ole Opry

Jim Ed celebrating 50 years on the Grand Ole Opry with the whole family—Leigh, Buster, Becky Oliver, Genevieve, Jim Ed, Isabella, Hampton, Mike and Kim

Jim Ed celebrating 50 years on the Grand Ole Opry with Genevieve, Jim Ed and Isabella

Girls trip to California—Dorothy Soto, Judy Taylor, Lynda Benson and Becky at Lake Tahoe

I washed all the mud off the Gator.

Becky and Betty Borth

Terry Tomlinson and Becky

Chapter Twenty

Thirty-five years had elapsed since Jim Ed released a solo project of his own. The title cut *In Style Again*, produced by Country Music Hall of Famer Bobby Bare, received rave reviews and once again garnered Jim Ed radio airplay—not bad for an eighty year old man.

Like J.E., I had an office downstairs in our home. Mine was more of an art studio really. It was the place where I have done (and still do) a lot of my painting. Many times, I'd be downstairs working on one of my projects and hear songs from J.E's new album make their way through the adjoining wall.

For a year, Jim Ed listened to new material—trying to find just the right songs to fit his voice and style. He wanted to record material that was meaningful on this new album—songs with a message that spoke to him. He knew if they touched him in some way, they would also touch his fans. I don't think anyone would argue with me when I say J.E. knew a good song when he heard it—and he knew how to deliver a song when he sang it.

For months he went into the studio with music journalist and historian Don Cusic, who produced the bulk of Jim Ed's album for Plowboy Records. Executive producer Shannon Pollard was taking a chance on them both.

For hours upon hours, J.E. would sit at his desk downstairs and listen to the music they recorded. He was very meticulous. If something didn't suit him, they would make changes until it did. He wanted this album to be just right, I think maybe deep down, he knew this album would be his last. He wanted it to be perfect. His gift to us all.

The single *In Style Again* was such a great song. You could listen to the song and grasp a different message every time—depending on what was going on in your life at the time. I think that's a quality that defines a great song—adaptability to circumstance.

The song could be a song about a romance that fades when a lover leaves his or her partner for a younger man or woman. Other friends told me they think of *In Style Again* as a metaphor for the music business. An artist gives his entire life to the industry he loves, only to be replaced on the radio and stage by a younger artist. It is the evolution of our industry, the evolution of life. However, even though we know that's the order of things, the knowing doesn't stop us from wishing our tomorrows could be more like our yesterdays. We all long to be needed—to be wanted. We remember the way it used to be when we were center stage in the spotlight bowing to the audience applause, and we'd like to feel in style again someday.

Jim Ed's friends Vince Gill, The Whites and Helen Cornelius joined him on individual selections, as did The Browns. As it turned out, *In Style Again* has the distinction of possessing the last recording of The Browns. The song is a beautiful selection that Jim Ed chose because it showcased the family harmony that he loved so dearly from the time he was a little boy growing up in Arkansas sitting around the radio singing with his sisters. The song is called *When The Sun Says Hello To The Mountain*.[48] It was one of Jim Ed's favorites.

Even with chemotherapy and radiation treatments, the album came out as scheduled in January of 2015. I think knowing the album was on the horizon made those treatments a little easier to take. Jim Ed had a goal. He needed to return to Opry center stage; after all, he had a new album to promote.

March 25, 2015 is a day I will always remember. That was the day the big announcement was made that Jim Ed and the Browns would become the newest members of the Country Music Hall of Fame! Jim Ed's dream, the dream he had dreamed for over sixty years, was coming true. This announcement was medicine for his soul. To be validated in such a big way for something you loved and worked so hard for is the pinnacle for any entertainer.

Years ago, artists were surprised when the announcement revealing the Hall of Fame Inductees was officially made. Now a days the only ones surprised are the press and the fans. The artists to be inducted have been told in advance so their families can be present for the ceremony.

Kim was the first to know in our family that J.E. would be among the Class of 2015 inductees. She was sworn to secrecy by Kirt Webster, J.E.'s publicist. For three days they concocted a scheme as to how the big reveal should be presented to her dad. Finally they agreed that Kim would tell her father that he was scheduled for an interview at Kirt's office—promoting his new album. She picked J.E. up and drove him to the interview that morning; however, when they arrived at the office, Kirt casually explained that the TV crew was shooting some footage at the CMA. It would be much easier on all if they just drove over there.

When they arrived at the CMA, they were escorted to the office of Sarah Trahern, Chief Executive Officer for the Country Music Association. Jim Ed was asked to take a seat in a comfortable recliner, and when he did, he began to question where the cameras were. They were noticeably missing. That's when Sarah told him that The Browns would be the newest members of the Country Music Hall of Fame!

I wish I had been there to see him throw up his hands and shed a few tears. Over and over again he said, "I don't believe it. I don't believe it." He had waited years for this honor—each year hoping the next year would be HIS year to be inducted. It was finally his time.

I will never know how Kim kept that secret from me. We don't keep secrets.

J.E. and Kim returned home, and were sitting at the kitchen table, when of all things, I bebopped through the kitchen door singing *Hallelujah*.[49] I had just won a tennis match, and I was feeling good. I noticed right away the somber looks on their faces. Kim said, "We have something important to tell you."

Oh my goodness! With looks like that—with everything we had recently been through—I thought this can't be good. I put my purse down and braced myself. That's when Kim's expression changed, and she blurted out, "Dad is going into the Country Music Hall of Fame!"

My hands flew to my face in surprise. I squealed with joy. "What? Are you serious? Who called? How did you find out?

I was having a hard time processing the information. I was so proud of J.E.! I was proud FOR him. We had made this journey from Arkansas to the Hall of Fame together. I wanted to hear every detail. I knew this was a day I would never forget.

It was then that we picked up the telephone and called Bonnie and Maxine. Like us, they were in surprised shock. This was wonderful news when we needed to hear wonderful news. The best kind.

At the press conference in the Hall of Fame Rotunda, Hall of Fame member Brenda Lee made the announcement that the newest members of the Hall of Fame in the Veteran's Era were The Browns. The press corps and their peers in attendance jumped to their feet in a standing ovation as The Browns made their way to the podium to give a speech. I was beaming as I watched the events unfold with my family. Buster and Leigh, Kim and Mike, and Bonnie's husband Dr. Gene "Brownie" Ring were by my side.

Jim Ed spoke first. He looked so handsome in his black jacket and hat.

> *I'm much more comfortable behind my guitar than this podium. I'm as nervous as a mosquito at a nudist colony. I know what to do, but I don't know where to start. (Everyone laughed.) Golly. Friends, it's been a long journey since Jim Reeves introduced us to Chet Atkins...to this wonderful journey at the Country Music Hall of Fame. No way could words express to you our feeling right now.*

Jim Ed went on to thank the people who were there for The Browns from the very beginning, and those who later made an impact on his own career. He understood you don't take a journey like the one he had traveled for sixty years by yourself. You have a lot of help along the way.

J.E. gave credit to Chet Atkins, Tom Perryman, Horace Logan, Jim Reeves, Jane Dowden, Bill Graham, Alan Reid, Bob Ferguson, Helen Cornelius, Tandy Rice, Ott Devine, Bud Wendall, Hall Durham, Bob Whittaker, Pete Fisher, Collin Reed, the CMA, Jo Walker-Meador, Ed Benson, Sarah Trahern, Felton Jarvis, and all of the musicians who had worked with him over the years both in the studio and on the road. They created and recreated the sound of The Browns. He then thanked me, his children and grand children for our love and support through the years.

He paused for a moment to get his bearings. His voice began to break as he continued.

> This past year has not been an easy one. (A long pause. J.E. was visibly shaken, and his face contorted with emotion.) Grown men aren't suppose to cry, are they?
>
> Cancer. (There is a catch in his voice. Brenda Lee standing to his left wipes away a tear.) Cancer is no fun. (Another pause. Bonnie to Jim Ed's right shakes her head and dabs at her own eyes. A slight smile appears on Jim Ed's face as he regains composure)
>
> But I made it through it. I'm in remission, and I can't thank my wife and family enough. Golly, the Lord has blessed me. I sure feel in style again.

The audience of old friends was pulling for him in more ways than one.

When Jim Ed concluded his speech, he heard their applause, but more than that, he felt their love.

That night, we certainly celebrated in style. Chef Dave prepared a glorious meal as we dined with family and friends, enjoying the moment of an honor earned. Don Cusic, Bill Anderson, Linda Davis and Lang Scott shared our happiness around the table. If life taught us anything at all, it taught us that time was a precious thing. We celebrated life's precious moments. We celebrated like there was no tomorrow.

In the months that followed, J.E. was in and out of the hospital. The cancer was taking its tole. I knew in my heart that I had taken my own cancer journey so that I was better prepared to help him with his journey. It all made sense to me now.

J.E. knew that only 1% of those diagnosed with small cell lung cancer live a year beyond the diagnosis. He was fighting a good fight, but if the Lord decided to bring him home, he was ready to go.

We talked about the future, and what the family's future would look like without him in it. I questioned whether I had the strength to go on. J.E. assured me that I was the strongest woman he knew. When the time came, I would have to take care of the family. We would take care of each other. Like I always had, he reminded me to trust in my faith. He marveled at my faith. He said, "Becky, I don't know where you get such faith, but you're going to be fine."

One morning we got up and had breakfast. J.E. looked at me across the table and said, "Rebecca Sue, I'm not going to be around much longer."

I put down my fork and asked, "Why do you say that?"

"It's just a feeling I have," he replied. "I can't explain it. I'm just tired.

We had a long conversation about death that day. We both wondered what happens when we die. I know one thing for certain, we have eternal life through Jesus Christ our Lord and Savior.

I asked him, if he died before I did, to send me a sign to let me know he was ok. Something to let me know he was in a good place. I asked him to send me butterflies. He said that he would.

I drove J.E. to the hospital. On the way, I was listening to a gospel CD in my car that The Browns recorded in 1996 titled *Family Bible*.[50] Throughout the years, this album had brought me great peace. It brought me peace on this day too.

Even though he wasn't feeling well, J.E. looked at me and his eyes twinkled when he said, "So what do you think? Were we any good?" I laughed and told him they were.

Many a time he would come up from his office and hear me playing *Family Bible* upstairs. I think of all his recordings, this album is my favorite. I told him when I listened to him sing, it felt like I had been to church. It felt like a month of wonderful Sundays.

I brought a portable CD player to his hospital room. I'd softly play that CD for him beside his bed. It seemed to bring him comfort too, although he enjoyed listening to the music of the many friends he made throughout the years. He loved listening to Ricky Skaggs and The Whites. These songs, these people kept him company when he couldn't sleep at night. They lessened his pain and lightened his heart.

J.E. was trying to hold on. The Hall of Fame induction was three months away, and he was growing weaker each day. He prayed that he would still be here to receive that Hall of Fame medallion around his neck.

I remember he turned to me once and said, "Becky, do you think the only reason they are inducting me into the Hall of Fame now is because they know I am dying?"

I was taken aback. I said, "J.E., would you like for me to give you a list of all the people who deserve to be in the Hall of Fame but are now deceased. I can give you a huge list. It overwhelms me. You are going into the Hall of Fame because you earned your place. It is an honor long overdue, and I am thankful you are getting your due. So, to answer your question, I think you are going into the Country Music Hall of Fame because you belong there."

On June 3, 2015 Kim posted this message on Jim Ed's facebook page:

This is a prayer request. They worked before, so I am hopeful they will work now too. Dad's cancer has returned (not in his lungs) and he is undergoing chemotherapy. We are hopeful for a positive outcome, but it is a combination of hope and prayers that will get him through this.

2015 inductees into the Country Music Hall of Fame—(back row) The Oak Ridge Boys: Duane Allen, William Lee Golden, Richard Sterban and Joe Bonsall (front row) The Browns: Bonnie, Jim Ed and Maxine

Luncheon at the Hall of Fame—2015
Becky, Kim, Jim Ed, Bonnie and Brownie Ring

Leaving the Ryman after the funeral of Jimmy C. Newman
Kim, Jim Ed and Becky—2014

Chapter Twenty-one

So here we are.

As I wrote in the introduction of this book, J.E. knew he didn't have long in this world. Over and over he prayed that God would allow him to live long enough to be inducted in the Country Music Hall of Fame. At one time his dream seemed within reach; now it seemed a million miles away. He knew he would be its newest member in October as part of The Browns, but the doctors predicted he only had a matter of days to live. He began to doubt that he would live to see the day when he would become an actual member of the Hall.

Still he continued to pray. I prayed too. We had faith.

Within hours of Kim making a few calls, Jim Ed's hospital room was filled with country music's elite: Pete Fisher and Bill Anderson from the Grand Ole Opry; Kyle Young, Lisa Purcell, Sharon Brawner, Jay Orr and Carolyn Tate with the Country Music Hall of Fame and the CMA's Sarah Trahern was accompanied by a small CMA entourage. How in the world did this happen so quickly?

As they wandered into his room within minutes of each other, each friend pretended like it was a coincidence they had chosen that exact time to visit him. For a moment, they visited like it was old home week. It took a while before Jim Ed realized it wasn't coincidence at all. They were there to induct him in the Country Music Hall of Fame. This was Jim Ed's big moment.

From a hospital bed, dressed in a hospital gown, florescent lights casting a pale greenish glow on a chosen crowd of 20, Jim Ed officially joined the ranks of country music's elite. It was a ceremony like no other before it or since.

June 4, 2015.

This moment, with these people—as unorthodox as it was—was absolutely beautiful. It was beyond beautiful. It was perfect.

The feeling of love in that room was almost tangible.

When Bill Anderson, in a voice that quivered, said, "Jim Ed, as a member of the Country Music Hall of Fame, I am here to make you it's newest member," I felt my heart lodge in my throat.

I don't think there was a dry eye in the room.

Through tears of my own, I watched my husband's face. His breathing was labored, but his eyes danced with excitement. I could see that he was tiring, but I could also see the happiness this moment brought him. He had waited a lifetime for this moment.

As part of the ceremony, a gold medallion was placed around Jim Ed's neck. This gold medallion to a country music performer is the equivalent of a gold medal to an Olympic athlete.

Just like every ceremony before it, Jim Ed's induction day concluded with everyone in the room joining in on a soulful rendition of *Will The Circle Be Unbroken*.[51] For a few seconds, his voice, so weak and raspy, was strong. As long as I live, I will never forget that moment.

Upon conclusion, photos were taken and congratulatory hugs were exchanged before the crowd of friends left the room so J.E. could rest. As soon as the door closed, and the last friends said their farewells, we began to replay this special day in our heads. We still couldn't believe what had just happened.

It all began that day with a private exchange between Opry President Pete Fisher and Jim Ed; Pete was one of the first friends to walk through his door that afternoon. In a moment of light-hearted banter, J.E. turned to Pete and said, "Pete, I want you to know, I only have one regret in life."

With a curious glance Pete inquired, "What's that?"

"Well, I was just thinking," he teased. "I've waited all my life to play the Grand Ole Opry stage as a member of the Country Music Hall of Fame. You know, Pete, when you play the Opry as a Hall of Fame member you get double scale. I don't think I'll ever make it to my Hall of Fame induction, and I don't think I'll ever be back to the Opry again. I'll never see that double scale."

I was glad to see that J.E. still had his sense of humor. Pete gave him a hearty chuckle, and more friends began to enter his room. That exchange between Jim Ed and Pete all but forgotten until Kim received a phone call from Pete several hours after the ceremony had concluded. He asked her if he could see J.E. one more time that day.

A short time later later Pete waltzed back into the room waving an envelope. "What's that?" J.E. asked.

"Well, I was thinking about what you said, Jim Ed. So when I got in the car I called accounting and had them cut you a check. After all, you are a Grand Ole Opry member AND a member of the Country Music Hall of Fame. You did sing *Will The Circle Be Unbroken* in an official capacity. I do believe that qualifies as double scale."

J.E. couldn't believe it! This was indeed a special day!

When Maxine and Bonnie made it in from Arkansas, J.E. couldn't resist teasing them. With a twinkle in his eye he said, "Sorry girls, but it looks like I beat you into the Country Music Hall of Fame, and I have the medallion to prove it."

For the next eight days you rarely saw him without that medallion around his neck. Nurses and doctors worked around it. It rested next to his chest on top of the hospital gown with wires and monitors beneath it. A Country Music Hall of Fame baseball cap topped his head. As its newest member, he was glowing with pride, and it was with great pride that he showed that medallion to every visitor who came in to say their goodbyes.

The country music community is like no other community I have ever known. At times it may appear to be a dysfunctional family, but it is indeed a family, and like a family, it rallies when another family member signals a distress call.

With just a few phone calls from Kim, the news spread that Jim Ed's curtain was about to come down. The hospital room number was passed along like falling dominoes to those who knew they had played an important role in his life as friends and colleagues. For the next several days a constant parade of people filed into his room. Kim let them in a few at a time so they could have private time with her dad. I think the hospital staff thought we were having a party. Instead of a barrage of wailing tears, laughter often rollicked through the closed door and down the hallway.

Once again, J.E. was right. Weeks ago, when I had asked him if given the choice to die unexpectedly or to know when his time was near, which would he chose? He said he wanted to know. He wanted to look his friends in the eyes and tell them how much knowing them meant to him. He wanted to hold their hands one last time. He wanted to know that when he left this Earth, his friends knew, without a doubt, that he loved them.

They came alone. They came in small groups. Friends. Neighbors. Family. Some famous. Some not so famous. No one took this visit for granted. They made every word—every second—count. This moment was precious—a rare opportunity.

Kim kept a list of all who walked through that hospital doorway: Russ Farrar, Jimmy Fortune, Donnie and Jacky Gregory, Diana Luster, Robbi Nash. Lang Scott and Linda Davis, Pete and Hope Fisher, Brenda Reed, Sarah Trahern, Brandie Simms, Martha Moore, Bill Anderson, Lee Willard, Lee and Karen Gillock, Kirt Webster, Jeremy Westby, Kyle Young, Sharon Brawner, Carolyn Tate, Lisa Purcell, from the Country Music Hall of Fame, Ralph Emery, The Whites, Billy Paul Jones, Don Cusic, Amber Gillock, Shane and Courtney Knoves, Norbert and Betty Borth, Dave and Marilou Barton, John Barton, Dina Johnson, Mike Baker, Tim Atwood, Steve Buchanon, Eddie Stubbs, Craig and Karen Morgan, Ed Reed, Bill Turner, Charlie Monk, Jody Rogers, Derrick Kinslow, Mike Manning, Ron Harman,

Nancy Jones, Buck White, T Graham and Sheila Brown, Rodney Fletcher, Beau Harland, Kyle Cantrell, Jeannie Seely and Gene Ward, Jan Howard, Helen Cornelius, Christie Cornelius, Rex Allen Jr., David and Trish Nichols, Bruce with All Over Landscaping, Emy Jo Bilbrey, Bob and Jean Whittaker, Ben Lampley, Jo Gregory, Chris Skinker, Lynn Gray, Robbie Wittowski, LuLu Roman, Daryle and Christie Hornberger, Roxane Atwood, Brenda Lee, Stu and Aldonna Phillips and their daughter, Ruth Elkins, Dorothy Soto, Terry Tomlinson, Pastor Boyd and all of our family members.

Our friend C Don Ladd visited J.E. every morning without fail. Because of circumstances beyond their control, some dear friends couldn't make it to the hospital at all, but they wanted him to know he was in their thoughts and prayers. Larry Black, Duane Allen and Joe Bonsall spoke to J.E. on the phone, and Blake Shelton sent a heartfelt text.

Sometimes friends lifted his spirits with the gift of song. It's the way most of our friends express themselves best.

LuLu Roman of *Hee Haw* fame entered J.E.'s hospital room with a smile on her face. It happened to be a time when he was sitting up in his chair. LuLu pulled a chair alongside J.E. and talked for a while. She had him laughing in no time. Before she left that day, she took both of his hands in her own, looked him in the eyes with kindness and love and began to sing. Her voice was calming and clear and filled with conviction.

> *Take my hand, Precious Lord. Precious Lord take my hand.*
>
> *Lead me on.*
>
> *Let me stand.*
>
> *I am tired. I am weak. I am worn.*
>
> *Through the storm, through the night*
>
> *Lead me on through the light.*
>
> *Take my hand, precious, Lord. Lead me home.*[52]

That was a moment.

A few days before J.E. passed, Kim talked with Cheryl White and her husband Billy Paul Jones on the telephone. They were about to leave for a month of tour dates and were heartbroken that they might not be in town when our family needed them most. On impulse, Kim asked if The Whites and Ricky Skaggs would come to the hospital and sing for her dad. Their music meant so much to him as he rested in his hospital bed. Their family harmonies playing from the tiny boombox on the table near him soothed his soul. Without hesitation, they agreed.

When they walked through the door, most of our family were gathered together talking about old times. Kim and Mike were there, along with Buster and Leigh, four of our five grandchildren, my sister Lynda, and my best friend from childhood Dorothy Vanlandingham Soto.

When Ricky walked in the room, he went straight for Jim Ed and gave him a loving hug. Ricky couldn't wait to tell him that he woke up that morning dreaming about him. (Now, before I go on, you have to know that when J.E. woke up that very morning he told Kim that he had the most wonderful dream. He was walking in a field of flowers.)

Ricky began to tell us about his dream. He said, "Jim Ed, I saw you in field of flowers. In my dream I asked you what you were doing. You said, 'I'm picking flowers for the Master's bouquet.'"

This moment was surreal. We all felt it was a sign from God above—another gift.

The Whites and Ricky confessed they'd been practicing *Amazing Grace*[53] all morning and wanted to sing it for him. As they crowded around his bedside, J.E. said he dearly loved that song, but he had a special request. He asked if he could hear them sing *The Old Rugged Cross*[54] one more time.

Just as they were about to begin, Rod Fletcher, bass singer at the Grand Ole Opry walked through the door. The group asked Rod to join them. I believe this was God's timing.

J.E. closed his eyes and just listened with the biggest smile on his face. As they were finishing his request, he turned toward Ricky, and in a voice barely above a whisper, he said, "Modulate for me."

It was one of the most touching—most awe inspiring—moments of my life.

Then Ricky, Sharon, Cheryl, Billy Paul and Rod began to sing *Amazing Grace*. Nurses, doctors, and a few passersby in the hallway stopped what they were doing for those few minutes and gathered outside J.E.'s door to listen. It truly was amazing. Everyone there that day, on both sides of his hospital door, were listening to those beautiful songs with their hearts.

Jim Ed knew he was loved.

His friends came to comfort J.E., but several times he found himself comforting them. When they did begin to cry by his bedside, he allowed them the luxury of their tears, but he asked them to remember the good times they shared, and then spent a few minutes reminiscing about those times. More often than not, they left his hospital room smiling as the next guest walked in. This was his routine for the next four days.

I believe the outpouring of love from his friends prolonged his life. He tried his best to stay alert to greet every one who walked through that door. J.E. was right. This special time with friends was truly a gift.

In quieter moments at the hospital, I would reflect on some of those friendships that meant so much to us. When the end really is near, you don't think about all of the awards you won or the money you have in the bank. You think about the people who made your life meaningful.

I thought about Grand Ole Opry legend Little Jimmy Dickens. Oh, how we loved that man. J.E. adored him. He often talked about the fishing trip they made together to the Alaskan wilderness. They caught a few fish and saw a few bears, but mostly they shared stories and memories of their time in the music business as only two Opry veterans could.

I thought about the Hobbs family. Business entrepreneur and family patriarch, John Hobbs, was a long time friend. When J.E. was diagnosed with lung cancer, he continued to go to John's supper club, John A's, and sing with John's house band after the Opry. Toward the end, he could only sing a song or two because he couldn't catch his breath, but that didn't matter to John or Jim Ed. It was something he had done for years, and something he continued to do for as long as he could.

 Afterward J.E., would make his way to the back of the restaurant and sit beside John in John's special booth. They didn't always say a lot to each other, but with good friends, long conversations aren't necessary. Sometimes all you needed with a good friend is to be in their presence.

Then there was Gus Arrendale, President of Springer Mountain Farms, producer of the best chicken in the world. He was such a good friend to us—he still is. In addition to the countless "just because" phone calls Gus made—just checking in to see how we were doing—we made so many wonderful trips together on his private jet. He flew us to Alaska to board an Opry cruise once, and then there was that trip to New York to see The Allman Brothers Band. The show canceled due to illness, but Gus made lemonade out of lemons and got us tickets to see the Blue Man Group.

When my sister's granddaughter was getting married in St. Kitts, we asked Gus and our friend Karen McEntyre to join us for the Caribbean nuptials. Gus and Karen were family. They fit right in with the rest of our family.

J.E. and I flew ahead on a commercial flight so we could spend a little extra time with the bride-to-be, my great niece Erika. Gus and Karen flew in a little later on their private plane. Even though we had round trip tickets, Gus convinced us to fly back to Tennessee with him. This was my first experience flying into our country on a private jet. It was amazing. We had to go through customs, but it was nothing like going through customs on a commercial flight. Once again, Gus made our lives easier—and so much fun!

Just a few weeks before J.E. entered the hospital for what would be the last time, Gus made it possible for us to attend the *Academy of Country Music Awards* in Arlington, Texas on April 19, 2015. We wouldn't have been able to make that trip if Gus hadn't attended the show with us.

I remember Martha Moore, a longtime friend and publicist, joined us in Arlington. On the day of the show, Martha took J.E. under her wing and personally escorted him from booth to booth in a large nearby building that housed the collective press core. She worked like the professional she is—making sure Jim Ed's new album, *In Style Again,* received the media attention it deserved. Then later that afternoon, right before showtime, Martha walked the red carpet with us. She paused every few feet, instructing Jim Ed where to deliver CD promoting sound bites for local news outlets and national entertainment shows. She was such a tremendous help to us.

My goodness, we had great friends! Good friends never go out of style.

When my longtime friend Dorothy Vanlandingham (now Dorothy Soto) heard the bleak news that J.E. was in the hospital for what could be the last time, she drove in from Arkansas with my sister Lynda to bring me comfort as only a childhood friend can. Dorothy was there the day I first met J.E. at the *Lions Club Minstrel Show* all those years ago. She had been with us since day one.

After a weekend of hospital visits, on Monday, June 8th we spent the day with J.E. and decided to meet Buster and Leigh for a quick dinner around 7pm. By 8:30 we were already home and getting ready for bed.

Lynda and I were sitting on the edge of the bed talking about J.E. and all that he had gone through, when Dorothy headed for the bathroom to take a shower and put on her pajamas. After some time elapsed, I remember thinking, that's odd, I don't hear the water running. Moments later I heard a thump. It wasn't very loud, but that thump was followed by complete silence.

Concerned, I cracked the bathroom door to see if Dorothy was ok. That's when I saw her lying on the floor. Her body must have hit the hamper on the way down. I knew right away it was a stroke.

I rushed down stairs yelling for Buster to call 911. He sat with Dorothy on the floor and tried to soothe her while I collected a few things she might need. We knew she must be scared. We told her she was going to be ok. The ambulance was on the way.

When we arrived at the hospital, the doctor confirmed our fears. Dorothy had a stroke, the worst possible kind. Because of the fragility of her condition, she couldn't make the drive back to Arkansas—not even in an ambulance. She would have to stay in Nashville for several weeks.

Dorothy was my family too. For the next three days, I made the drive back and forth between St. Thomas Hospital in Nashville to be with Dorothy and Williamson Medical Center to be with my husband. There were days that it felt like I was swimming in quicksand, but I knew that God wouldn't let me drown. Knowing God loved me, I kept paddling.

On June 11, 2015 Jim Ed passed away.

News of Jim Ed's passing spread quickly through the country music community. It was a Thursday--the first day of the CMA Music Festival. J.E. looked forward to this event every year. Since Jim Ed died one hour before the official start of Fan Fest, Sarah Trahern opened the festivities with a moment of silence in his honor.

Country superstar and fellow Opry member Alan Jackson kicked off the first night of big shows to a sold out, multi-artist concert at LP Field. Thousands of fans were in attendance. He concluded his set by performing a bit of *Pop A Top*. Alan said, "We're gonna miss you, Jim Ed. God bless you." Then he walked off stage. The crowd went wild.

Every artist that took the stage that first night mentioned Jim Ed in tribute. They tipped their hats to him as an industry patriarch and mentor. Several fans at the show extended their stay in Nashville through Monday morning so they could attend his funeral.

We decided to have J.E.'s funeral at The Ryman. It was where he first became a member of the Grand Ole Opry fifty-one years ago. He called the Opry home. Today he would trade one home for another—his eternal home.

By 10am, as they opened the doors to The Ryman for friends and fans, the line for Jim Ed's funeral wrapped around the Auditorium and stretched up Fourth Ave. It was so obvious: Jim Ed is loved.

Before the service started, I had several offers from friends who were willing to supply me with medication designed to calm me and help me through the morning ahead. I declined. I wanted to remember every detail of this day. I wanted to feel the emotions inside me. I wanted to share in the laughter as friends relived funny stories about their times with J.E. through the years. I wanted to share in the tears too.

I was his wife. I could do this.

When the family was seated, I looked around at the scene before me.

Someone started a recording of The Browns. They were singing *When They Ring Those Golden Bells*.[55] You could have heard a pin drop in The Ryman. Everyone was listening intently—in awe of that perfect sibling harmony. I think we all felt a little closer to Heaven with each and every note. I remember glancing over at Bill Landers, director of *Going Our Way*. He was nearby on the front row with Garth Brooks and Trisha Yearwood. The expression on Garth's face as The Browns sang, touched my heart.

The Ryman stage was bathed in soft purple lights. A spotlight shone on Jim Ed's familiar red show jacket with the black appliqued lapels. It hung on a mannequin frame to the right of a large easel positioned center stage. The easel displayed a large picture of him Center stage right where he belonged.

The stage was clean. Simple.

A grand piano rested downstage—waiting to be played, and upstage stood two microphone stands with the vertical Grand Ole Opry boxed logos covering their lengths. As it always has been, the announcer's podium was stage right.

A huge spray of white roses rested atop Jim Ed's casket was positioned directly in front of center stage. It was elegant.

The room was quiet

The mood was reverent.

There was no applause after an artist sang. No applause after brief eulogies and remembrances.

Once artists finished their songs, they respectfully announced the next artist to talk or sing. No fancy introductions. Simply a name.

There were no egos on stage that day. This day wasn't about anyone else. This day was about one man only. Those participating knew it. They could feel it.

Grand Ole Opry General Manager Pete Fisher spoke from the heart when he said, "Harmony was a thread throughout the entirety of Jim Ed's legacy." Pete remembered how Jim Ed could be found backstage visiting with his fans, or introducing himself to a first timer on the Opry—making that artist feel like they were part of the Opry family. Brenda Lee recalled that when she toured with the Browns they were her "road family," and former Opry General Manager Bob Whittaker reminded everyone that Jim Ed's voice mail greeting began with a cheery, "Hello, Friends!"

Sarah Trahern talked about the day she told JE he was going into the CMHOF. Colin Reed, CEO of Ryman Entertainment, talked about their numerous hunting trips and Jeannie Seely very graciously read what Kim had written for the service about her Dad and what she wanted us to remember. Kim wanted everyone to carry on his legacy and try to be more loving, and forgiving and be more willing to ask, "What can I do to help?"

The Oak Ride Boys performed an a capella rendition of *Life's Highway*,[56] followed by songs of faith by Craig Morgan, Vince Gill, Lady Antebellum, Hillary Scott, Lang Scott, Linda Davis, The Gatlin Brothers, Rhonda Vincent and The Isaacs. Crystal Gayle, who made her TV debut alongside Jim Ed on *The Country Place*—back when she was a teenager—sang one of his favorite songs, *When I Dream*.[57]

The pacing of the service was perfect. Flawless. Pastor Sam delivered a sweet eulogy and message.

Some lighthearted stories were told. Some laughter followed.

There was no lengthy biography read about Jim Ed's career. Although the artist was part of the man, all in attendance were there to honor the man not the artist.

From the Opry podium, the reoccurring theme of the day seemed to center around Jim Ed's friendships and his faith in God. What a glorious legacy!

Final prayers. All heads bowed.

His band The Gems, the men and women who stood beside him on stage, served as his pallbearers. For years they had carried each other through thick and thin. We asked them to carry Jim Ed one more time.

As mourners filed out behind the casket, large screens on stage displayed a montage of video clips and photos of Jim Ed through the ages. The music enhancing the pictorial was a song by Jim Ed himself—a new song, from his new album—*It's a Good Life.*[58] I couldn't help but think to myself, "Yes it was."

Jim Ed and Becky on the red carpet at the 2015 Academy of Country Music Awards

"Jim Ed spent his whole life doing what he loved to do, with people he loved, for people he loved."—Becky Brown

Jim Ed receives a senate proclamation from the State of Tennessee pictured with Senator Jack Johnson, 23rd senatorial district

Kim was always content in her daddy's arms —circa 2015

One of Jim Ed's Favorites—Trisha Yearwood, with our beautiful daughter, Kim, and Garth Brooks

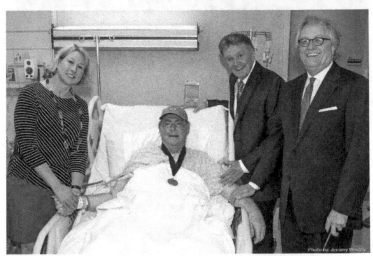

History made. Jim Ed inducted into the Country Music Hall of Fame in his hospital bed—Sarah Trahern, Jim Ed, Bill Anderson and Kyle Young
photo by Jeremy Westby

Chapter Twenty-two

Sunday evening, October 25, 2015, was the night Jim Ed had waited for all of his life—the night he would become an official member of the Country Music Hall of Fame. Happily, in an unprecedented gesture, the Hall of Fame made him a member of country music's elite on June 4, 2015 in a special ceremony from his hospital room. He relished the knowledge that he stood on top of the mountain for eight days before his death. Now I would stand in his place before friends and colleagues and publicly accept the greatest honor that can be bestowed on a country music entertainer. I knew I wouldn't be alone. I would stand alongside Maxine and Bonnie; however, the thought of having two hands to hold, did nothing to squelch my nerves at the thought of speaking publicly to J.E.'s peers.

For days I sat at the kitchen table and tried to put my thoughts in writing. I knew I needed at least an outline to get me through my speech. Extemporaneous speaking was not my strong suit, and I didn't want to humiliate myself or my family by stuttering and stammering through the acceptance speech. As Jim Ed's representative, I wanted this acceptance speech to be meaningful. As his wife, I wanted it to be perfect. He spent sixty-four years of his life earning this award. Surely I could take a few hours to gather my thoughts and write what needed to be said.

Speech after speech was crumpled up in a tiny ball and thrown into a trash basket. Back space and delete seemed to be my two favorite keys on the computer keyboard. I was frustrated and overwhelmed.

Once again, Kim came to my rescue. She said, "Mom, let's do this together. Why don't you start from scratch? I'll sit right here with you. Remember. You're just the wife. Let's voice this speech from your point of view. But let's keep this in mind: What would Dad want you to say on his behalf?"

Suddenly, I knew what to do. I knew what to say. All I had to do was speak from the heart.

It was mid afternoon when the limousines began to arrive at the house. The Country Music Hall of Fame sent long, black Mercedes Sprinters to pick up all of the new inductees and their families. I proudly observed my family members and friends as they boarded those prestigious vehicles. Everyone looked so beautiful—so handsome—dressed in a style fitting for such a monumental occasion. My childhood friend Gloria Miley Williams flew in from Florida to attend the ceremony. Lynda drove over from Arkansas. Closer to home, my friends Terry Tomlinson, Dave and Marilou Barton joined me in our vehicle.

I was nervous. I was excited. I couldn't stop smiling. All I could think about was how much J.E. would have loved this day.

The limousines arrived at the Hall of Fame, and we made our exits onto a red carpet lined with press. Along the perimeters of barricaded streets and sidewalks, fans called out the names of some of country music's greatest ambassadors—hoping to secure a treasured photo of their beloved artists.

The Country Music Hall of Fame inductees were escorted into the Hall of Fame room known as the Rotunda, while our friends took their places in the theater, mixing and mingling with the other guests. Inside, in a private moment, we were greeted by current Hall of Fame members who personally welcomed us to this exclusive club. I looked around the room and was astounded by the talent I saw. As Jim Ed's representative, I posed in a group photograph with those Hall of Famers in attendance: Bobby Bare, Harold Bradley, Garth Brooks, Roy Clark, Ralph Emery, Vince Gill, Emmylou Harris, Ray Walker of the Jordanaires, Brenda Lee, Charlie McCoy, Randy Owen of Alabama, Kenny Rogers, Connie Smith and E.W. "Bud" Wendell. Jim Ed would have been right at home.

We then made our way into the state-of-the-art CMA Theater for the actual induction ceremony.

As I walked to my seat, I clutched my purse a little tighter. Inside, hidden from view, was the speech I had written on Jim Ed's behalf. I knew my time at the podium was drawing near.

The 800-seat CMA Theater was full. Since each Hall of Fame inductee was allotted a specified amount of tickets to give to their family and friends, this night was 100% personal. Every filled seat represented someone special in an inductee's life. Those in attendance traveled our journeys with us. We made it to this destination because of these people.

One of the coolest things about a Hall of Fame induction is the surprise factor. The families of the inductees do not know what songs will be performed at the induction ceremony or which stars will perform those songs.

As part of the Hall of Fame Class of 2015, The Browns shared their induction night with The Oak Ridge Boys who were being inducted in the Modern Era Category and studio session guitarist Grady Martin who would be posthumously inducted in the Musician Category. Marty Stuart, Vince Gill, Duane Eddy, Mandy Barnett, Pete Wade, Buddy Miller and Brenda Lee had just participated in Grady's induction. It was finally time to make Jim Ed and the Browns members.

The ceremony for Veterans' Era started with a spirited rendition of the song that first brought Jim Ed and Maxine to the dance, *Looking Back To See,* performed by swing artist Carolyn Martin and musician Chris Scruggs. Then gospel favorites, The Isaacs, known for their tight family harmonies, sang The Browns' signature song *The Three Bells*. I thought back to the last time I heard The Isaacs sing. It was at J.E.'s memorial service, 136 days earlier. Oh, how he would have loved to hear The Isaacs sing this classic. Since he was a little boy singing with his sisters around the kitchen table in Arkansas, family harmonies had been dear to his heart. The Browns built a career on those harmonies.

In a nod to Jim Ed's fifty year career as a solo artist, fellow Opry member Dierks Bently performed his version of Jim Ed's 1967 hit *Pop A Top*. Dierks lovingly referred to him as "Opry Dad." In a way, J.E. watched Dierks grow up backstage.

Next, it was time for the actual induction. As is tradition, an actual Hall of Fame member welcomes the newest member into the Country Music Hall of Fame. Bill Anderson did the honors four and a-half months ago in Jim Ed's hospital room, but tonight Bill was ill at home. Our longtime friend Bobby Bare served as pinch hitter for the October honors.

With a smile on his face, and a "no hurry," super relaxed manner for which Bare is known, Bobby loped to the microphone and began to drawl. "I met The Browns in the summer of 1961 at a big fair up in Iowa. They were big stars. I had just seen them the week before on *The Ed Sullivan Show."*

Bare reminisced about family dinners that he shared with The Browns whenever he passed through Arkansas in the 1960s, and the audience chuckled when he started in on Maxine. "Maxine has a mouth on her. If you don't want to know the answer to a question, don't ask Maxine. She's gonna give you the full answer. That's why we love her."

As the audience laughed, I thought about the truth of that statement. There was no telling what Maxine would say, or how she would say it. I thought back to when the kids were younger. Whenever Kim and Buster found out she was coming to town, they'd jump up and down and say, "Yay! Aunt Maxine is coming!" I'd think to myself, "Oh No! Maxine is coming!" Then I'd give a minute long lecture on why we don't talk like Aunt Maxine.

I heard Bobby say, "Please help me welcome the newest members of the Country Music Hall of Fame, my friends, The Browns." I took my speech out of my purse and nervously headed for the podium. I knew I would be the first to speak. It was a little daunting being first, but at least I didn't have to follow Maxine!

I took a deep breath, then I began.

> *I'm in the midst of country music royalty, and I just need to get my composure."*

My heart was beating so fast. I thought surely it was going to beat right out of my chest. I could feel my knees knocking. So many different emotions were swirling in my head. I was filled with gratitude.

I wasn't sure I could get through these next few minutes without breaking down. But this was for J.E. I would do my best.

Another deep breath—and I continued.

> Jim Ed spent his whole life doing what he loved to do, with people he loved, for people he loved. He felt so blessed every day. We heard him say so many times, God has been so good to me. Yes, he was right; we were blessed with a great family, friends and colleagues, and many of you are here tonight. Without you this award would not have been possible.
>
> If Jim Ed were here right now, he would want to hug every single one of you and thank you from the bottom of his heart, but he is not here, so I will keep this short. My family, my son Buster and daughter Kim, would like to thank the CMA, the Hall of Fame and Bill Anderson for coming to the hospital and presenting him with his medallion. He was so excited and thankful. He couldn't believe that you took the time to do that.
>
> I was married to Jim Ed for 54 years, and we did have a blessed life. For that, I give God the praise and the glory.

Somehow I made it through that speech. I glanced up to the balcony and saw Jim Ed's band and Christy sitting there, and just knowing that our dear friends Tom and Billie Perryman were in the audience added to my resolve to do well. As a long time manager of The Browns, J.E. would have shared his success with the Perrymans.

When Maxine got up to speak, she acknowledged that Tom and Billie had driven in from Texas. With a mischievous twinkle in her eyes she said, "Tom and Billie are nearing ninety, and they still have their own teeth and hair." Maxine had the wives of the Oak Ridge Boys rolling with laughter. Almost everything she said that night resulted in someone saying under his or her breath, "I can't believe she said that!" Today when I run into one of the Oaks' wives, I playfully greet her the same way. "Hello, my name is Becky Brown. I'm Maxine's sister-in-law."

After the ceremony, everyone made their way upstairs for a wonderful buffet dinner and visits with friends. When we were ready to leave, the limo whisked us back to Brentwood where I began to wind down after what had to be the most amazing affair I had ever attended.

I was on a natural high like no other, and I really didn't want to come down. I was completely exhausted, but so happy. I replayed the day over and over in my head. As I reflected back on the night, I touched the shadow box that was presented to me during the ceremony. The box encased J.E.'s medallion—the very medallion Bill Anderson presented him at the hospital that made him an official member of the Hall back in June. I remember how much that medallion meant to him, and how he wore it proudly from his bed. J.E. never made it home, but that medallion did, and through it, another piece of Jim Ed will live on.

I remember J.E. said to me once that if he made it into the Country Music Hall of Fame, his memory would live on forever. I put on my pajamas and crawled into bed. "You did it, J.E.!" I thought to myself. I went to sleep that night smiling.

Since J.E.'s death, there have been so many wonderful tributes and honors that have been bestowed in the name of Jim Ed Brown. Our family appreciates every one of them, and we thank all of those who remember him fondly.

SAG-AFTRA, the Screen Actors Guild-The American Federation of Television and Radio Artists—a performer's union of approximately 160,000 actors, journalists, recording artists, singers, voice-over talent and other media professionals worldwide—placed a plaque at the Nashville Local naming their conference room *The Jim Ed Brown Board Room*. Jim Ed joined AFTRA early in his career. He was a long time member and for a time served on the board.

During a special presentation at Nashville nightclub 3rd and Lindsley, Bobby Bare presented our family with the Plowboy Records 2017 Legacy Award. The award reads:

> *In recognition of Jim Ed Brown's contribution to the enduring legacy of Eddy Arnold and to the legacy of Plowboy Records.*
>
> *Jim Ed will always be in style.*

Gus Arrendale, a chancellor at Piedmont College, asked his assistant Susan Wade to send me a letter. When I read it, I was overwhelmed at the extent of his kindness.

> *Dear Becky,*
> *Gus thought so much of Jim Ed that he wanted to do something special to not only honor him and his contribution to country music, but to also help Jim Ed's legacy live on in the music world that he helped create.*
>
> *Therefore, Gus has made a gift to Piedmont College to establish "The Jim Ed Brown Scholarship" which will be awarded to a deserving vocal or chorale student from this point forward.*

Of all of his many honors, I think this honor touches my heart the most. Jim Ed encouraged young artists to study their craft and to go after their dreams. He was a dreamer too, but he worked hard to make those dreams a reality. As he traveled his journey, there were people along the way who gave him a hand up. To think Gus will continue to give young adults a hand up, bringing them a step closer to fulfilling their own dreams through this scholarship in Jim Ed's name, is the ultimate honor.

J.E. would have loved it. It is perfect.

Piedmont College with Karen McEntyre, Gus Arrendale, Kim, Isabella, Becky and Mike

Becky receiving Plowboy Records 2017 Legacy Award for Jim Ed from Bobby Bare

Mike and Kim, Becky, Leigh and Buster, Genevieve, Oliver and Hampton at the naming of the SAG-AFTRA Jim Ed Brown Boardroom

Isabella, Becky and Kim enjoying a concert

Becky and Kim at the CMA's

Going on…

It's hard to imagine that the diagnosis of lung cancer hit one family twice in one year, but it did. Seven weeks before the Medallion ceremony at the Country Music Hall of Fame, Bonnie made an appointment with her doctor for a series of tests. She thought she was having troubles with her heart. The September 2, 2015 diagnosis stopped her in her tracks: Stage 4 Adenocarcinoma right lung cancer.

She broke the news to her fans at a Medallion luncheon for the media at the Hall. She said, "This news came as a shock to our family as we are still mourning the loss of my big brother, Jim Ed." When Bonnie accepted her award at the Medallion Ceremony in October, she was in the middle of treatment for her cancer.

Her husband Brownie had a few health issues of his own, and his one wish was to stay healthy enough to see his wife of fifty-six years through the fight of her life. I haven't said much about Brownie in this book, but let me tell you, he was a good man. Like me, he was the spouse that sat in the wings while The Browns took center stage.

Dr. Gene "Brownie" Ring practiced medicine in Dardanelle for thirty-eight years and co-owned the Dardanelle Family Practice Clinic. In his early days of practice, he delivered over two-thousand babies into this world. A fifty-four year member of the First Presbyterian Church, he was a kind man who loved animals. He and Bonnie raised thoroughbred horses, Longhorn cattle, Bantam chickens and Fainting goats. Brownie also enjoyed landscaping and once planted over 3,000 daffodils on a hill on his farm so those who drove by could enjoy the beautiful color.

Brownie passed away in his favorite chair at home on January 16, 2016. Bonnie continued to fight her cancer without her best friend by her side.

Bonnie herself joined him in the Here After just six months after his death. She died at Baptist Health Medical Center in Little Rock on July 16, 2016 due to complications from the lung cancer. J.E. proceeded Bonnie in death by thirteen months. Ironically, their oldest sibling Maxine, who had suffered from a variety of health issues throughout the years, was the last Brown standing.

One of J.E.'s greatest joys was living long enough to watch his grandchildren grow up. Before he died, he knew each child was enrolled in college. He was so proud.

Isabella graduated Magna Cum Laude from Piedmont College in Demorest, Georgia with a degree in Arts Administration with a concentration in music. She is currently pursuing her passion for songwriting and performing in Nashville, Tennessee.

Hampton studied biology and graduated from Georgia Southern. He now works in a lab in Atlanta. Biology is not something I know much about, but I am so proud of his accomplishment.

Both Oliver and Genevieve continue their college pursuits. Oliver studies Architectural Design at Kennesaw Mountain, and Genevieve is earning a degree in Fashion at the University of Arkansas. Like her Poppy, her blood runs Razorback red.

Catherine attends the University of South Carolina. Next year she hopes to attend graduate school in Europe.

All of our grandchildren have grown into wonderful human beings. Buster and Leigh, Kim and Mike, did such a good job raising them. I like to think J.E. and I helped too. Each of these young adults has a love for God, they understand the value of a good education, and the reward of hard work.

Buster works for Colonial Pipeline, and he and his wife Leigh live in a suburb of Atlanta. Kim is opening a Hot Yoga studio in Donelson, Tennessee while her husband Dr. Mike Corwin continues to run his successful veterinary practice in Nashville.

I miss not having J.E. by my side when the grandchildren accomplish so many monumental firsts as adults. There are times I long to turn to him and discuss something they did or tell him something they said, and he's not here.

And as for me...Well, for fifty-four years, I shared my life with my husband, but I also shared my husband with the world. I knew from the beginning, that scenario would only be possible, if I created a life of my own. I couldn't just sit around and wait for J.E. to walk through the door before I began to live. Life didn't stop for me when he left the house. I had a life to live when he was on the road, attending a meeting, giving an interview or making records. Together we had dreams. I hope one of the things I have taught my own children by example, is that when you marry, you work together as a team, but don't get so caught up in the oneness of the team that you lose your true self.

I have always found fulfillment in the arts. Teaching dance, choreography, modeling and painting bring me joy. I consider myself an athlete. I enjoy snow skiing and water skiing. Playing tennis with my friends is a passion. Being a homemaker was always important to me, and it still is. I enjoy an active lifestyle that centers around the love I have for my children and grandchildren, and I am so thankful for God's love for me.

Occasionally, I'll think of something I'd like to share with him when he gets home from the road. Just for a split second, it's like nothing has changed. But then I remember.

He isn't on the road, and he isn't coming home. I remember I am alone. But I am not lonely. God is my constant companion. My life is full of family and friends, and I have a life of many interests to sustain me. But mostly, I have my faith and my music.

I am so thankful I have The Brown's music. I listen to their albums and every song brings back a sweet memory.

Before he passed away, I asked J.E. to send me butterflies to let me know he was in a good place. My life is now filled with butterflies.

I'm not sure how fast butterflies can fly, but one day I was driving my car down Edmondson Pike, and a kaleidoscope of butterflies continued to fly in front of my car as I traveled down the road. It was amazing.

Another time, I was playing tennis with a friends, and a butterfly began to dance around me. It continued to flutter around me during the match. After one good volley, I reached down to pick up the tennis ball, and the butterfly was waiting patiently for me, perched on top of the ball. In all of my days playing tennis, I had never seen anything like it.

The time that stands out most in my mind was the time shortly after J.E.'s death. I was alone, deep in thought, sitting outside on a step on my back porch. Out of no where ten bright yellow butterflies appeared. They hovered a few feet from my face. They flitted to the right and then to the left, I was surrounded by butterflies.

I sat very still, and a couple of those delicate creatures actually landed on my arms and legs. They kept me company in complete trust. I couldn't believe it. I was overwhelmed. I knew in my heart this was a sign from J.E. He remembered his promise. If he were in a good place, he would send me butterflies. He was Home. I was sure of it.

Writing this book has been a journey of reflection. Through these pages, I have relived memories and moments that I haven't thought about in years. I was amazed at how fast the past bubbled to the surface once I directed my thoughts in a backward motion. I did my best to be truthful throughout.

Now, as I redirect my thoughts once again to the present and future, I remember the words to one of the last songs J.E. ever recorded, and I smile with satisfaction. Through all the laughter and the tears, it was, is and always will be, a good life. Thank you, God, for the lessons and the blessings.

> *It's a good life,*
> *blessed in so many ways.*
> *It's a hard life;*
> *It's been tough some days.*
> *It's a sweet life*
> *That's come my way.*
> *It's a good life in so many ways.*

It's been a long life.
I couldn't count the days.
It's been a short life.
Time has slipped away.
It's my life,
and I have to say;
It's been a good life in so many ways.

I've looked at life from a mountain top.
I gave my all, for all I got.
Through the good times or when times were bad,
I always gave it all I had.

I've had dreams come true,
Dreams fall away.
I've cried tears of joy and tears of rage.
I've had things go right and things turn out wrong,
But the best of life,
I've found in a song.

Life's been good to me.
Life has hurt me deep.
I've laughed a thousand times.
I've cried myself to sleep.
I still have regrets,
Some debts to pay,
But it's been a good life in so many ways.

It's been a good life in so many ways.

References

[1] *O Holy Night*; hymn; by Adolphe Adam; 1847—page 10

[2] *Softly and Tenderly*; hymn; by Will L. Thompson; public domain; 1880—page 11

[3] *Farther Along*; hymn; by W.B. Stevens; arranged by Barney Elliott Warren; <u>Select Hymns for Christian Worship and Church Gospel Service</u>; 1911—page 15

[4] *Can't Stop Loving That Man*; by Jerome Kern; and Oscar Hammerstein II; <u>Showboat</u>; 1927—page 29

[5] *The Three Bells*; by Jean Villard Gilles and Bert Reisfeld; recorded by Jim Ed Brown and The Browns; <u>Sweet Sounds</u>; producer Chet Atkins; RCA Victor; 1959—pages 33, 221

[6] *Twilight Time*; by Buck Ross; Marty Nevins; Al Nevins and Artie Dunn; recorded by The Platters; <u>The Flying Platters Around the World</u>; Mercury Records; 1958—page 36

[7] *Are You Missing Me?*; recorded by Jim Ed Brown and The Browns; 1955—page 48

[8] *Looking Back To See*; by Jim Ed and Maxine Brown; recorded by Jim Ed Brown and The Browns; <u>Jim Edward, Maxine and Bonnie Brown</u>; 1954—pages 48, 78, 195, 221.

[9] *Scarlet Ribbons*; by Evelyn Danzig and Jack Segal; recorded by Jim Ed Brown and The Browns; <u>Town & Country</u>; producer Chet Atkins; RCA Victor; 1959—page 49

[10] *The Old Lamplighter;* by Nat Simon and Charles Tobias; recorded by Jim Ed Brown and The Browns; <u>Town & Country</u>; producer Chet Atkins; RCA Victor; 1960—page 49

[11] <u>Baptist Hymnal</u>; Lifeway Christian Resources (formally Sunday School Board of Southern Baptist Convention); 1956—page 53.

[12] *I'll Be Home For Christmas*; by Kim Gannon and Walter Kent; recorded by Bing Crosby; DECCA; 1943—page 55.

[13] *A Bushel and a Peck*; by Frank Loesser; <u>Guys and Dolls</u>; RCA Victor; 1950—page 56.

[14] *Send Me The Pillow You Dream On*; by Hank Locklin; recorded by Jim Ed Brown and The Browns; <u>The Essential Jim Ed Brown and The Browns</u>; 1960—pages 62, 221.

[15] *Once a Day*; by Bill Anderson; recorded by Connie Smith; <u>Connie Smith</u>; producer Bob Ferguson; RCA Victor; 1964—page 63.

[16] *Mexican Joe*, by Mitchell Torok; recorded by Jim Reeves; <u>Jim Reeves Sings</u>; producer Fabor Robinson; RCA Victor; 1953—page 78.

[17] *Bimbo*; by Glenn O'Dell; recorded by Jim Reeves; <u>Bimbo</u>; RCA Victor; 1956—page 78.

[18] *The End of The World*; by Arthur Kent and Sylvia Dee; recorded by Skeeter Davis; producer Chet Atkins; RCA; 1962—page 86.

[19] *Still*, by Bill Anderson; recorded by Bill Anderson; producer Owen Bradley; DECCA; 1963—page 88.

[20] *The Blizzard*; recorded by Jim Reeves; <u>Tall Tales & Short Tempers</u>; 1961—page 94.

[21] *Four Walls*, by Marvin Moore and George Campbell; recorded by Jim Reeves; <u>The Best of Jim Reeves</u>; producer Chet Atkins; RCA Victor; 1957—page 94.

[22] *He'll Have to Go*; by Joe Allison and Audrey Allison; recorded by Jim Reeves; <u>He'll Have To Go</u>; producer Chet Atkins; RCA Victor; 1960—page 94.

[23] *Welcome to My World*; by Ray Winkler and John Hancock; recorded by Jim Reeves; <u>Touch of Velvet</u>; RCA; 1964—page 94.

[24] *The Night Watch*; by Cindy Walker; recorded by Jim Reeves; <u>We Thank Thee</u>; 1962—page 94.

[25] *I Heard From a Memory Last Night*; by Ralph Freed and Jerry Livingston; recorded by Jim Ed Brown; <u>Alone With You</u>; RCA Victor; 1965—page 97.

[26] *Pop a Top*; by Nat Stuckey; recorded by Jim Ed Brown; <u>Just Jim</u>; producer Felton Jarris; RCA Victor; 1966—pages 97, 98, 110, 114, 173, 174, 214, 221.

[27]*Harper Valley PTA*; by Shelby Singleton and Tom T. Hall; recorded by Jeannie C. Riley; Harpeth Valley PTA; Plantation Records; 1968—page 105.

[28]*You Don't Know Me*; by Cindy Walker and Eddy Arnold; recorded of Eddy Arnold; The Best of Eddy Arnold; RCA Victor; 1955—page 106.

[29]*Back in the Saddle Again*; recorded by Gene Autry; The Essential Gene Autry; 1939—page 107.

[30]*Rudolph the Red-Nosed Reindeer*; by Johnny Marks; recorded by Gene Autry; Rudolph the Red-Nosed Reindeer and Other Christmas Classics; Columbia; 1949—page 107.

[31]*Do Not Forsake Me*; High Noon; by Dimitri Tiomkin and Ned Washington; recorded by Tex Ritter; 1952—page 108.

[32]*I'll Be A Sunbeam For Jesus*, recorded by Tex Ritter—page 108.

[33]*Country Sunshine*; by Dottie West, Billie Davis and Dianne Whiles; recorded by Dottie West; The Essential Dottie West; RCA Records; 1973—page 109.

[34]*Black Mountain Rag*; traditional—page 116.

[35]*Alabama Jubilee*; by George Cobb and Jack Yellen; Remick Music Corp.; 1915—page 116.

[36]*Orange Blossom Special*; by Ervin T. Rouse; Columbia; 1938—page 116.

[37]Morning; recorded by Jim Ed Brown; RCA Victor; 1970—page 118.

[38]Angel's Sunday; recorded by Jim Ed Brown; RCA Victor; 1971—page 118.

[39]Evening; recorded by Jim Ed Brown; RCA Victor; 1972—page 118.

[40]It's That Time of Night; RCA Victor; 1974—page 118.

[41]Corrie Ten Boom; John and Elizabeth Sherrill; The Hiding Place; (Netherlands: Chosen Book Publishers); 1974—page 119-120.

[42]*Kiss An Angel Good Morning*; by Ben Peters; recorded by Charley Pride; Charley Pride Sings Heart Songs; producer Jack Clement; 1971—page 128.

[43]*I Don't Want To Have To Marry You*; by Fred Imus and Phil Sweet; recorded by Jim Ed Brown and Helen Cornelius; I Don't Want To Have To Marry You; producer Bob Ferguson, RCA Victor; 1976—page 140.

[44]*He Stopped Loving Her Today*; by Bobby Braddock and Curly Putman; recorded by George Jones; producer Billy Sherrill and George Jones; EPIC; 1989—page 154.

[45]Unknown source; attributed to Dr. Suess or an anonymous proverb—page 161.

[46]*Big Foot Rides With Santa*; by Jack Franzen with Jim Ed Brown; producer Gene Kennedy; 2004—page 173.

[47]*In Style Again*; by Lance Miller and Austin Cunningham; recorded by Jim Ed Brown; In Style Again; producer Don Cusic; Plowboy Records; 2015—pages 194-195, 201.

[48]*When The Sun Says Hello To The Mountain*; by Harry Pease and Larry Vincent; recorded by Jim Ed Brown and The Browns; In Style Again; producer Don Cusic; Plowboy Records; 2015—page 202.

[49]*Hallelujah*; by Leonard Cohen; producer John Lissauer; Columbia; 1984—page 203.

[50]*Family Bible*; by Willie Nelson; Goldstar Studios; 1957; 1996—page 205.

[51]*Will The Circle Be Unbroken*; by Ada R. Habershon; publisher Don Cusic; 1907—page 208.

[52]*Precious Lord, Take My Hand*; by Thomas Andrew Dorsey; Warner-Tamerlane Publishing Corp.; 1938—page 210.

[53]*Amazing Grace*; hymn; by John Newton; 1779—page 211.

[54]*The Old Rugged Cross*; hymn; by George Bennard; 1913—page 211.

[55]*When They Ring Those Golden Bells*; recorded by Jim Ed Brown; public domain; 1965—page 214.

[56]*Life's Highway*; by Richard Leigh and Roger Murrah; produced Tony Brown and Jimmy Bowan; MCA Nashville; 1986—page 215.

[57]*When I Dream*; by Sandy Mason Theoret; recorded by Crystal Gayle; producer Allen Reynolds; United Artists; 1979—page 215.

[58]*It's a Good Life*; In Style Again; by Don Cusic; recorded by Jim Ed Brown; Plowboy Records; 2015—pages 216, 227-228.